SCI-FI

DAYS OF FEAR AND WONDER

Edited by James Bell

A BFI Compendium

BFI
21 Stephen Street
London W1T 1LN

www.bfi.org.uk

First published 2014

© 2014 BFI

ISBN 978-1-84457-849-8

A CIP catalogue record for this book
is available from the British Library

Typeset in Caecilia, and Foundry Gridnik.
Designed by chrisbrawndesign.com
Printed in England by Colt Press
Image retouching by DawkinsColour

Front cover:
Sigourney Weaver in 'Alien' (1979)

Back cover:
'Close Encounters of the Third Kind'
(1977)

Inside front cover:
'It Came From Outer Space' (1953)

Inside back cover:
'Metropolis' (1927)

This page:
'The Day the Earth Stood Still' (1951)

CONTENTS

PREFACE

BY HEATHER STEWART,
CREATIVE DIRECTOR, BFI

Sci-fi is the world's most popular film genre, and there's a simple reason why: at its best it is pure onscreen magic. Great sci-fi cinema and television at once offer challenging new ways of looking at the world, venture questions on what it is to be human, and provide a thrilling visual spectacle that no other artform can match. Over the century-and-a-bit that the cinema has existed, sci-fi has propelled onscreen visions into new realms, firing the imagination of our most creative filmmakers, visual effects wizards and television writers to show us things that we cannot see ourselves, whether that's Georges Méliès taking early film audiences to outer space in *A Trip to the Moon*, (still regarded as one of the most influential visual effects of all time) Stanley Kubrick taking us 'beyond the infinite' in *2001: A Space Odyssey*, Jonathan Glazer imagining how our world might look through an alien's eyes in *Under the Skin*, or Ridley Scott giving us *Alien* and *Blade Runner*, two of the best sci-fi films ever made. In fact, British creativity has been right at the forefront of the genre since H.G. Wells, with *Doctor Who* our biggest sci-fi export, and the boldness of vision and talents of award-winning British visual effects artists making the UK a world leader.

Sci-fi cinema and television are great litmus tests for social unease, from the alien invasions that expressed Cold War paranoias in the 1950s to our contemporary anxieties about whether artificial intelligences will eventually make us humans redundant. Sci-fi probes our deepest fears, but it can also fill us with awe at the majesty of the universe and the scale of human achievement, evoking the sublime in truly grand fashion. But sci-fi – though it prevails with audiences – has also often been consigned to the cultural margins, patronised as juvenile: we want to bring these spectacular films back to the big screen, but we also want to celebrate them as representing a cinema of ideas.

All of which is why we at the BFI are thrilled to be presenting 'Sci-Fi: Days of Fear and Wonder', the biggest sci-fi season ever mounted, on TV, DVD and online, and with more than 1,000 screenings and events in cinemas across the UK, all accompanied by a range of new sci-fi related Film Classic books and this BFI Compendium you have in your hands, the perfect accompaniment to it all. So come, let's boldly go and explore strange new worlds...

(Opposite)
Harrison Ford in Ridley Scott's
'Blade Runner' (1982).

INTRODUCTION

BY JAMES BELL

Is it just a coincidence that the cinema and science fiction as we know it were both born in the same year? In 1895, the year in which H.G. Wells – following in the footsteps of writers of 'scientific romances' like Jules Verne and Mary Shelley – first published his science-fiction novel *The Time Machine*, over in France the Lumière brothers held the first public screenings of their new *cinématographe* machine to enraptured audiences. If Wells's story dazzled the imaginations of his readers with its giant leaps across expanses of time and into the Earth's distant future, the *cinématographe*, with its ability to capture moments in the past and replay them in the present, and, through editing, seemingly accelerate or slow the passing of onscreen time, was quickly hailed as a sort of time machine itself. If science fiction would be the genre that would most imaginatively reflect our fear and wonder at the things to come in the new modern age, then the new artform of the cinema would be the means by which its visions would be most vividly and popularly depicted. The potential the moving image held for the telling of science-fiction stories was recognised right away, when the British director R.W. Paul approached Wells about collaborating on an adaptation of *The Time Machine*, and the ties between science fiction and cinema have been unbroken ever since.

The chapters that follow chart a course through the great history of sci-fi film and television, and are grouped into three organising sections. We start with 'Tomorrow's World', and depictions and speculations of future societies and technologies, move on to 'Contact', heading out of this world and on to others, and finish with 'Altered States', where we consider how sci-fi film has dealt with the post-Darwinian world, and the new cyberspaces where we can't even be sure what is real and what is not. The chapters themselves take us from the magical invention of early cinema pioneers like Georges Méliès, whose *A Trip to the Moon* still has the capacity to thrill, and onwards past the grand speculative visions of epics such as *Metropolis* and *Things to Come*. We depart for the flying saucers, forbidden planets and Martian invaders of 1950s Cold War sci-fi, with titles like *The Day the Earth Stood Still*, and return home to the apparent safety of our sitting rooms, where we in fact face the terrifying revelations of *The Quatermass Experiment*, the grand conspiracies of *The X-Files* and the adventures in space and time of *Doctor Who*. We're cast deep into the virtual realities of the *The Matrix,* and plunged into the nightmarish visions of future dystopias like *1984* and *The Hunger Games*. We meet advanced artificial intelligences in *Blade Runner*, biological mutations on the *Island of Lost Souls* and in the mind of David Cronenberg, and alien lifeforms hostile, gentle and superior in *Alien, E.T. the Extra-Terrestrial* and *2001: A Space Odyssey*. We also learn that, though onscreen sci-fi can astound us with the visual splendour of special-effects-laden, galaxy-spanning spectacles like *Star Wars*, great sci-fi films have also been made on a shoestring, for it is a genre that is finally and most importantly fuelled by ideas, by asking the great 'what if?' questions about the human experience and our place in the grand scheme of things – it probes the inner spaces of the human mind as much as it does the outer reaches of the universe.

Sci-fi films have thrilled us and expressed our sense of fear and wonder for more than a century now, and they look set to continue to do so long into the future – on this planet or beyond.

TOMORROW'S WORLD

Future shock

by Mark Fisher

During the television broadcast of the Superbowl in 1984, a commercial for Apple computers was screened for the first time. Directed by Ridley Scott, who had recently updated science fiction with *Alien* and *Blade Runner*, the advert is virtually an inventory of totalitarian tropes (both visual and verbal) from dystopian science fiction. It shows visored cops and shuffling grey drones, slack-jawed and stupefied in front of an enormous screen dominated by a monochrome talking head, intoning authoritarian platitudes ("We have created, for the first time in all history, a garden of pure ideology – where each worker may bloom, secure from the pests purveying contradictory truths"). The one dash of colour comes from a female athlete, who throws a sledgehammer into the screen, causing it to explode.

The success of this commercial shows how, by the 1980s, the dystopian mode had become so familiar that it could be called upon to instantly trigger a set of associations. Scott's film – only a minute long – mines these associations, playing on a set of oppositions (between the individualistic and the conformist, between the innovative and the established, between the bureaucratic and the creative). In 1984, its images of dreary, centralised control would naturally have triggered thoughts of the Soviet empire (since it drew upon stereotypes of the Eastern bloc), but the cleverness of the commercial lies in the way it conflated the authoritarianism of state socialism with the stuffiness of corporate capitalism (we were supposed to think of IBM as well as the USSR). There's a parable here about the uses of dystopian imagery. Today, we are controlled not by an authoritarian patriarch, but by corporations such as Apple, which appeal to our individuality and our creativity.

The major reference in Scott's commercial was, of course, George Orwell's *Nineteen Eighty-Four*. Orwell's vision of a future Britain – Airstrip One – dominated by an Inner Party, which subjects the population to intensive surveillance and controls not only language but thought itself, is one of the major templates of dystopian fiction. The distinction between the anti-utopian and the dystopian has been much discussed, but for our purposes here, I will argue that, to count as anti-utopian, the system that is being depicted must bear the traces of a positive political project. The anti-utopia is not simply a totalitarian society; its totalitarianism is held to result from the utopian impulse itself. Consequently, the anti-utopian mode has often functioned as a critique of the utopian.

The dystopian, by contrast, carries with it no sense of any betrayed utopian promise. Authoritarianism and social control are pursued for their own reasons, without any serious reference to political ideals (such ideals may be invoked, but only in a cynical and propagandistic fashion). If *Nineteen Eighty-Four* provides the model for the dystopian, then we can find a prototype for the anti-utopian in Aldous Huxley's *Brave New World*. Significantly, both of these novels emerged in the first half of the 20th century, a moment haunted by grand visions of total social transformation. The fear that animates them is one of excessive regulation, and both are accordingly about the dangers of conformity, homogenisation and subjugation. In the 1930s and 40s, governments and corporations could call upon new industrial and media technologies, capable of manipulating desires, engineering personality and manufacturing what counted as reality itself. In *Nineteen Eighty-Four*, the only point of the surveillance and other authoritarian machineries is their own reproduction. In *Brave New World*, the citizens achieve a kind of happiness, but the anti-utopian question is: what price happiness? Is a happiness emerging out of hypnosis and drugs worthy of the name? Both Andrew Niccol's *Gattaca* (1997) and Kurt Wimmer's *Equilibrium*

(2002) are riffs on these *Brave New World* themes. They emerged at a moment when genetic engineering seemed to offer exactly the kind of micro-manipulation of identity that Huxley had anticipated, and the widespread use of anti-depressants such as Prozac threatened to vindicate his vision of a population subdued by pharmaceuticals. These films are about a genetic and affective uniformity, in which behavioural deviation and extremes of emotion are screened out in advance, yet both *Gattaca* and *Equilibrium* are as strangely neutralised as the societies they portray, and lack the power to haunt.

The most disturbing vision of social control via drugs and hypnotic control remains the Ludovico Technique sequence of Stanley Kubrick's *A Clockwork Orange* (1971), in which the violent gang leader Alex (Malcolm McDowell) is subjected to a new system of aversion therapy that completely reconstructs his personality. In *A Clockwork Orange*, anti-utopian elements are embedded inside a larger dystopian frame – although the dystopia is not one of over-regulated social control, but one of social breakdown, in which Alex's droogs can rape and steal with impunity. In effect, *A Clockwork Orange* asks if Huxleyan anti-utopian techniques would be the solution for a dystopia.

Huxley claimed that *Brave New World* had been inspired by reading some of H.G. Wells's utopian works, such as *A Modern Utopia*. But with *The Time Machine*, Wells himself was responsible for inventing one of the most enduring forms of the dystopian. The book (adapted into a flawed but compelling film adaptation by George Pal in 1960, and a travesty of a remake in 2002) offers a pessimistic vision of the decline of human civilisation into barbarism and ultimately extinction. Here, the problem is not excessive control but the lack of any guiding vision. No doubt Wells envisaged the novel as a warning of what would happen if the positive political programmes he outlined in his utopian works was not followed: in this sense, it might be considered an example of an anti-anti-utopian fiction. In the future society to which the time-traveller journeys, social stratification has become so pronounced that humanity has effectively devolved into two species: the effete, imbecilic yet beautiful Eloi, and the monstrous, brutish Morlocks. Yet this grim vision of decline – on which the 1960 film concentrates – is only a foretaste of the bleakness with which the novel concludes. When the time traveller ventures further into the future he finds an Earth from which all traces of human life have been removed, a burned-out planet that is ruled by crustaceans, a vision worthy of William Burroughs, and one shied away from by both of the film adaptations.

Yet another version of the dystopian can be found in the work of Franz Kafka. Kafka's writing is more ambivalent and oneiric, less readable in

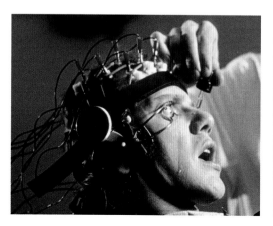

terms of clear polemical intentions, than that of Huxley, Orwell or Wells. Kafka's major fictions are structured like anxiety dreams, in which the protagonist is constantly frustrated and obstructed, his pursuit of justice and personal vindication perpetually deferred. Kafka's version of dystopia is a centreless labyrinth, in which domestic space, the bureaucratic and power connect up in unpredictable ways. So much of the agony in Kafka comes from the anxiety-dream dynamics of things happening when or where they shouldn't (not knowing the time and place that your trial hearing is due to take place, then stumbling into proceedings halfway through; sexuality suddenly erupting in public places; corporal punishment for corrupt officials taking place in an office cupboard).

This dream topography was captured brilliantly in Orson Welles's superb 1962 adaptation of *The Trial*, which made great use of brutalist architecture in Zagreb to create the impression of an interminable, impersonal office space. Anthony Perkins was perfectly cast as Josef K: irredeemably awkward, bewildered, occasionally outraged, yet never convinced that he is innocent of the charges which hang over him – which are never specified.

Kafka's work is haunted by the feeling of being in the wrong place, or (which might amount to the same thing) of not having a place in the world. Jean-Marie Straub and Danièle Huillet's 1984 film *Class Relations* (*Klassenverhältnisse*), a version of Kafka's unfinished novel *Amerika*, centres on lead character Karl Rossmann's thwarted attempt to set this right, to finally find a place for himself in the world. Straub refused to see Rossmann as a 'protagonist', referring to him instead as a 'recurring character'. Rossmann does not have enough agency to be a protagonist. Exiled from the world with which he was familiar, Rossmann finds himself among the dispossessed, making temporary friendships and alliances with drifters and service staff. The 'Amerika' he discovers is not so much a land of opportunity as a world of perpetual anxiety, in which everyone fears losing whatever status they might have achieved. There are echoes of silent-era comedies in *Class Relations* – apt, since Kafka's own novels, with their mood of quiet panic, their pratfalls and the leering omnipresence of a pitiless law, feel as if they could be grim versions of a Chaplin or Keaton film.

The Insurance Man, a 1986 BBC film directed by Richard Eyre from a script by Alan Bennett, offers another angle. As you would expect from Bennett, this is a minor-key dystopia, pitched in some indeterminate space between a biography of Kafka and an adaptation of his work, and saturated in awkwardness. *The Insurance Man* roots Kafka's imagined world in the time he spent working at the Workers' Accident Insititute in Bohemia, and the television film creates a frustrating series of corridors at the end of which sits yet another functionary. In keeping with Kafka's novels, the space is always cramped, confined – a deliberate contrast with the large open-plan offices Welles used in *The Trial*.

Political worlds

If dystopian fictions have inspired much film and television, then the same could not be said of the utopian form. The standard explanation for this is the supposed lack of drama in utopia. Absence of antagonism, it is argued, might produce social harmony, but it is inimical to dramatic spectacle. Yet this seems to have affected cinema more than literature. The utopian was perhaps first of all a literary genre, one with a long history. Thomas More might have coined the term in 1516, but Plato's *The Republic* could be considered the first example of a work about a perfect society. Modernity didn't staunch the utopian impulse in literature,

(Above)
Anthony Perkins (left) as Josef K. in Orson Welles's Kafka adaptation 'The Trial' (1962).

(Below)
The world is cramped and awkward in Alan Bennett's minor-key dystopia 'The Insurance Man' (1986), starring Daniel Day-Lewis.

even if it has often served as a kind of foil or negative inspiration, as it does in works such as William Morris's *News from Nowhere* and the feminist ecotopias imagined by Marge Piercy and Ursula Le Guin, where the polluted, the industrial and the urban are figured as the despoiled spaces from which the various utopias offer an escape.

Cinema and television have, however, found the dystopian much more congenial. *Nineteen Eighty-Four* was adapted for the BBC by the great science-fiction author Nigel Kneale in 1954, in a production starring Peter Cushing. A big-screen adaptation directed by Michael Anderson followed in 1956, and a further cinema version, directed by Michael Radford and starring John Hurt as Winston and Richard Burton as O'Brien, was released in 1984 itself. In 1968 Nigel Kneale himself would go on to write a dystopia, *The Year of the Sex Olympics*, a prescient anticipation of 21st-century reality TV and its commodification of intimate experience. Here we have a strand of the dystopian in which social control is maintained via entertainment rather than by the machinery of a repressive state apparatus alone. In films such as *Death Race 2000* (1975), *Rollerball* (1975) and *The Running Man* (1987), violent spectacle serves as a form of distraction from authoritarian rule and as a symbolic ratification of the controlling powers. Tensions that might otherwise have exploded in political antagonisms are instead deflected into the vicarious enjoyment of others' suffering, or – as in *The Running Man* – the entertainment actually stages a display of political power, the game functioning as a kind of televised punishment.

A more direct return to the *Nineteen Eighty-Four* model was Volker Schlöndorff's dutiful if somewhat pedestrian version of Margaret Atwood's *The Handmaid's Tale* (1990). The future North America here is not subdued via libidinal spectacle, but by a more conventional authoritarianism. Yet what makes *The Handmaid's Tale* distinctive is the centrality of gender to its dystopia, and its related fears that the gains of the 60s counterculture would be erased by resurgent reactionary forces.

The novel was an unambiguous response to the coming to power in the US of Ronald Reagan and the religious right. In *The Handmaid's Tale*, this victory of the right becomes absolute: a catastrophe that causes most of the population to become sterile allows the suspension of the constitution and the ascent of a neo-puritan ruling class. Women in the subjugated class find themselves deprived of their agency, their sexuality and their names, and turned into breeding machines to be used by the ruling elite.

James McTeigue's *V for Vendetta* is similarly inspired by the fear of a reactionary revival – perhaps because the graphic novels on which the film was based, written by Alan Moore, came out in the early 1980s and could therefore be considered part of the same anti-Reaganite moment as *The Handmaid's Tale*. The ruling Norsefire party in Moore's dystopian future Britain is imperialistic, religious and homophobic. Apart from this resonance with late 20th-century reactionary movements, however, *V for Vendetta* – both in the original and in the film – adds little to the familiar model of dystopia established by Orwell. Perhaps the film's most enduring contribution has been the influence of its imagery on real-life protest, with many anti-capitalist activists wearing the Guy Fawkes mask that the anonymous rebel V uses to conceal his identity.

Paul Verhoeven's *RoboCop* (1987) is another anti-Reaganite dystopia. Here, the emphasis is not so much on the repudiation of the counterculture as on the quasi-militaristic tooling-up of the forces of reaction, and on the privatisation of functions previously controlled by the state. The film turns on a deal by the beleaguered city government of Detroit and a large corporation to sell off the policing of the city to the Omni Consumer

Products corporation. The heavily armoured, virtually invulnerable cyborg policeman RoboCop has walked straight out of right-wing authoritarian fantasy, and the film confronts us with a dialectic that has become increasingly familiar under neoliberal governance. As the services and systems that previously enabled social cohesion are stripped away, it becomes easier to justify the implementation of ever more violent and ruthless authoritarian measures. Verhoeven was reputedly inspired by the Judge Dredd comic strip (itself the subject of two unsatisfactory adaptations, *Judge Dredd* [1995] and *Dredd* [2012]). The Dredd comic strip actually preceded the Reagan years – it was originally published in 1977 – but prefigured their authoritarian rhetoric. (It was also heavily indebted to cinematic sources – Dredd is clearly inspired by the Dirty Harry series, and the look of the character was initially based on *Death Race 2000*.)

After the fall

If these dystopias are primarily political, there are also dystopias rooted in natural or human-caused catastrophe – even if this opposition is somewhat misleading, as many if not most of the political dystopias also depend upon catastrophe. *Nineteen Eighty-Four* takes place after a nuclear war; the society in *The Handmaid's Tale* is structured around the illness that brings about widespread sterility, etc. In these cases the catastrophe functions as a pretext for the imposition of authoritarian control.

There are other dystopias, however, that emerge from the disappearance of political authority caused by catastrophe. In the BBC TV series *Survivors* a virus has wiped out most of the human population, reducing society to a Hobbesian war of all against all. Or so it initially seems. *Survivors* quite clearly shows the influence of feminist and ecological struggles, and explores the possibility that a catastrophe might allow society to be rebuilt in a more collective, egalitarian and sustainable way, as well as the threats these efforts might face. (The recent BBC remake of *Survivors* was sadly bereft of any of these utopian traces.)

A more unambiguously bleak post-catastrophe dystopia was the 1984 BBC television drama *Threads*, which begins in a simulated documentary style, depicting the impact of a nuclear attack on Sheffield, and ends up as a vision of the near-total disintegration of human society. The nuclear apocalypse not only destroys people and infrastructure, it also irredeemably corrodes the virtual 'threads' – the various forms of commonality – that hold society together. The film is loaded with nightmare images of searing vividness. A woman – her eyes coal black and totally devoid of affect – clings onto the shrouded corpse of a baby. Soldiers frisk the dead body of a freshly shot looter for a packet of crisps. "Salt and vinegar. It would be. I hate those." A woman gives birth in a filthy abandoned hangar, with only a chained-up barking dog for company. *Threads* concludes with an image of England as a medieval country, the massively reduced population hoeing an unyielding earth… Language is diminished, devolved into rough, guttural injunctions, reflecting a new harshness in social relations. No compassion, which is yet another luxury from a bygone age no one can even remember any more.

Few films can compete with the intensity of this bleakness, but Alfonso Cuarón's *Children of Men* (2006), based on the novel by P.D. James, is a recent highly accomplished post-catastrophe dystopia. Here, as in *The Handmaid's Tale*, social collapse has been precipitated by a sterility crisis. No babies have been born for a generation. This makes for a fascinating temporality of catastrophe: in one sense this is a *post*-catastrophe dystopia; in another, the film shows the catastrophe as it is being lived through. One of the most powerful scenes takes place inside Battersea Power

(Top)
The cyborg policeman as right-wing fantasy in Paul Verhoeven's anti-Reaganite dystopia 'RoboCop' (1987).

(Above, middle)
Nuclear attack has led to the disintegration of human society in Barry Hines's bleak BBC drama 'Threads' (1984).

(Above, bottom)
Battersea Power Station functions as the Ministry of Art in Alfonso Cuarón's 'Children of Men' (2006).

(Top)
Steven Spielberg's 'Minority Report' (2002) anticipated our current immersion in banal communicative capitalism.

(Above)
The young clones in Mark Romanek's 'Never Let Me Go' (2010) are taught to accept their grim fate.

Station, now functioning as a Ministry of Art, in which the elite preserve and enjoy cultural treasures (Picasso's *Guernica*, Velasquez's *Las meninas*, Pink Floyd's inflatable pig). The lead character, Theo (Clive Owen) asks his cousin Nigel, one of the Ministry's curators, what the point of it all is if, in 100 years, there won't be anyone left to see any of it. Nigel's answer exemplifies a kind of suave nihilism: "You know what it is, Theo. I just don't think about it." Without any possible connection to the future, cultural objects become museum pieces, a set of decontextualised ornaments.

John Hillcoat's 2009 adaptation of Cormac McCarthy's novel *The Road* does not even hold open the picturesque pleasures of dereliction offered by *Children Of Men*. Here, as in Cuarón's film, the catastrophe is never explained; but whereas the malaise in *Children of Men* affects only humans, leaving nature intact, in *The Road* it is nature itself that dies. The ultimate effect is the same, however: there is no future, and the past is in the process of being erased. When the two lead characters, the unnamed 'man' and his son, discover a can of Coke, it is a holy relic from a lost age of commodity fetishism. There is no escape. To reproduce means only to extend the process of extinction, and there is no possibility of reconstruction, since both living nature and the products of labour are close to being totally used up, with no prospect of replenishment.

Precarious existences

What do contemporary dystopian films have to tell us about the technologised present? In most respects, 21st-century culture falls disappointingly short of the futuristic vistas to which 20th-century science fiction accustomed us. Perhaps it is only communications technology that has kept pace with those expectations, but its ubiquity has produced a banal dystopia in which we are always connected and – as a consequence – always in a state of distraction. With its walk-through, pop-up blipverts and corporate graffiti, it was perhaps Steven Spielberg's *Minority Report* (2002) which most effectively anticipated our current condition of banal immersion in communicative capitalism.

The most powerful contemporary dystopias concern the experience of precariousness to which communications technology has contributed. Mobile telephones allow arrangements to be made and unmade instantly; we can be called into work or sacked at a moment's notice. But the anxiety of precarity stems principally from the dismantling of social-security provision and the proliferation of short-term, casual employment. Andrew Niccol's *In Time* (2011) is perhaps the first dystopia to be expressly about this sense. In the future United States in which the film is set, time, rather than money, is the major asset. Society is stratified into time zones, with the super-rich having effectively infinite time to waste, and the poor always only a few hours away from death.

Mark Romanek's *Never Let Me Go* (2010), adapted from the novel by Kazuo Ishiguro, is similarly infused with an anxious sense that time is desperately short. The premise here is remarkably similar to that of Michael Bay's *The Island* (2005). Both focus on an underclass of clones who have been specially bred and trained to provide spare-part organs for the general human population. However, while Bay serves up a familiar slew of action-film tropes of car chases and shoot-outs, Romanek – in keeping with the novel – offers only fatalistic submission. The clones in *Never Let Me Go* accept their fate, never rebelling or looking to escape, seeking instead only some bureaucratic reprieve from the authorities themselves. The film is ultimately about the power of ideology – it begins in an English school where the clones are taught to accept their fate. The

(Above)
Generational conflict and class
antagonism sit at the heart
of the massively sucessful
'The Hunger Games' (2012).

film resonates with the contemporary sense that there is nothing to be done, a fatalism that the young in particular must fight, partly because they are disproportionately affected by precarity. (The clones in *Never Let Me Go* are all young, because they don't get the opportunity to live to be old.)

A sense of generational conflict is also at the heart of the most popular contemporary dystopia, *The Hunger Games* series. As with *In Time* and *Never Let Me Go*, *The Hunger Games* is also about class antagonism. Closely adapted from Suzanne Collins's young adult dystopian novels, *The Hunger Games* films cleverly return to earlier cinematic dystopias, but with a distinctively 21st-century edge. In their fusion of entertainment and violence, the films recall *Rollerball* and *The Running Man*, but the entertainment form at work is reality TV. In Panem, the future society in which the films are set, society is stratified into 12 'districts', all ruled over by the authoritarian Capitol. Every year, each district is required to offer up two human 'tributes' who will engage in a fight to the death with tributes from the other districts, live on television: the spectacle of extreme precarity as entertainment. In addition to engaging in the base-level struggle to stay alive, the tributes, like the participants in any other reality TV show, must also worry about how they present themselves, because the most popular of them will receive additional weapons, medical supplies and tools.

The Hunger Games is about the way in which individuals are required to collude in the commodification of their own personalities, and a mediatised logic of competition is taken to an extreme – as in *The Apprentice* and *Big Brother*, there can (normally) only be one winner. Yet the Capitol's dependence on media also makes it vulnerable to attack, something exploited in the second film, *Catching Fire* (2013), in which the revolutionary insurrection begins with an attack on the televisual spectacle. The massive success of the *Hunger Games* films shows that the dystopian imagination remains powerful. Do the rebellions against the Capitol presage revolts against capital in the world outside the cinema? We must wait and see. ●

SILENT RUNNING: EARLY SCI-FI CINEMA

by Bryony Dixon

Cinema's greatest attribute may be to show us reality, but its greatest trick is to show us the imaginary. Visualising the impossible has been one of the great drivers of development in film across the century-and-a-bit of its existence, leading to ever-more convincing evocations of the future. Science fiction and film were closely associated from the beginning. The incorporation of science in envisioning fictional future worlds in 19th-century writing, most notably by Jules Verne and H. G. Wells, was given a tremendous boost by the arrival of film in the 1890s.

Even before the first commercial film shows in 1895 and early 1896, plans were afoot to use moving image to show scientifically possible (if improbable) futures. In 1894, as soon as H.G. Wells's *The Time Machine* was published in serial form, R.W. Paul and Wells had discussed an entertainment – a so-called 'dark ride' – which took an audience on a journey based on the book, combining moving image, oscillating seats, wind machines and lighting effects to visualise the future. The 'conductor' would then pretend to 'overshoot' on the return journey, taking the audience into the past.

The most famous early science-fiction film, Georges Méliès's *A Trip to the Moon* (1902) also derived from a 'ride' of the same name, first shown at the Pan-American Exposition in Buffalo in 1901, as well as including elements of Jules Verne's *From the Earth to the Moon* (1865), Jacques

R.W. Paul's 'The ? Motorist' (1906)

Offenbach's stage operetta inspired by Verne's story, and Wells's *The First Men in the Moon* (1901). Film proper, when it arrived, proved uniquely able to deliver science-fiction stories. With their ability to portray, with greater 'realism', otherworldly landscapes, alien creatures, and their use of rudimentary special effects, film adaptations were a game-changing improvement on the stage and fairground versions of these works.

Initially science fiction in film had much in common with what we would now distinguish as 'fantasy' – that is, a story in which the agency of change or transformation is magical rather than scientific – and they shared space typically in short comedies and trick films. Trips to space and the planets in films such as Méliès's *Le Voyage a travers l'impossible* (1904) and R.W. Paul's *The ? Motorist* (1906) overlapped with fantasy, with 'space' as just another setting.

Georges Méliès's 'Le Voyage a travers l'impossible' (1904)

Comedies involving scientific inventions – imagined or real – abounded; an early example, G.A. Smith's *The X-Rays* (1897), in which we see a couple reduced to their bones, exploited the X-ray mania sweeping the media at that time. Other comedies imagined scientific innovations not yet invented, such as in *La Vie intense* (1910), in which a scientist produces a test-tube baby who, due to miscalculation, lives a massively accelerated life (cradle to grave in six minutes, only bettered by the banned X-Box advert *Champagne* of 2002, which did it in 52 seconds). All kinds of things we now associate with science fiction can be traced back to such silent comedies: invisible men, robots, gigantism, miniaturisation, cryogenics, anti-gravity devices, rockets, space travel, aliens, time travel and so on.

As films became more sophisticated, science-fiction ideas moved into adventure serials, dramas and animation and later, feature films. An increasingly serious tone expressed contemporary anxieties about the future: the development of airborne machines dispensing death from the skies was seen in *The Airship Destroyer* (1909); catastrophes from space in films such as *Halley's Comet* (1910), which deals with human survivalism in as bleak a way as many a later post-apocalyptic film; and the end of the world was portrayed in *Ever Been Had?* (1917), an ostensibly light animation that shows us a glimpse of an imagined future during the darkest days of World War I, where humankind has fought itself to the last man and where sentient tanks roll over the ruins of London in scenes that anticipate *The Terminator* (1984).

World War I of course left innumerable psychic scars, and in the films made during the fighting and in its aftermath the emergence of several dystopian science-fiction tropes can be traced: unstoppable robots in André Deed's *L'uomo meccanico* (*The Mechanical Man*, 1921); soulless men in Stellan Rye and Paul Wegener's *The Student of Prague* (1913); man-made monsters such as *The Golem* (1920); and capitalism gone mad in the greatest of all the silent science-fiction films, Fritz Lang's *Metropolis* (1927), in which the majority of mankind is enslaved by the machine city while the elite play with their advanced technological toys.

Film in the late silent period was a test-

Maurice Elvey's 'High Treason' (1929)

André Deed's 'L'uomo meccanico' (1921)

René Clair's 'Paris qui dort' (1925)

bed of ideas for societies of the future; British director Maurice Elvey's *High Treason* (1929) was unusually prescient in predicting a world of continental alliances threatened by terrorists and controlled by arms dealers, with an aerial attack on New York skyscrapers and the blowing up of the Channel Tunnel (which wouldn't be opened for another 65 years). *High Treason* had its lighter, more utopian side, with a progressive society (even a really wacky idea: gender equality!) and a plethora of gadgets such as all-over dryer attachments in the shower and videophones.

Likewise French director René Clair's wonderful *Paris qui dort* (aka *The Crazy Ray*, 1925), which played with the idea of a city frozen in time by a paralysing ray, providing delicious opportunities for the few survivors to help themselves to everything in the shops – scenes that anticipate films such as *The Omega Man* (1971) or *28 Days Later* (2002).

Aesthetically too, science-fiction cinema and TV of today owes a debt to the silent film days, in which we see the first glimpses of shiny futuristic clothing with lots of metallic strapping, silver lamé and asymmetric styles. From the imaginative costume design of Soviet director Yakov Protazanov's *Aelita: Queen of Mars* (1924), *Metropolis* or *High Treason* to the iconic outfits seen in *Star Trek* is not such a giant leap.

Finally, there is one more link between science fiction and silent cinema that is becoming ever more pronounced. As cinema advances ever further towards making visions of our possible futures more 'realistic', watching early film (such as the non-fiction films of Mitchell & Kenyon) increasingly functions as a form of time travel. As the distance increases between us and a distant past that is recorded in moving images, that great attribute film has – of showing reality – can evoke the same feeling strived for by science-fiction film in its depictions of the future: convincing immersion in another place and time. ●

The cinema of catastrophe

by John Clute

It may be a bridge too far to claim that the catastrophe-raddled 20th century and cinema were born for each other, but it might be worth reiterating a truism: that the apocalyptic eventfulness of the 20th century profoundly shaped the most significant artform to have been born within it. Cinema could not have so rapidly become a viable commercial medium without a spectacular world to record, and from 1900 onwards the residents of this planet have not been short of inspiring spectacle (catastrophe is spectacle wrought to its uttermost). So the world can be said to have, in a sense, *enabled* cinema.

Later in the century, and even more in our current age, a reverse flow can be detected – that the cinema of catastrophe enables real-life disasters to come. This intuition is most plausible when the rapidly increasing repertoire of science-fiction films is taken into account: nowadays film catastrophes tend to anticipate – and perhaps actually to shape – the anguishes and disasters that daily scar our planet. A film like *Independence Day* (1996), whose comedic exuberance almost seems to forgive in advance the death of billions in Manhattan and elsewhere, cannot exactly have shaped the terrorist assault on Manhattan just five years later, but for anyone familiar with movie catastrophes in the 20th century, the terror and shock of witnessing 9/11 must have been accompanied by a terrible sense of recognition.

Last men standing

But planetary terrors do not appear until we begin to be able actually to imagine a planet at risk. Before a time very roughly datable as *circa* 1800, the human imagination, as housed in the West, tended to restrict the felt compass of what could be envisioned or literally *seen* to what one might call the world itself: a stage as encompassing as the air we breathe, but like air, invisible. The ingredients for a new perspective had been brewing together for very many years. Astronomy and geology and biology and physics bore potentially estranging messages. And although globes had existed from the time of Mercator, a significant change can be detected when, in *The Ruins* (1791), the French philosopher Comte de Volney (1757-1820) is able to imagine his spirit yoicked into actual orbit, where it observes the planet spinning beneath him. What then happens is bad science and good spectacle (some things never change): the faster Volney spins around the planet, the deeper into the future he is able to gaze. It is a future full of event. Empires rise and fall. Great catastrophes topple civilisations. It is the next thing to the movies.

The sheer number of crises endured by the human race over the past century does warrant and perhaps explain our attentiveness to the cinema of disaster, over and above the pleasures of vicarious calamity. But a genuinely good disaster needs to threaten the planet. Volney starts the ball rolling with his extremely popular text, but we do not really begin to experience the end of the world in fiction or other arts for several decades after *The Ruins* was published; and most catastrophes of this sort tended not to be depicted directly. (We will speak of the Biblical Flood in due course.)

Though Mary Shelley's Frankenstein Monster seems quite capable of creating a revolutionary new world, as many critics have recently noticed, she is content to bid him farewell as he disappears around the curve of the planet into Arctic mists, his destiny (and ours) unknown. (Sadly, no *Frankenstein* film yet made addresses his world-changing potential.) Shelley's own planetary disaster tale, *The Last Man* (1826) was itself never directly filmed until a little-seen, low-budget adaptation by James Arnett in 2008, though her visionary description of a last survivor

trekking through the deserted, demolished streets of London is the primal source for every subsequent film to depict a similar scene, the first of these probably being Felix E. Feist's *Deluge* (1933), loosely based on British author S. Fowler Wright's 1928 novel, but with events moved from London to New York, followed by many other examples such as Ranald MacDougall's *The World, the Flesh and the Devil* (1959), starring Harry Belafonte, and very loosely inspired by M.P. Shiel's classic 1901 novel of global apocalypse, *The Purple Cloud*, and Val Guest's *The Day the Earth Caught Fire* (1961), whose prelude in a depopulated London has haunted viewers ever since; and whose ominous, gritty documentary verisimilitude – not to mention global warmind parallels – still evokes a sense of planetary terminus. Its continuing influence can almost certainly be detected in 21st-century releases such as Danny Boyle's *28 Days Later* (2002).

But with the honourable exceptions, most films of this sort seem to avoid action rather than augur its effects. They do not depict the catastrophe. Philosophical (or at least brooding) conversations tend to be featured, lectures and musings on the nature of the catastrophe: all of which may be estimable, but which seems to make inadequate use of the film medium. Arnett's aforementioned *The Last Man* in fact takes off more closely from Richard Matheson's *I Am Legend* (1954). The result is dispiriting. (Zombie apocalypses are for the most part poor relations of the genuine catastrophe film, depending almost entirely upon splatter effects on aftermath survivors, rather than upon argument, however weak.)

When we return to the real beginning of the 20th century, which is to say as soon as World War I begins to transform the Western world, we return to the heart of the matter: a present-tense vision of our world at risk. The cinema of 1914 and later, with its rapidly evolving technical facility, was well designed to dramatise and exploit the new world, and to envision apocalypse now. The first great catastrophe film appears almost immediately. Though it ostensibly depicts 'only' the fall of Babylon, the scenes of apocalyptic demolition that climax D.W. Griffith's *Intolerance* (1916) are a synecdoche for the demolition of the known world, in front of our eyes.

Griffith was much influenced by the work of the most cinematic (and nakedly entrepreneurial) painter of the 19th century, John Martin (1789-1854), in particular *Belshazzar's Feast* (first version 1820), which Griffith replicated directly in his spectacular orgy sequence – maybe

(Previous page)
New York lies in ruins in Felix E. Feist's 'Deluge' (1933).

(Above)
Cillian Murphy wakes to find London deserted in Danny Boyle's '28 Days Later' (2002).

(Below, left)
Will Smith as the last man in Robert Neville's adaptation of 'I Am Legend' (2007).

(Below, right)
Edward Judd walks through a deserted London in 'The Day the Earth Caught Fire' (1961).

(Above)
Harry Belafonte wanders
alone through deserted
New York streets in Ranald
MacDougall's 'The World, the
Flesh and the Devil' (1959).

not the first orgy to prelude and morally justify scenes of terminal disaster, but certainly a template sedulously followed by almost every filmmaker ever since. (It is almost certainly under Martin's influence that the Babylon sections of *Intolerance* in the four-tint original version are given a conspicuous reddish aura: as of the fire to come.)

Much of Griffith's film is, of course, set in the deep past. The actual holocaust of World War I, for political and cultural reasons, and because the extent of the disaster of the Western Front only slowly became recognised, was not so much visualised as heard in our bones. We still hear World War I somewhere deep inside, deeper than plummet sounds. A sense that we live on a planet where something dreadful has happened that we cannot quite visualise may help us grasp the emotional power of 20th-century disaster films, in which the actual events of the past 100 years are displaced into cartoon catastrophes that shake us deeply. It is not simply that a visual medium like film does destruction better than peace; the truth is that the most garish Hollywood spectacle, in which a cardboard California is inundated, tells something more radically true about the human race than any number of art films.

The main exception may be the astonishing *La Jetée* (1962) by Chris Marker, where the destruction of the West is conveyed in a sequence of still shots, the rest being a deeply tragic prolepsis of aftermath. As with that extraordinarily influential film – Terry Gilliam's *Twelve Monkeys* (1995) standing out by being an explicit homage – 20th-century disaster movies almost certainly needed to gain distance on the unendurable through a tense change in the narratives of the West first found in

(Top)
Catastrophe comes by stealth
as the Pod people take over
in Don Siegel's 'Invasion of
the Body Snatchers' (1956).

(Above)
Based on H.G. Wells's novel,
'Things to Come' (1936) vividly
anticipated the destruction
of the coming World War II.

(Opposite, top)
The poster for Byron Haskin's
'The War of the Worlds' (1953),
which relocates the events of
H.G. Wells's story to California.

(Opposite, bottom)
Catastrophes in British cinema,
as in Steve Sekely's adaptation
of 'The Day of the Triffids'
(1963), are typically visualised
with less grand spectacle
than Hollywood productions.

science fiction (indeed as long ago as Volney's tract): futures that could be lived in. A film such as August Blom's *The End of the World* (*Verdens Undergang*, 1916), though it clearly responds to real (but unmentionable) contemporary terrors, depends on an arbitrary comet to wreak destruction worldwide some time hence. A later film, Abel Gance's *End of the World* (*La Fin du monde*, 1931), of which no uncut English-subtitled version exists, also makes use of a comet some day soon – though this time a sententious moral is drawn: the comet has come to purge Earth of sin.

Gance based his film (very roughly) on Camille Flammarion's *La Fin du monde* (1894); as far as English-language cinema is concerned, acknowledged retrofittings of 19th-century literary tales of disaster seem almost exclusively restricted to versions of H.G. Wells's scientific romances, primarily *The War of the Worlds* (1898). The most famous version of Wells's story – after Orson Welles's radio broadcast of 1938 – is Byron Haskin's 1953 adaptation, which relocates events to California, the home of special effects and backlots. One reason for the difference between UK and American catastrophe films, certainly in the second half of the century, may be as simple as this. Britain, being set at the heart of a four-season temperate zone, where change is slow and the Earth recovers itself annually, is a fit venue for aftermath tales such as John Wyndham's *The Day of the Triffids* (adapted for cinema and television several times) or John Christopher's *No Blade of Grass* (adapted by Cornel Wilde in 1970) – movies in which tinpot gangsters and marauders are cheap synecdoches for spectacles of collapse.

Southern California, on the other hand, is located smack in the middle of a desiccated geological and climate zone where violent change is normal – with the effects of drought and flood and volcanic action and earthquakes and innumerable tornadoes everywhere visible. The landscape that houses Hollywood is *already* a catastrophe, as Mike Davis argues in his brilliant *Ecology of Fear: Los Angeles and the Imagination of Disaster* (1998), which includes descriptions of backlot film after film. A California backlot today is a snapshot of the world tomorrow. A film like *Them!* (1954) could not have been filmed in England; and Haskins's *War of the Worlds* seems also to occupy a venue almost uniquely designed to permit images of a convulsed world on the cheap.

The uses to which Wells's great minatory tale have been put neatly demonstrate some of the transformations in the understanding of catastrophe over the last century. The original text of the novel clearly presents the Martian invasion as an analogue of British imperialism, and his English cast is no more successful at fending off Martians than non-high-tech Africans were when forced to face modern artillery, which must have seemed Martian to them. Welles's 1938 radio version is a parable of a world waiting for the next war, one which will surely make World War I seem local; it is a central model for the 'dreadful warning' catastrophe film, in which catastrophe assaults a world unworthy through its unpreparedness.

Haskins for his part presents his Martians as equivalent to treacherous Cold War Russians in our midst, and his Americans as culpably ill-prepared to defend their homeland against this infection. It is part of a cluster of Cold War films – of which Don Siegel's *Invasion of the Body Snatchers* (1956) is the *locus classicus* – in which catastrophe is something that comes by stealth (in Philip Kaufman's 1978 remake it might be fair to define 'catastrophe' not as the Red menace but as 'late capitalism'). But when we reach Steven Spielberg's version of *War of the Worlds* (2005), we find almost a return to Wells's *fin de siècle* pessimism, for it is a typically 21st century attempt to supply catastrophe with an understory so abyssal and massive that contemporary politics seem to be froth on the

daydream. Spielberg's film returns in spirit to the opening paragraph of Wells's novel, in which *Homo sapiens* are envisioned as being scrutinised, "perhaps as narrowly as a man with a microscope might scrutinise the transient creatures that swarm and multiply in a drop of water."

After his great scientific romances of the 19th century, Wells wrote one further catastrophe text that influenced the cinema. *The Shape of Things to Come* – filmed faithfully by William Cameron Menzies as *Things to Come* (1936) – vividly depicts the disaster of World War II, which Wells presciently describes as beginning in 1940 with a German invasion of Poland. But this film spawned no immediate successors. For obvious reasons, there would be no further movies depicting the destruction of civilization due to World War II until well after the conflict ended. Humphrey Jennings's great quasi-documentary *The Silent Village* (1942) is an allegory of the Nazi atrocity at Lidice, Czechoslovakia, retold as if it happened in Wales. Only later would we see a film like Kevin Brownlow's *It Happened Here* (1965), which depicts the alternative future of a Nazi-ruled UK.

A further problem with *Things to Come* lies in Wells's preoccupation with the inevitability of a World State. This shifts the second half of Menzies's film into a saga of reconstruction: a mistake very few catastrophe films repeated. Hope may be expressed about rebuilding a new civilisation (or, in American terms, reuniting a family), but only if that hope is restricted to the very last sequences of a film. A rainbow or two may blush demurely in

(Above)
One of a series of stills
that depict the collapse of
civilisation in Chris Marker's
'La Jetée' (1962).

(Below, left)
Viggo Mortensen and Kodi
Smit-McPhee as father
and son in John Hillcoat's
adaptation of Cormac
McCarthy's 'The Road' (2009).

(Below, right)
Stanley Kubrick's fierce
satire of the nuclear threat
'Dr Strangelove, Or: How I
Learned to Stop Worrying
and Love the Bomb' (1964).

the middle distance, as in Darren Aronofsky's *Noah* (2014), after the Deluge has dramatically washed the planet clean except for Noah and his children. But these are films of the 21st century, where any requisite sign of hope for the future tends to be heavily ironised. The last moments of *Noah* do little to counter Noah's conviction that familial love for his grandchildren – whom he had needed (but was unable) to kill in order to prevent humanity from spreading again – has simply doomed the planet to more catastrophes. Perhaps this is the exact world of constant crisis we now inhabit, if the film's ominous prologue, with its CGI vision of a dystopian near-future city about to bite the dust after despoiling the world, is to be taken literally.

Both *The War of the Worlds* and *Noah*, which are closely based on books (or Book) with a message, convey a clear sense of the blameful inadequacy of the human species to cope with disaster – and *Noah* is explicit that the Deluge is a punishment. These films stand at the end of a long tradition in catastrophe cinema *not* to envision terminal disaster as due to anything as savagely impersonal as the blind malice of the universe, or as realistic and likely as human error, the two honourable exceptions being Sidney Lumet's *Fail-Safe* (1964) and Stanley Kubrick's *Dr. Strangelove, or: How I Learned to Stop Worrying and Love the Bomb* (1964), though much of the power of the latter lies in its comic-inferno refusal to exculpate anyone from complicity in the inevitable apocalypse, whose effect on viewers may be all the greater because the end of things only begins to happen, abstractly, as the film closes. But these films, along with *La Jetée*, are exceptions because they present human nature as culpable but not exactly *blamable*.

New dawns

The habit of creating a film universe governed by blame may represent some covert disquiet about the true century of disasters lying beneath the plenitude of faked disasters we now face – more than can be described, almost more of them than can even be listed. In American movies, blame for the disaster itself – a comet, an invasion, a plague, a flood, a Godzilla from the depths – can normally be laid at someone's door; though the final sequence, in which a nuclear family is saved, can seem almost cheery. In British films, the aftermath of disaster – ecological decay, balkanised tinpot tyrannies, dystopias – is similarly addressable in terms implying moral judgement.

Indeed, on reflecting upon a century of disasters, it is impossible to

reduce (or elevate) the end of the world into an impersonal visitation of natural law. For nearly a century now, no volcano has destroyed an innocent city; no monster has got away with some monstrous version of the *acte gratuit* and just simply demolished the set: King Kong falls off the tower; Godzilla is driven back into the deep waters; James Bond's foes need to fail just short of the end of the world.

A very rare exception is Stanley Kramer's 1959 film version of Nevil Shute's novel *On the Beach*, in which, though the cast is alive at the end, what one might call a planetary doom continues to descend in the form of an inevitable progression of radiation-bearing winds into the southern hemisphere. This is singularly tough-minded; elsewhere, it all seems too easy somehow. After a century of self-censorship about the nature of a hard-rain real world where history happens, our catastrophe films continue to allegorise us out of Dodge City; we are still burdened with all too many movies in which spring-heeled narrative leaps carry us into an unargued happy ending (even *Dr. Strangelove* implies a morally reversed form of survival, though its savage guying of an anthemic song of hope puts it all in perspective). Villains do not win in movies, unless a sequel is in the offing. The world does not end, unless a flower can be seen to bloom in some crack – the binding distinction between Cormac McCarthy's *The Road* (2006) and John Hillcoat's 2009 adaptation is that the book ends bracingly, without hope, opening our eyes to what may befall us, and the movie ends with a bromidic hint of continuance. The moment near the end of *WALL-E* (2008) when human beings, inspired by the love between two robot critters, begin to restore the Earth to which they have returned, tells us no more than that another movie, which is right now telling us another lie, is about to end.

So, we need catastrophe films for several reasons, because they provide the most natural-seeming excuses for cinema to cloak us in the spectacular. But more importantly, because they seem to talk to us about the real world we are forced to inhabit, but in truth talk about almost anything but. Which is to say we need catastrophe films because they console us. ●

BETWEEN TWO WORLDS: SCI-FI LITERATURE AND CINEMA

by Graham Sleight

Shortly after the death in 1982 of Philip K. Dick, the sf writer Thomas M. Disch wrote a memorial poem for him entitled Cantata '82'. Disch wondered whether, at Dick's funeral, there would be a wreath from "the studio that did its level best/ To level his best book". Dick's "best book" was *Do Androids Dream of Electric Sheep?* (1968), filmed as *Blade Runner* (1982), and Disch's acid remark exposes a paradox. On the one hand, science-fiction film has brought many tropes and ideas from written sf to far greater prominence than they would otherwise have. On the other, sf film is often accused of dumbing down the nuances of the written works – whether in direct adaptations or more generally. *Blade Runner* is perhaps the most-discussed sf film ever, yet it's also very significantly different from the source text, in ways some admirers of the original find difficult to stomach.

In some cases, such transformations are almost understandable. Dick, for instance, was often a chronicler of the lives of those defeated by the world; his story *The Minority Report* (1956) begins as follows: "The first thought Anderton had when he saw the young man was that he was: *I'm getting bald. Bald and fat and old.*" When this story was turned into a movie with Tom Cruise as Anderton, those words were unlikely to remain applicable. To take another example, Harlan Ellison has achieved acclaim both as a sf writer and a screenwriter. He wrote the teleplay for *The City on the Edge of Forever* (1967), perhaps the most acclaimed episode of the original *Star Trek* series. Yet he was so incensed by the rewrites forced on him by the producers that he eventually republished his screenplay with a 45-page introduction explaining the whole saga. Similarly, he produced a remarkably thoughtful screenplay adaptation of Isaac Asimov's 'Robot' stories; but its *Citizen Kane*-influenced flashback structure bore no resemblance to what was eventually made into the 2004 movie *I, Robot*.

It has to be said that direct adaptations of sf novels do not always succeed. David Lynch's *Dune* (1984) was, famously, a commercial disaster although it arguably preserved the strangeness of Frank Herbert's imagined world. Kevin Costner's self-directed adaptation of David Brin's *The Postman* (1997) was, if anything, even less successful. But for every example of this kind, there are reasonably faithful, thoughtful adaptations of sf works that are generally considered to succeed in their own terms – for instance, *Never Let Me Go* (2010), *The Handmaid's Tale* (1990), or *Children of Men* (2006). A special case of a screenplay being developed by a sf writer working closely with a director is *2001: A Space Odyssey* (1968), considered by Stephen Baxter elsewhere in this volume. Equally, some less faithful adaptations of sf originals, like Paul Verhoeven's *Starship Troopers* (1997) apply a new spin to their source and create a work that finds an interested public.

However, the line from written sf to the filmed version can't only be followed in

Francesca Annis, Kyle Maclachlan and Frank Herbert on the set of 'Dune' (1984)

'Blade Runner' (1982) differs significantly from its source, Philip K. Dick's book 'Do Androids Dream of Electric Sheep?' (1968)

direct adaptations of works. There are numerous examples of filmed sf taking its lead – more or less directly – from predecessors in the written word. For instance, one of the first widely popular works in the US sf pulp tradition was a series of stories by A.E. van Vogt, following the adventures of the crew of the *Space Beagle*. Beginning with *The Black Destroyer* (1939), these stories chronicled the adventures of a spaceship whose crew was tasked with understanding alien life in the galaxy – much like the crew of Darwin's *Beagle*. The episodic format, and its wide potential for different kinds of stories, were acknowledged sources for the original *Star Trek*. Similarly, the inventor-heroes of Jules Verne and H.G. Wells are clear ancestors of *Doctor Who*. Sometimes influences can be argued to be more specific: Ellison claimed that James Cameron's *The Terminator* (1984) drew from works of his including an episode of *The Outer Limits* entitled 'Soldier' (1964). Following a legal dispute around this issue, later prints of Cameron's film carry a credit acknowledging Ellison's work.

Influence is not a one-way street, either. As an example, from the mid-1980s, a strain of large-scale 'new space opera' began

to emerge in British written sf – initially in the work of the late Iain M. Banks, and subsequently through younger writers such as Alastair Reynolds. This subgenre took unalloyed kinetic joy in, for instance, the idea of vast spaceships battling – the writing was much more visual than in previous British works. It's surely a kind of writing that was enabled by the visual possibilities of *Star Wars* and its successors.

Apart from Ellison, there have been a few writers who have made their home in the worlds of both sf and Hollywood. Perhaps the most striking example is Leigh Brackett, who helped establish the template for the first wave of space opera fiction in the 1940s and 50s. At the same time, she began work as a Hollywood screenwriter, assisting William Faulkner with the screenplay for

'The City on the Edge of Forever' (1967)

The Big Sleep (1946). She subsequently continued to work with Howard Hawks, writing or co-writing films such as *Rio Bravo* (1959) and *El Dorado* (1966). The last work she undertook before her death in 1978 was to prepare the first-draft screenplay for *The Empire Strikes Back* (1980) – a return to the roots of her writing.

Careers like Brackett's, though, are very much the exception rather than the rule. Science fiction writers and those who work on sf movies tend to be two distinct groups. Arguably, both fields are the poorer for this. There are many fine sf works that might well make striking movies; and the lessons of film pacing and editing could have a much fuller impact on written sf. Indeed, it's striking that there are a number of figures who have had this kind of dual career in the fantasy rather than the sf field, such as Clive Barker, Neil Gaiman, and George R.R. Martin. Perhaps there is something specific about the disciplines of sf writing that makes the transition between the two difficult. It's very striking, for instance, how much Russell T. Davies talked about eschewing the overtly 'sci-fi' in his revival of *Doctor Who*. Maybe, in the end, written and visual sci-fi are two different worlds. ●

Visions of wonder
by Helen Lewis

"We used to look up in the sky and wonder at our place in the stars," says Cooper, the lead character in Christopher Nolan's *Interstellar* (2014), in the film's third trailer. "Now we look down and worry about our place in the dirt."

It's an intriguing statement, given the pessimism of Nolan's career so far: the jumbled lowlife world of *Memento* (2000), the guilt-ridden hallucinations of *Insomnia* (2002), and the bleak vision of a modern metropolis in the Batman films. But it could also stand as a comment on the progress of science fiction over the last century. Where once we dreamed of building utopias, now we are obsessed with the possibility of losing what we already have. *Interstellar* bucks the downbeat trend; although it is set in a future where food shortages have crippled the earth, the trailer ends with its lead character offering hope: "We'll find a way. We always have."

Cooper's statement gets to the heart of one of science fiction's fundamental questions: is this as good as it gets? Is our planet a rare oasis in a hostile universe, at risk of attack from extraterrestrials that will treat us much like we treat lower species here on earth? Or is space, the final frontier – a place of mystery and opportunity – something to aim for and marvel at?

In *Interstellar*, Christopher Nolan seems to be intent on recapturing some of the wonder that used to be attached to the idea of space travel. It is a return to the ideas Tom Wolfe explored in his 1960s essays about test pilots and early astronauts. Going into space is terrifying, of course, but also exhilarating. (Wolfe coined the phrase "post-orbital remorse" to explain how walking on the moon is such a transcendent experience that nothing else can ever quite match up to it.)

In this vision, it is only by leaving earth that you can truly appreciate it. If you talk to astronauts they will happily recount the times they spent staring out of the window. "It was always different, always amazing," said Tom Jones, who flew four space shuttle missions between 1994 and 2001. Commander Chris Hadfield, whose version of 'Space Oddity' went viral on YouTube, lived through many minor re-enactments of *Gravity* (2013) as pieces of debris hit the International Space Station. "Yeah, I've heard one ricochet off the window," he told me. "It's an interesting reminder of where you are in the shooting gallery. You see the holes, like a little bullet hole." With a level of laconic understatement only available to those with NASA training, he added: "That was interesting."

In cinema, space often stands in for the unknown. So the attitudes of writers and directors towards it becomes a useful proxy for whether the prevailing mood is optimistic or pessimistic. In *2001: A Space Odyssey* (1968) – released a year before Neil Armstrong and Buzz Aldrin landed on the Moon – conquering space is represented as the final step on a great human journey, one that started with apes scratching in the dirt. Although we might have to contend with murderous computers when we get there, space is our destiny.

Nine years later, that mood of wonder is still evident in Steven Spielberg's *Close Encounters of the Third Kind*; yes, the aliens might have indulged in a little light abduction, but they kept all their abductees safe – not even allowing them to age – and were a dab hand at the Clavinova. The aliens are so benign that the film ends with a human willingly stepping aboard the Mothership, a spangly light-covered disc that puts the viewer in mind of a Las Vegas nightclub chandelier. The film dwells lovingly on it, and the little aliens that emerge, as well as on the faces of the scientists. They are overawed by this experience: we are supposed to be too.

Contrast that with the vision of space in Duncan Jones's 2009 film *Moon*. Here, space is *boring*. Sam Bell is a lonely office drone; it's just that he is trapped on a sterile lunar base instead

(Above)
Brand (Anne Hathaway)
in Christopher Nolan's
'Interstellar' (2014), which
attempts to recapture
the sense of wonder
at space travel.

(Previous page)
Roy Neary (Richard Dreyfuss)
boards the alien Mothership
at the climax of Steven
Spielberg's 'Close Encounters
of the Third Kind' (1977).

(Below)
Roy Neary (Richard Dreyfuss)
looks to the sky in amazement
in 'Close Encounters of
the Third Kind' (1977).

of inside an open-plan cubicle. What's more, he is – even more than most of us under capitalism – literally replaceable.

James Cameron's *Avatar*, released the same year, offers a sweeping vision of a lush tropical world inhabited by nine-foot-tall Navi, but its core is still pessimistic. Humans have only ended up on Pandora because they have exhausted their own planet; given an opportunity to start again, their leaders still want to put profit above the lives of indigenous people. The strangeness of the setting serves to highlight a fundamental truth about human nature: we are greedy and destructive. (Shades of Agent Smith in *The Matrix* (1999): "Human beings are a disease, a cancer of this planet. You're a plague and we are the cure.")

Paradise lost

One way that wonder is rarely used now is in the context of utopian visions – an idea that, with rare exceptions such as *Star Trek* and Iain M. Banks's 'Culture' novels – has fallen out of fashion. If asked to name great dystopian fiction of the 20th or 21st century, the examples come tripping off the tongue: *Children of Men, The Hunger Games, Battle Royale, Divergent, The Handmaid's Tale, Tank Girl*. Narrow it down only to films with a number in the title and you can still get into your stride: *1984, 28 Days Later, Fahrenheit 451, Twelve Monkeys*. But utopias? That's much harder.

Partly this reflects a change in how we see ourselves. Thomas More's *Utopia* presented a humanist society as a reproach to his Renaissance contemporaries; Bacon's *New Atlantis* was designed to show the benefits of the scientific method. Edward Bellamy's *Looking Backward: 2000-1887* – a runaway bestseller when it was published in 1888 – inspired a political movement and a rash of sequels championing the idea of socialist paradises. Unfortunately, this burgeoning optimism was badly bruised by collision with reality: the rise of Communism in the early 20th century showed the world what collectivism and a planned economy could become. Suddenly, the bland conformity of utopias seemed oppressive, rather than merely troubling: being ordered to be happy makes unhappiness an act of political resistance. Our civilisation seems fragile now, precarious; "the end of history" turned out not to be the triumph of Western liberal democracy, but more of the same old grievances and secular conflicts. We also might run out of oil, or water; and we have biological, chemical and nuclear weapons that can cause destruction on a scale that was unthinkable in the time of Francis Bacon or Jules Verne.

But the turn against utopia was also caused by another simple problem: if drama is conflict, then utopias are inherently static – and therefore boring. (As the American essayist Roxane Gay puts it: "Perfection lacks texture".) In the absence of drama, all the artist can do is create a sense of wonder; but as anyone who has been on a long guided tour of a museum can tell you, our deposits of awe are quickly mined.

Many early utopian narratives involve little more than a traveller arriving in a strange land, where a helpful native unloads paragraph after paragraph of exposition. This means even the most intellectually interesting examples – such as Charlotte Perkins Gilman's feminist epic *Herland* – struggle to work as fiction. In the early 20th century, H.G. Wells tried to invoke wondrous visions of the future with several novels, including *The First Men in the Moon* (1901) and *A Modern Utopia* (1905), but they never struck a chord with readers in the way the blighted Morlocks in *The Time Machine* (1895) or the invading Martians in *The War of the Worlds* (1897) did. "Horror stories are easier to write than gay, exalting stories," he wrote in 1934. And by that point, Wells didn't even want to try any more – looking at the rise of Hitler in Germany, he was "tired of talking in playful parables to a world engaged in destroying itself".

And if holding the audience's attention is an issue with literature, where authors have the luxury of raining down exposition on the reader as a substitute for plot, even if they really, really shouldn't – then with cinema, there really is nowhere to hide.

What many directors have found is that the best way to deploy wonder in their films is to make it a counterpoint to a story that otherwise relies on fear and suspense to drive it forward. Think of the lingering zero-G shots in *Gravity*, showing the utter strangeness of a setting without a force we take completely for granted: they turn a relatively simple story into an epic struggle.

Shock and awe

This is film's advantage over literature: where written texts have to describe what you should be amazed by, cinema can make it a casual backdrop to the "real action". Here is Arthur Conan Doyle describing the explorers' first sight of dinosaurs in *The Lost World*: "There were, as I say, five of them, two being adults and three young ones. Even the babies were as big as elephants… I do not know that I can bring their appearance home to you better than by saying that they looked like monstrous kangaroos, twenty feet in length, with skins like black crocodiles."

Conan Doyle is hobbled twice over: first, by having to resort to existing creatures in order to describe something strange and new; second, by having his characters speak at all. We assume that a sign of being truly awestruck is to be speechless: look out for how many shots of upturned faces, bathed in eerie light, there are in *Close Encounters*. Wonder is wordless.

Or compare *The Lost World* with the 1993 film *Jurassic Park*, adapted from Michael Crichton's book: in one early scene, there is a full 45 seconds of Sam Neill and Laura Dern's faces as they gaze in awe at… something. Then the camera pulls round to reveal a 30ft brachiosaurus, hooting and cropping leaves from the tops of trees. I remember seeing that film as a ten-year-old: my face probably held a similarly slack-jawed look at those groundbreaking special effects.

Again, this deployment of wonder is tactical. Gazing out over the park, to the accompaniment of a typically epic John Williams soundtrack, Dr Alan Grant realises that his earlier theoretical assumption about a smaller species of dinosaur is right: "They *do* move in herds." The story is more affecting because it is not about a greedy entrepreneur trying to create a prehistoric theme park where he can gouge you out of £20 for a locker and a souvenir photograph: Jurassic Park is built with the noblest of intentions. Its failure is a tragic, Shakespearean fall, born from hubris.

Rewatching *Jurassic Park* or *Close Encounters* now feels a little like time travel. They seem to come from a less complicated, less self-aware, less cynical time – we wouldn't just gaze in awe at the dinosaurs or the aliens any more; we'd be trying to get them in the background of a selfie. Jurassic Park would have one of those chummy corporate Twitter accounts that tries to act like your best mate when you tweet an official complaint about having your leg bitten off by a velociraptor.

In such an age, perhaps we need cinema to make the case for wonder all over again. "We've always defined ourselves by the ability to overcome the impossible," says Cooper in the first *Interstellar* trailer. "But we lost all that. Or perhaps we've just forgotten that we are still pioneers. And we've barely begun. And that our greatest accomplishments cannot be behind us, because our destiny lies above us." ●

(Above)
Groundbreaking special effects made possible the spectacular, lifelike dinosaurs in Steven Spielberg's 'Jurassic Park' (1993).

(Below)
Tim Murphy (Joseph Mazzello) gazes awestruck at a dinosaur in 'Jurassic Park' (1993).

The truth is out there

by George Watson

Society's infiltration by shadowy external forces or its manipulation by an evil ruling elite have provided some of the most unforgettable science-fiction cinema and television. The specifics may have changed from decade to decade (Cold War paranoia replaced by a growing disillusionment with governments and big business, then by other pre-millennial anxieties), but the essential truth remains the same – 'They' are out there and 'They' are running the show.

In the earliest years of the Cold War, as the House Un-American Activities Committee switched its hunt for Nazi spies to communist infiltrators with the rise of McCarthyism, Hollywood produced a series of low-budget features such as *The Red Menace* (1949) and *Invasion U.S.A.* (1952) that connected with the palpably fearful atmosphere of the times. Although wildly implausible, they were realistic in the sense that the villains were clearly human – spies, assassins or Russian soldiers in disguise – following conventional plans of subversion and conquest. Science-fiction films of that era also thrum with this paranoid energy, but the communist threat has become something far stranger and richer in its shift from the literal to the allegorical.

Instead of the recognisably alien invaders of *The Thing from Another World* (1951), *The War of the Worlds* (1953) or *Invasion of the Saucer Men* (1957), mankind also came under threat from creatures that looked just like us. In place of communist doctrine, saboteurs were recruited to the alien cause through the use of electronic implants, the resurrection of the recently dead, or simply by replacement with a compliant double. The aliens of *Invaders from Mars* (1953), *War of the Satellites* (1958) and *The Cape Canaveral Monsters* (1960) took over or replaced human beings to sabotage military rocket programmes. The hapless hosts of *The Brain Eaters* (1958), the impostors from *I Married a Monster from Outer Space* (1958) and the pod people of *Invasion of the Body Snatchers* (1956) staged a takeover bid of small-town USA, one person at a time.

In the UK, we were also under attack from cosmic fifth columnists, but the various iterations of *Quatermass* and even John Krish's *Unearthly Stranger* (1964) were far more pessimistic about the ability of our authorities to take charge and prevail against an alien invasion. Witness the armed response to the masters of the remotely controlled townsfolk of *Invaders from Mars*, and compare it with the far bleaker tone of the film adaptation of *Quatermass 2* (1957). In the former, the US Army defeats the enemy with an onslaught of tanks, bazookas and flamethrowers. In the latter, the establishment has already fallen to the invading creatures and the army is now little more than a puppet directed by the alien threat.

Many Cold War alien invasion allegories relied on a single plot point – that unwilling or unsuspecting individuals could be subverted and repurposed through the use of mind control. John Frankenheimer's *The Manchurian Candidate* (1962), based on Richard Condon's novel, dispensed with aliens and took the idea of brainwashing in a more realistic direction that explicitly recalled the forced 'confessions' made by US PoWs during the Korean War. Programmed through drugs and hypnotism to assassinate a presidential nominee, Laurence Harvey's Sergeant Raymond Shaw is a pawn in the plans of both the communists and his mother's bid to secure the presidency for her husband. Foreshadowing a decade of political assassinations, the film fuelled many of the conspiracy theories that emerged around the deaths of JFK, RFK and Martin Luther King. At various times, their killers, Lee Harvey Oswald, Sirhan Sirhan and James Earl Ray, have all been identified as 'Manchurian Candidates' by the conspiratorially minded.

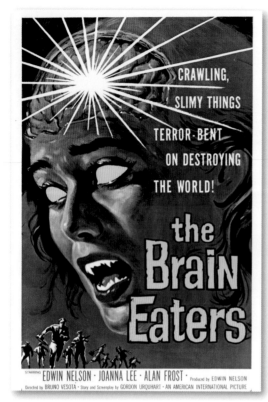

CRAWLING,
SLIMY THINGS
TERROR·BENT
ON DESTROYING
THE WORLD!

the
Brain
Eaters

STARRING EDWIN NELSON · JOANNA LEE · ALAN FROST · Produced by EDWIN NELSON
Directed by BRUNO VESOTA · Story and Screenplay by GORDON URQUHART · AN AMERICAN INTERNATIONAL PICTURE

(Previous page)
David Duchovny as Agent
Mulder and Gillian Anderson as
Agent Scully in Chris Carter's
hugely influential 'The X-Files'
(1993-2002), which weaves
every popular conspiracy into
a Grand Unified Theory.

(Above)
Alien mind-control as
allegory for communist
takeover in Bruno VeSota's
'The Brain Eaters' (1958).

From the mid 60s onwards, those already in a position of power became the new masterminds plotting to pacify the masses and quash dissent. Alien pod people were supplanted by corrupt government agencies and multinational corporations. Frankenheimer followed up *The Manchurian Candidate* with *Seconds* (1966), in which a jaded man's reinvented new life turns out to be just another cog in the self-perpetuating business model of The Company. In *The President's Analyst* (1967), The Telephone Company plans to implant Cerebrum Communicators into everybody's skulls. In the years that followed, the elderly were processed into food in *Soylent Green* (1973), the production of programmed assassins was opened to the free market in *The Parallax View* (1974), and advertising crossed the line into overt mind control in *Looker* (1981). The government faked Mars landings in *Capricorn One* (1977), covered up their interactions with aliens in *Close Encounters of the Third Kind* (1977) and pacified their citizens with rigged gladiatorial spectacles in *Rollerball* (1975).

By the 1980s, the invaders had returned, and made the conquest of these earthbound antagonists their first priority. The aliens in *V* (1983-84) only reveal their true nature as flesh-eating reptiles once they have taken control of the media and the government, created their own line of action figures and recruited an army of disaffected teenagers. The titular parasitic organism in Larry Cohen's *The Stuff* (1985) hides in plain view as a delicious, highly addictive dessert marketed by an unscrupulous food company. The most interesting film of this time is John Carpenter's *They Live* (1988), which is at once a throwback to the alien invasion narratives of the 1950s, but also dabbles with the symbols and imagery associated with the then current fears of an impending New World Order. Humankind is kept in a state of happy, unthinking compliance in a sea of subliminal messages transmitted by agents of a voracious alien corporation. Television, radio, newspapers and advertising covertly reinforce the aliens' message of obedience. In a smart rethink of the belief that dollar bills hold secret Illuminati/occult symbology, all paper money is printed with the hidden message 'This Is Your God'. Like much of the best science fiction, a serious point is being made in the guise of pulpy, B-movie entertainment. Carpenter takes issue with unthinking consumerism, the ubiquity of advertising and the growing social inequalities of Reagan-era America.

Conspiracies can often be very convoluted, complex constructions that are hard to fully explore in the length of a feature film, so here the television series can come into its own. Although there were shows that paralleled the paranoid content and concerns of the cinema of the time, such as *The Twilight Zone* (1959-64), *The Outer Limits* (1963-65) and *The Invaders* (1967-68) in the US, or Gerry Anderson's *Captain Scarlet and the Mysterons* (1967-68) and *U.F.O.* (1969-73) in the UK, they all remained largely episodic in nature. A notable early exception to this rule was *Quatermass II* (1955), later turned into a feature by Hammer, which ran for six episodes.

The full potential of the story arc was finally realised by Chris Carter's *The X-Files* (1993-2002). Embracing everything that had come before it and adding a vital injection of pre-millennial anxiety, the series became a runaway mainstream hit. The ever-more convoluted investigations of Agents Mulder and Scully managed, with varying degrees of success, to weave every popular (and sometimes downright obscure) conspiracy into a paranoid Grand Unified Theory. At least two competing groups of aliens struggled to colonise the world with the assistance of human co-conspirators and the use of mind control, genetic manipulation, implant technology and secret 'supersoldier' programmes. Flying saucer crashes, Area 51, alien abductions, alien autopsies, cattle mutilations

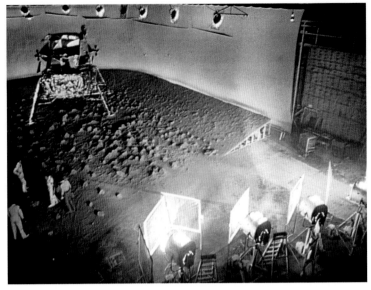

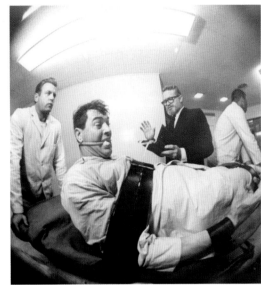

and black helicopters, all popular images of 1990s conspiracy belief, shared the same space as more traditional supernatural material such as vampires, witches and the Jersey Devil. Obscure secret projects, both real and imagined, such as Majestic 12, MK-ULTRA, Unit 731 and Operation Paperclip were namechecked and incorporated into an increasingly labyrinthine mythology. Supporting characters 'Deep Throat', 'X' and 'The Lone Gunmen' took their names from Watergate and JFK's assassination. After nine seasons, the show collapsed under the weight of its own plot twists and contradictions, but its impact on television science fiction cannot be underestimated. Without *The X-Files*, it's likely that such conspiracy-tinged fare as *Nowhere Man* (1995-96), *Dark Skies* (1996-97), *Dark Angel* (2000-02), *Warehouse 13* (2009-), *Dollhouse* (2009-10), *Lost* (2004-10) and *Fringe* (2008-13) would have had a hard time getting commissioned. In the UK, *Ultraviolet* (1998), *Invasion: Earth* (1998), *Torchwood* (2006-11), the remake of *Survivors* (2008-10), *Utopia* (2013-) and Steven Moffat-era *Doctor Who* all recall the same dark paranoia of Chris Carter's show.

When *The X-Files'* Lone Gunmen got their own eponymous spin-off series in 2001, the pilot episode, broadcast in March 2001, dealt with a plot to crash an airliner into the World Trade Center. A significant number of viewers thought that *Alternative 3* (1977), a *faux* documentary about kidnapped scientists being transported to a secret Moon base, was real, even though it was actually a rescheduled April Fool's Day hoax. To this day, more extreme conspiracy theorists still maintain that the programme contained an element of truth. Just as *The Manchurian Candidate* appeared to predict the string of assassinations in the 1960s, these seemingly coincidental intersections between fiction and reality have proven to be fertile ground for both serious research and wild conjecture.

There is one last conspiracy left to consider that skirts the border between the real world and the fictional: the films discussed here are part of a scheme to dupe us all. Bruce Rux, author of *Hollywood Vs. the Aliens: The Motion Picture Industry's Participation in UFO Disinformation*, has suggested that the film industry in both the US and the UK has been co-opted by intelligence agencies for their own nefarious purposes. It's a grand scheme that takes work as disparate as *Close Encounters of the Third Kind*, *Star Trek* (1966-) and *Plan 9 from Outer Space* (1959), and incorporates them into a plot worthy of inclusion in the Grand Unified Theory of *The X-Files*. ●

(Above, left)
Mistrust of authority was manifested in such films as 'Capricorn One' (1977), in which the government fakes a Mars landing.

(Above, right)
Rock Hudson as Antiochus Wilson, the jaded man misled by The Company in John Frankenheimer's 'Seconds' (1966).

(Below)
An alien corporation keeps unwitting humankind in a state of unthinking compliance in John Carpenter's 'They Live' (1988).

FANDOM

by Kevin Lyons

Perhaps more than any other genre, science fiction has enjoyed a fruitful and synergetic relationship with its fan base. From the early days of the Los Angeles Science Fantasy Society in the 1930s to the rise of the San Diego Comic-Con since the 1970s, from the earliest mimeographed fanzines to the advent of Kickstarter and Indiegogo as avenues for involvement, science-fiction fans have been less passive consumers than active and enthusiastic creators.

The Los Angeles Science Fantasy Society – part of Hugo Gernsback's Science Fiction League – was a hotbed of talent from its early days, numbering eager young fans like Forrest J. Ackerman, Ray Bradbury, Ray Harryhausen, Robert Heinlein and Leigh Brackett – all of whom would go on to make their names as science-fiction writers or filmmakers – among those who gathered to sing the genre's praises. In the late 1950s Bjo and John Trimble, key figures in *Star Trek* fandom in the USA, helped to revive the flagging group with a series of art shows, conventions and fashion shows. In 1967 they initiated the 'Save *Star Trek*' campaign, credited with returning the series for a third season after the NBC network threatened to cancel it following poor viewing figures for season two. It was one of the earliest and most effective examples of how 'fan power' has swayed the professionals and it would be far from the last.

From the 1930s onwards the ambitious fan's most potent weapon was the fanzine, produced in great numbers in all shapes and sizes from around the world. They ranged from letters-only publications (the analogue equivalent of today's online bulletin boards) to fiction zines where soon-to-be-famous names practised their skills. Ray Bradbury produced four issues of *Futuria Fantasia* between 1939 and 1941, and the likes of John Christopher, Harlan Ellison, Michael Moorcock, Christopher Priest, Robert Silverberg and many others published some of their earliest work in fanzines.

Producing and distributing fanzines was relatively cheap and easy – all you needed was time, a few contacts and access to spirit duplicators, mimeographs and, later, photocopiers. Other areas of the media were altogether different propositions. Films, for example, cost money and were solely the province of the professional.

Things began to change in 1965 when Eastman Kodak introduced Super 8 film, a small-gauge format that allowed budding filmmakers to shoot their own movies at a fraction of the cost of a 'real' production. It wasn't long before a generation of young fans, inspired and fuelled by Ackerman's influential *Famous Monsters of Filmland* magazine, with its captivating mix of old film stills, terrible puns and articles singing the praises of science fiction and horror

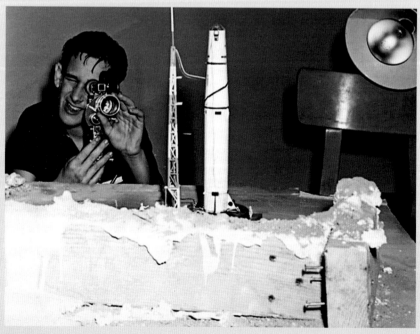

Steven Spielberg, aged 16, at work on his first science-fiction film, 'Firelight' (1963)

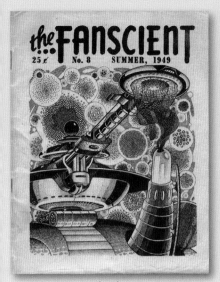

A vintage fanzine (left); A fan-written Doctor Who novel (right)

film history, were seizing the opportunity to express themselves on celluloid. Before his breakthrough with *Dark Star* (1974), a youthful John Carpenter made the likes of *Terror from Space* (1963) and *Gorgon, the Space Monster* (1969); Tim Burton practised animation on super 8 with films such as *The Stalk of the Celery Monster* (1979); Peter Jackson produced his small-gauge vision of a post-apocalyptic future in *The Valley* (1976); and the ever-ambitious Steven Spielberg shot the 140-minute science-fiction epic *Firelight* (1963), long before he reused elements of the film in *Close Encounters of the Third Kind* (1977) and *E.T. the Extra-Terrestrial* (1982).

Analogue video replaced 8mm in the 1980s and 90s, leading to a glut of shot-on-video backyard epics, many of which received legitimate video releases, among them *Death Run* (1987), *Things* (1989) and *Feeders* (1996). The subsequent arrival of digital video in the 2000s opened up whole new vistas for the wannabe Hollywood mogul. Soon anyone with a smartphone, a handful of apps and a Vimeo account could create and distribute their own films – many of them as polished as anything their Hollywood counterparts were making.

Television has traditionally proved a harder nut to crack for aspiring fans wanting to forge a career, but they still have opportunities to exert influence. The letter-writing campaign that saved *Star Trek* was echoed by fans of Joss Whedon's *Firefly*, who in 2002 campaigned to

revive it after it was cancelled after one incomplete series with several episodes unbroadcast. This time they were less successful, but their online campaign led to the release of a DVD box set (complete with the 'missing' episodes) and eventually to one last hurrah for the crew of Serenity as the world of the series was revived for a big-screen outing in 2005.

Star Trek itself has used fan-submitted scripts and ideas in its many manifestations, and a thriving fan film community – some of their efforts crowd-funded through Kickstarter and Indiegogo – has kept Starfleet alive over the past decade while the television incarnation has seemingly been laid to rest. On the big screen, the moribund franchise was raised from the dead by long-time fan J.J. Abrams when he directed the 2009 reboot to great acclaim.

But no discussion of the importance of fandom would be complete without

mentioning *Doctor Who*. In the UK, when *Doctor Who* went off air in 1989, one group of fans made shot-on-video spin-offs featuring favourite monsters and actors associated with the series, including Jon Pertwee, Colin Baker, Sylvester McCoy, Louise Jameson and Caroline John; another congregated around the long-running series of 'missing adventures' novels published by Virgin; and yet another group used CDs to keep the programme alive via Big Finish Productions. Their long-running and popular range of audio-only adventures brought several Doctors back to life and helped keep the much-loved character in the public consciousness.

When in 2005 another lifelong fan, Russell T. Davies, successfully resurrected the Doctor for the small screen, it felt like he had never been away. Davies eventually handed the reins to Steven Moffat, another devotee, and he in turn cast Peter Capaldi as the Twelfth Doctor. Capaldi is an avowed fan of the series, and his youthful letters to the 1970s *Radio Times* and impressive teenage *Who*-related fanzine artwork was exhumed in the wake of his casting.

Today the distinction between fan and professional is more blurred than ever, and the levels of influence fandom exerts is impressive. These days it's a foolhardy production company or television network that tries to launch a new sci-fi film or TV series without first courting the attendees of the San Diego Comic-Con. Once a source of fun for local television news, today it's a vital weapon in the marketers' arsenal. Fans, it seems, have successfully stormed the citadel and assumed a level of control that even the most starry-eyed of those early enthusiasts could only have dreamed of. ◉

Joss Whedon's 'Serenity' (2005)

A brief history of time travel

by Adam Roberts

We start with H.G. Wells's *The Time Machine* (1895) because this is where 'time travel' itself starts as a fictional form. This doesn't mean there were no time-travel stories before Wells. On the contrary, there are numerous examples. Wells himself published an earlier version of his story under the less euphonious title *The Chronic Argonauts* back in 1888. A few years earlier Edward Page Mitchell published *The Clock That Went Backward* (1881) about a magic grandfather clock that enables characters to go back to the siege of Leyden in 1572 and save the city. In Dickens's *A Christmas Carol* (1844), magic spirits gift Scrooge glimpses of his past and future. But it was Wells's *The Time Machine* that set in motion an entire genre of time-travel stories, novels and films.

This starting point, though, raises puzzling questions. We might wonder how it is that time travel came from nowhere in 1894 to become one of the most popular modes of fantastical and science-fiction storytelling of the 20th and 21st centuries? It is the standing start nature of this runaway success that is most intriguing. For more than a generation now, time travel has been something of a dominant cultural force. TV has seen the extraordinary popularity of the BBC's *Doctor Who* (1963-) and *Star Trek* (1966-), a show that stands with *Who* in the most globally impactful science-fiction TV series' stakes. The latter very often included time-travel stories in its narrative and many of its spin-off movies involved time travel, from *Star Trek IV: The Journey Home* (1986) to J.J. Abrams's rebooted *Star Trek* (2009). Contemporary box-office successes include many such texts, from *The Time Traveller's Wife* (2009) to the Harry Potter movies (which include a 'time turner' among their magical props). At the end of the first *Superman* movie (1978), the hero undoes Lex Luthor's villainy and resurrects his dead girlfriend by turning back time. Latterly, superhero movies out of the Marvel or D.C. franchise have come to dominate global box office, and one of the most recent of these, *X Men: Days of Future Past* (2014), is a time-travel drama.

What those pre-Wells stories have in common is the arbitrariness of their temporal pretexts: magic, dreams, spirits. There's no interest there in futurological speculation or historical research, and no sense that time travel could belong to the material world of science and technology. The significance of Wells's *The Time Machine*, in other words, is not its narrative motion but its mechanism – its device, its in-story vehicle. This is why it made sense for Wells to alter his title from *The Chronic Argonauts* to name-check the actual machine that enables his tale. We're not primarily interested in the temponaut, we're interested in his car. As Marty McFly put it so memorably in *Back to the Future* (1985), his voice freighted equally with wonder and material envy: "You built a time machine... out of a DeLorean?!" For *Doctor Who* fans the TARDIS is as much a character as any of the doctor's interchangeable assistants.

One reason for this new focus on the machine part is that it makes dirigible something that had, hitherto, been imagined as beyond our capacity to control or steer. Dreams and magic happen to us, inflicting upon us a Scrooge-like passivity. Memory plagues us, or grants us wistful pleasure, but we can do nothing about the events that the memory recalls. A time machine, on the other hand, is something we can control. This, it turns out, is the specific dream that captures the imagination of the 20th century.

A complete survey of time-travel short stories, novels and films would be beyond the scope of the present essay; but we can note that by the 1950s and 60s hundreds of 'time travel' stories had been written, effectively codifying the parameters of the conceit. These cluster around two main varieties of temporal paradox that time travel, were it actually possible, might generate. Firstly, there's the 'time loop' paradox theme, whereby

(Previous page)
George Wells (Rod Taylor)
at the controls of the titular
machine in George Pal's
adaptation of H.G. Wells's
'The Time Machine' (1960).

(Above)
Arnold Schwarzenegger as
the cyborg assassin from the
future in James Cameron's
'The Terminator' (1984).

it might be possible for me to go back and become my own ancestor, or even my own parent. Second is the so-called 'grandparent paradox' (if I went back in time and killed my grandparents, my parents would never be born, so I would never be born; but then I wouldn't exist to be able to go back in time and kill my grandparents, in which case they would exist and I would have been born able to go back in time and kill …) And so on.

The key texts as far as the first paradox is concerned are two Robert Heinlein short stories: *By His Bootstraps* (1941) and *All You Zombies* (1958). In the latter the contortions of a temporally dislocated plot result in the main character impregnating a sex-change earlier version of himself who thus gives birth to himself. This is, we could say, a kind of limit case of 'control': the ultimate male fantasy of perfect self-reliance and self-containment, bare existence itself created out of the self unsullied by interaction with others. That there is something claustrophobic and even psychopathological about this fantasy hasn't stopped it becoming a staple of the genre. Cinema has been particularly taken with the structural neatness of this loopy trope: *Groundhog Day* (1993), *Donnie Darko* (2001), *Déjà Vu* (2006), *Source Code* (2011) and the aptly named *Looper* (2012) all rehearse this structure.

A paradox invites attempts at solution, and this one has most commonly been 'solved' in fiction with the possibility that travelling back in time results in an alternate reality or 'time line' branching off from the moment of one's arrival. An influential and much-parodied version of this is Ray Bradbury's *A Sound of Thunder* (1952), in which a time-travelling big game hunter travelling back to a licensed Tyrannosaurus Rex hunt accidentally steps on a butterfly, and then returns to his own time to find everything is different.

In some key works, this 'control' appears to be sacrificed, but even in these cases time travel works to reinforce the importance of the protagonist. In A.E. van Vogt's *The Weapon Shops of Isher* (1951) a time traveller loses control of his craft and ends up shuttling back and forth across huge stretches of time, building up a form of temporal-friction energy the whole while, before ultimately shooting back to the dawn of time and exploding as the Big Bang that creates the cosmos. As a fantasy of the potential catastrophic omnipotence of the time traveller figure, even as he loses control, this could hardly be bettered.

Books are machines to facilitate our access to narrative. Cinema and television rely on newer and more intricate machines for doing much the same thing. The difference is not merely that the latter present moving pictures and the former static words (this is hardly a difference, in point of fact, since words are never 'static'). Indeed, the conceit of time travel makes clear what the difference inheres: the facility with which visual texts can move backwards as well as forwards can accelerate or decelerate the apparent passage of time. The visual text locates itself between the motionless still photograph on the one hand, and the ceaseless fluency of pure flow on the other. Perhaps it is for this reason that visual narratives of time travel so often revert to, or are formally structured by, still photographs.

Cinema's treatments of time travel have been extremely numerous, although the vogue only really got started with George Pal's 1960 adaptation of Wells's cornerstone time-travel story, *The Time Machine*. This took as much pleasure in the fixtures and fittings of its (by the 60s) quaintly retro Edwardian clothes and props as in its science-fictional features. BBC TV serials like *Doctor Who* and *Adam Adamant Lives!* (1966-68) also construed a fundamentally cosy, Edwardian text out of their science-fiction conceits. A 1980s resurgence in time-travel cinema was occasioned by a different

sort of blockbuster, an exercise not in nostalgia but high-tech cyber terror. James Cameron's *The Terminator* (1984) connects time travel with a sense of the danger posed by mechanisation, both the alarming implacability of the big machines that have increasingly come to dominate life in the West, and the nascent fear of the possibilities of what was in the 80s a new kind of technology: computers. Both, in other words, look back to the Wellsian logic of the Edwardian machine, although with different emphases.

Key cinematic texts, though, not only work through the 'loop' and 'paradox' conceits of time travel as a genre, but do so in ways that give a visual pride of place to still photography. Chris Marker's *La Jetée* (1963) starts after a devastating World War III. A prisoner (Davos Hanich) is sent decades back in time to pre-war Paris, where he uncovers the truth behind a memory he has been obsessively rehearsing from his own childhood – standing with a woman (Hélène Chatelain) on the observation pier or 'jetty' of Orly Airport and seeing a man die. The film is composed almost wholly of black-and-white still images, a mode that resists the 'temporal' fluidity of conventional cinema, and also invokes the habit of consulting still photos of one's own past – because this is a film about childhood memory and trauma working itself out, on a global scale, in adulthood. The key to the memory (the dying man the child saw is that same child as a time-travelling adult) is a surprisingly resonant semiotic knot. It speaks to the way our anticipation of our death folds back into our past; time travel figures as a kind of feedback loop.

Arnold Schwarzenegger in *The Terminator* plays the future-built humanoid robot of the movie's title, sent back in time by a malign, intelligent computer system to kill a woman called Sarah Connor who, in 1980s Los Angeles, will give birth to John Connor, the child who will grow up to defeat the computer system in its global war against humankind. Future humanity sends one of their own to protect Sarah Connor. The twist is that Kyle Reese, the future-human, and Sarah Connor fall in love; he is John Connor's by-his-bootstraps father, and by attempting to snuff-out the threat of Sarah Connor the wicked 'Skynet' computer system is actually guaranteeing the birth of the very man it was trying to prevent. Reese's love was kindled by a photograph of the young Sarah that he carried with him through the future wastelands.

As with *La Jetée* the narrative loop has a pleasing symmetry to it, and it flatters our (human) sensibilities to think that 'chronology', however it is messed about with, will shake down into a timeline in which human beings win. The first film is about implacability. Reese describes the Terminator to its target, Sarah Connor: "It can't be bargained with. It can't be reasoned with. It doesn't feel pity, or remorse, or fear. And it absolutely will not stop, ever, until you are dead." This draws its imaginative heft from the cultural traditions of *memento mori* – the 'true form' of the Terminator, stripped of its ersatz human flesh, is that of a chromium skeleton

(Above)
Scenes from Chris Marker's 'La Jetée' (1963), composed almost entirely of black-and-white still images.

(Below)
Joseph Gordon-Levitt as the time traveller in Rian Johnson's 'Looper' (2012).

(Above)
Film editing can effortlessly
suggest huge leaps across
time, as in the celebrated edit
between the prehistoric man's
tossed bone and the spaceship
in Stanley Kubrick's '2001:
A Space Odyssey' (1968).

complete with grinning death's head. The implacability of death used to figure in human culture as a feature of the natural world, through plague, famine and old age. Now it is embodied by a man-made device, as if we actually are terrified of the future because of what we will make of it.

The other big time-travel franchise of 1980s cinema was Robert Zemeckis's *Back to the Future*, which played complex and satisfying plot games with the paradoxes of time travel; grounding its appeal in the opportunity to revisit one's family's own past, back to that sinkhole in US collective nostalgia, the *Happy Days* vision of 1950s small-town America. Its sequel attempted a minimally satirical vision of a commodified near-future, and is the less successful, a fact underscored by the final film in the trilogy, which reanimated the nostalgia and offered a cleaned-up vision of 'How the West was won'.

Yet despite tonal differences the through-line of this immensely popular series is not unlike that of *The Terminator*. 'History' in the larger sense must not be changed – the timeline registers such change slowly, and marks its occurrence by slowly rubbing out the hero Marty McFly from a photograph (shades again of *La Jetée*) to signify his existential un-becoming. Instead what must change is individual personality. In particular, Marty's Dad must learn to stand up to bullies and not be a coward, while Marty himself must learn something like the opposite – he must learn to control his temper, not to rise to taunts that he is 'chicken' and generally behave himself in a less belligerent, unconsidered manner. Both men learn these lessons, and are rewarded – not only does the 'present' of Marty's Dad see him much more materially successful, but his childhood dream of becoming a writer of science fiction is realised. Marty gets the girl, and avoids annihilation. There is, in other words, a kind of existential conservatism to the cinematic time-travel story, something that links back to its own form.

Several critics have explored the analogues between the formal qualities of cinematic representation and time travel. Films can easily speed up or slow down the apparent passage of time; running film backwards gives a sense of how the exterior world might look like to somebody travelling against the vector of the arrow of time. Cutting between shots effortlessly disposes of intervening time (perhaps the most famous edit in cinema – between the prehistoric man's bone tossed into the air and the spaceship falling through its orbital path in *2001: A Space Odyssey* (1968) – is a nicely extreme illustration of this). While watching a film we do not, of course, literally travel forward in time thousands of years; but the illusion is more compelling for the viewer because it has been visually rendered.

We can see this if we step back to the early history of the mode, and watch a film like René Clair's *Paris qui dort* (1925), a 35-minute silent picture released in anglophone countries under the title *The Crazy Ray*. A man wakes one morning, at the top of the Eiffel Tower, to discover that most (though not all) of the population of Paris has been frozen in place. Though not specifically a time-travel narrative, its ludic exploitation of the possibilities of the camera's eye: the same machine that creates the illusion of movement can stop it, slow it down, speed it up and reverse it. The relationship between the *La Jetée*-esque still photograph and the kinetic always-in-motion drive of the *Terminator* films is embodied in the interaction of moving and frozen Parisians in this delightful film. It is, of course, a movie about movies, as all the best time-travel films are. We start the history of time travel in the 1890s with H.G. Wells; but it is no coincidence that this is also the decade when motion pictures themselves begin as a serious form of art. There are metaphorical, as well as actual, points of comparison between photons and tachyons. ◉

METRO-GOLDWYN-MAYER PRESENTS THE SPECTACULAR GEORGE PAL PRODUCTION OF H.G. WELLS'

THE TIME MACHINE

WHIRLS YOU TO A WORLD OF AMAZING ADVENTURE IN THE YEAR 800,000!

IN FUTURISTIC METROCOLOR

starring
ROD TAYLOR · ALAN YOUNG · YVETTE MIMIEUX · SEBASTIAN CABOT · TOM HELMORE

Screenplay by **DAVID DUNCAN** Based on the Novel by H. G. WELLS Directed by **GEORGE PAL**

(Above)
The poster for 'The Time Machine' (1960), George Pal's adaptation of H.G. Wells's cornerstone time-travel story.

(Right)
"You built a time machine... out of a DeLorean!?" Christopher Lloyd as Dr Emmett Brown and Michael J. Fox as Marty McFly in 'Back to the Future' (1985).

Future tech
by Simon Ings

Science fiction is about escape, about transcendence, about how, with the judicious application of technology, we might escape the bounds of time, space and the body. Technology's playing the same game, but because technology has to work, it tends to lag behind the sci-fi prop-shop design curve. The gestural interfaces of *Minority Report*, with Tom Cruise, were still a decade away when the film was released in 2002. Nike says it'll deliver Marty McFly's self-tying laces to shops in 2015 – 25 years after the release of *Back to the Future Part II*. The hoverboards from that movie still elude us, but dreams of magnetic levitation are what drive superconductivity researchers out of bed each morning.

Long before we can build something for real, we know how it will work, and what it will require by way of materials and design. The young steampunk genre gorges on Victorian designs for steam-powered helicopters and the like (yes, there were such things), with films like *Hugo* (2011) and gaming apps like *80 Days* (2014) telescoping the hard business of materials science into the twinkling of a mad professor's eye. Always, our imaginations run ahead of our physical abilities.

At the same time, science fiction is not at all naive, and almost all of it is about why our dreams of transcendence through technology *fail*: why the machine goes wrong, or works towards an unforeseen (sometimes catastrophic) end. *Blade Runner* (1982) didn't so much inspire the current deluge of in-yer-face urban advertising, so much as realise our worst nightmares about it. *Short Circuit* (1986) knew what was wrong with robotic warfare long before the first Predators took to the skies.

So yes, sure: science fiction enters clad in the motley of costume drama: polished, chromed, complete, not infrequently camp. But beware: there's always a twist, a tear, a weak seam. Science fiction takes what in other movies would be the set dressing – finery from the prop shop – and turns it into something vital: a god, a golem, a puzzle, a prison. In science fiction, it matters where you are, and how you dress, what you walk on and even what you breathe. All this *stuff* is contingent, you see. It slips about. It bites.

Sometimes, in this game of "It's behind you!" less is more. Futuristic secret agent Lemmy Caution explores the streets of the distant space city *Alphaville* (1965) and the strangeness is all in Jean-Luc Godard's cut, his dialogue and the sharpest of sharp scripts. Alphaville, you see (only you don't; you never do), is nothing more than a rhetorical veil cast over contemporary Paris.

More usually, you'll grab whatever's to hand: tinsel and Pan Stick and old gorilla costumes. Two years old by 1965, at least by Earth's reckoning, William Hartnell's Doctor was tearing up the set, and would, in other bodies and other voices, go on tearing up, tearing down and tearing through his fans' expectations for the next 24 years, production values be damned. Bigger than its machinery, bigger even than its protagonist, *Doctor Who* (1963-) was, in that first, long outing, never in any sense realistic, and that was its strength. You never knew where you'd end up next: a comedy, a horror flick, a western-style showdown. The Doctor's sonic screwdriver was the *point*: it said, We're making this up as we go along.

So how did it all get going? Much as every other kind of film drama got going: with a woman in a tight dress. It is 1924: in a constructivist get-up that could spring from no other era, *Aelita: Queen of Mars* (actress and film director Yuliya Solntseva) peers into a truly otherworldly crystalline telescope and spies Earth, revolution, and Engineer Los. And Los, on being observed, begins to dream of her.

You'd think, from where we are now, deluged in testosterone from franchises such as *Transformers* and the *Terminator* series, that such

(Above)
David Butler's 'Just Imagine'
(1929) speculated on the
technology to come in its
vision of New York in 1980.

(Previous page)
Tom Cruise in Steven
Spielberg's 'Minority Report'
(2002), which predicted the
touch-screen technology now
ubiquitous in the real world.

(Below)
Ridley Scott's 'Blade Runner'
(1982) visualised our worst
fears about the in-yer-face
urban advertising of the future.

romantic-comedy beginnings were an accident of science fiction's history: a charming one-off. They're not. They're systemic. Thea von Harbou wrote novels about to-die-for women and her husband Fritz Lang placed them at the helm of science-fiction movies like *Metropolis* (1927) and *Frau im Mond* (1929). The following year saw New York given a 1980s makeover in David Butler's musical comedy *Just Imagine*. "In 1980 – people have serial numbers, not names," explained *Photoplay* magazine. "Marriages are all arranged by the courts… Prohibition is still an issue… Men's clothes have but one pocket. That's on the hip… but there's still love! "*Just Imagine* boasted the most intricate setting ever created for a movie. Some 205 engineers and craftsmen took five months over an Oscar-nominated build costing $168,000. You still think this film is marginal? *Just Imagine*'s weird guns and weirder spaceships ended up reused in the serial *Flash Gordon* (1936).

How did we get from musical comedy to Keanu Reeves's millennial Neo shopping in a virtual firearms mall? Well, by rocket, obviously. Science fiction got going just as our fascination with future machinery overtook our fascination with future fashion. Lang wanted a real rocket launch for the premiere of *Frau im Mond* and roped in no less a physicist than Hermann Oberth to build it for him. When his 1.8-metre tall liquid-propellant rocket came to nought, Oberth set about building one *eleven* metres tall powered by liquid oxygen. They were going to launch it from the roof of the cinema. Luckily they ran out of money.

What hostile critics say is true: for a while, science fiction *did* become more about the machines than about the people. This was a necessary excursion, and an entertaining one: to explore the technocratic future ushered in by the New York World's Fair of 1939-1940 and realised, one countdown after another, in the World War and Cold War to come. (Science fiction is always, ultimately, about the present.) H.G. Wells wrote the script for *Things to Come*; by the time the film came out, in 1936, the world war his original novel had predicted with such eerie accuracy (not to mention its apocalyptic, bombed-out aftermath) seemed all but inevitable. In 1950, *Destination Moon* picked the brains of sf writer Robert Heinlein; he'd spent part of Wells's war designing high-altitude pressure suits, and created a preternaturally accurate forecast of the first manned mission to the moon. George Pal's *Conquest of Space*, five years later, based its technology on writings and designs in *Collier's* magazine by former Nazi rocket designer Wernher von Braun. In the same year, episode 20 of the first season of Walt Disney's *Wonderful World of Colour* was titled *Man in Space* and featured narration from Braun and his close (anti-Nazi) friend and colleague Willy Ley.

Another voice from that show, TV announcer Dick Tufeld, cropped up a few years later as voice of the robot in the hit 1965 series *Lost in Space*, by which time science fiction could afford to calm down, take in the scenery and even crack a smile or two. The technocratic ideal might seem sterile now, but its promise was compelling: that we'd all live lives of ease and happiness in space, the Moon or Mars, watched over by loving machines: the Robinson family's stalwart Robot B-9, perhaps. Once clear of the frontier, there would be few enough places for danger to lurk, though if push came to shove, the Tracy family's spectacular *Thunderbirds* (1965-66) were sure to come and save the day. *Star Trek's* pleasant suburban utopias, defended *in extremis* by phasers that stun more than kill, are made, for all their scale and spread, no more than village neighbourhoods thanks to the magic of personal teleportation, and all are webbed into one gentle polis by tricorders so unbelievably handy and capable, it took our best minds half a century to build them for real.

(Above)
The unknowably strange, almost organic-seeming technology of the long-dead Space Jockey, as imagined by H.R. Giger for 'Alien' (1979).

(Below)
Examples of the technology of the future predicted and designed for Stanley Kubrick's '2001: A Space Odyssey' (1968): a 'tablet' computer, video communications, and a 'Visionphone'.

Once the danger's over though, and the sirens are silenced – once heaven on earth (and elsewhere) is truly established – then we hit a quite sizeable snag. Gene Roddenberry was right to have pitched *Star Trek* to Desilu Studios as "*Wagon Train* to the stars", for as Dennis Sisterson's charming silent parody *Steam Trek: the Moving Picture* (1994) demonstrates, the moment you reach California, the technology that got you there loses its specialness. The day your show's props become *merely* props, is the day you're not making science fiction any more. Forget the teleport, that rapelling rope will do. Never mind the scanner: just point.

Realism can only carry you so far. Pavel Klushantsev's grandiloquent model-making and innovative special effects – effects that Kubrick had to discover for himself more than a decade later for *2001: A Space Odyssey* (1968) – put children on *The Moon* (1965) and ballet dancers on satellite TVs (I mean TV sets *on board* satellites) in *Road to the Stars* (1957). Such humane and intelligent gestures can only accelerate the exhaustion of 'realistic' SF. You feel that exhaustion in *2001: A Space Odyssey*. Indeed, the boredom and incipient madness that haunt Keir Dullea and poor, boxed-in HAL on board Discovery One are the film's chief point: that we cannot live by reason alone. We need something more.

The trouble with utopias is they stay still, and humanity is nothing if not restless. Two decades earlier, the formal, urban costume stylings of *Gattaca* (1997) and *The Matrix* (1999) would have appeared aspirational. In context, they're a sign of our heroes' imprisonment in conformist plenty.

What is this 'more' we're after, then, if reason's not enough? At very least a light show. Ideally, redemption. Miracles. Grace. Most big-budget movies cast their alien technology as magic. *Forbidden Planet* (1956) owes its plot to *The Tempest*, spellbinding audiences with outscale animations and meticulous, hand-painted fiends from the id. The altogether more friendly water probe in James Cameron's *The Abyss* (1989) took hardly less work: six months' team effort for 75 seconds of screen time.

Arthur C. Clarke, co-writer on *2001*, once said: "Any sufficiently advanced technology is indistinguishable from magic." He was half right. What's missing from his formulation is this: sufficiently advanced technology can also resemble nature – the ordinary weave and heft of life. Andrei Tarkovsky's *Solaris* (1972) and *Stalker* (1979) both conjure up alien presences out of forests and bare plastered rooms. Imagine how advanced their technology must be to look so *ordinary*!

In *Alien* (1979) Salvador Dali's friend H.R. Giger captured this process, this 'vanishing into the real', half-done. Where that cadaverous Space Jockey leaves off and its ship begins is anyone's guess. Shane Carruth's *Upstream*

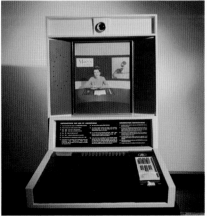

Color (2013) adds the dimension of time to this disturbing mix, putting hapless strangers in the way of an alien lifeform that's having to bolt together its own lifecycle day by day in greenhouses and shack laboratories.

Prometheus (2012), though late to the party, serves as an unlovely emblem to this kind of story. Its pot of black goo is pure Harry Potter: magic in a jar. Once cast upon the waters, though, it's life itself, in all its guile and terror.

Where we have trouble spotting what's alive and what's not – well, that's the most fertile territory of all. Welcome to Uncanny Valley. Population: virtually everyone in contemporary science fiction cinema. *Westworld* (1973) and *The Stepford Wives* (1975) broke the first sod, and their uncanny children have never dropped far from the tree. In the opening credits of a retrodden *Battlestar Galactica* (2004-09), Number Six sways into shot, leans over a smitten human, and utters perhaps the most devastating line in all science-fiction drama: "Are you *alive?*" Whatever else Number Six is (actress Tricia Helfer, busting her gut to create the most devastating female robot since Brigitte Helm in *Metropolis*), alive she most certainly is not.

David Cronenberg is a regular visitor to the Valley. For 20 years, from *The Brood* (1979) to *eXistenZ* (1999), he showed us how attempts to regulate the body like a machine, while personalising technology to the point where it is wearable, can only end in elegiac and deeply melancholy body horror. Cronenberg's visceral set dressings are one of a kind, but his wider philosophical point crops up everywhere – even in pre-watershed confections such as *The Six Million Dollar Man* (1974-1978) and *The Bionic Woman* (1976-1978), whose malfunctioning (or hyperfunctioning) bionics repeatedly confronted Steve and Jaime with the need to remember what it is to be human.

Why stay human at all, if technology promises More? In René Laloux's *Fantastic Planet* (1973) the gigantic Draags lead abstract and esoteric lives, astrally projecting their consciousnesses on to distant planets to pursue strange nuptials with visiting aliens. In *Pi* (1998) and *The Fountain* (2006), Darren Aronofsky charts the epic comedown of characters who, through the somewhat injudicious application of technology, have glimpsed their own posthuman possibilities.

But this sort of technologically enabled yearning doesn't have to end badly. There's bawdy to be had in the miscegenation of the human and the mechanical, as when in *Sleeper* (1973), Miles Monroe (Woody Allen) wanders into an orgasmatron, and a 1968-vintage, the evil Dr Durand-Durand's 'Excessive Machine', that Barbarella (Jane Fonda) causes to explode.

For all the risks, it may be that there's an accommodation to be made one day between the humans and the machinery. Sam Bell's mechanical companion in *Moon* (2009), voiced by Kevin Spacey, may sound like *2001*'s malignant HAL, but it proves more than kind in the end. In Spike Jonze's *Her* (2013), Theodore's love for his phone's new operating system acquires a surprising depth and sincerity – not least since everyone else in the movie seems permanently latched to their smartphone screen.

"…But there's still love!" cried *Photoplay*, more than 80 years ago, and *Photoplay* is always right. It may be that science-fiction cinema will rediscover its romantic roots. (I hope so.) But it may just as easily take some other direction completely. Or disappear as a genre altogether, rather as Tarkovsky's alien technology has melted into the spoiled landscapes of *Stalker*. The writer Antoine de Saint-Exupéry, drunk on his airborne adventures, hit the nail on the head: "The machine does not isolate man from the great problems of nature but plunges him more deeply into them."

You think everything is science fiction now? Just you wait. ●

(Above)
The future smartphone?
Theodore (Joaquin Phoenix)
has a relationship with his
operating system in Spike
Jonze's 'Her' (2013).

(Opposite)
Marty McFly (Michael J. Fox)
with hoverboard and self-lacing
Nikes in the 2015 of 'Back to
the Future Part II' (1989).

(Above)
Jane Fonda gets an unexpected
sexual thrill from Dr Durand-
Durand's 'Excessive Machine'
in 'Barbarella' (1968).

(Below)
The crew of the USS Enterprise
teleport in the original
'Star Trek' series (1966-).

Cheap thrills: sci-fi on a shoestring

by Vic Pratt

Where better to explore fantastic worlds of boundless possibility than the cinema screen? The technological advances of recent decades have seen science-fiction film become ever more epic in scope and, thanks to CGI, startlingly plausible in realisation. But it wasn't always so easy. In those dim and distant pre-CGI days, analogue ingenuity was required to create a truly futuristic vision. A big budget helped, of course. Decades after that elaborate spectacle *2001: A Space Odyssey* (1968) stunned audiences, devotees still debate the finer details as to how those famous special effects were achieved; what's certain is that much money was spent on them. No standard prop wires and harnesses for Mr Kubrick; his jogging astronaut, seemingly defying gravity, was actually running around an enormous and costly 'hamster wheel' centrifuge constructed mid-set. But it wasn't just big stuff that had time and money lavished upon it, but little details too. Even a tiny prop, like a pen – glimpsed floating in mid-air – was a prototype 'atomic pen' painstakingly designed for the production; and, according to Parker Pens' publicity, "equipped with a tiny isotopic packet… to produce power which is then converted to heat." The company made it clear, however, there was "no point in going to your dealers now – Parker doesn't expect to put this pen on sale until the next century!" Yet the expensive, perfectionist detail of *2001* was the exception, rather than the rule: historically, science fiction had predominantly been the province of the low-budget filmmaker. For many of Kubrick's predecessors, blessed with fantastic visions, but without fantastic bankrolls, sand-pit planets, rubber monsters and hub-cap flying saucers just had to do.

Back in the early days of cinema, moving pictures themselves had seemed a lot like science fiction. But as audiences became ever more sophisticated, it grew harder to convince them that the strange futuristic worlds they saw on screen could conceivably be real. Studio bosses in the 1930s hoped that kids, at least, could be convinced and cheaply made science fiction became a staple of cinema's 'supporting programme', with a string of thrilling cliff-hanger serials, screened in weekly instalments. Universal's *Flash Gordon* serials (1936, 1938, 1940), based on Alex Raymond's renowned newspaper strip, caused a sensation. Interplanetary adventurer Flash, played by buff Larry 'Buster' Crabbe, seemed to face certain death at the end of each action-packed episode, only to miraculously overcome the odds the following week. Buster was everything a leading man should be. Blond corkscrew locks bouncing across his determined brow, he nimbly swashbuckled about, fists flailing, sorting out the villainous inhabitants of Planet Mongo; while his nemesis, the bald, moustachioed, impressively collared Ming the Merciless, played by tremulously toned Charles Middleton, tirelessly attempted to destroy the Earth. It was a tough gig, though, to cost-effectively transpose the intergalactic wonders of Raymond's imagination from strip to screen, so a sand-pit doubled for extraterrestrial terrain; from which fragile, dart-like model rocket-ships were jerkily tugged aloft on piano wires to circle in clouds of smoke, emitting showers of indoor-firework sparks, and whining like enraged mechanical bees.

If budgetary limitations sometimes showed through, the cheapness only added to the charm. The *Flash Gordon* serials and the similar *Buck Rogers* (1939) – also starring Crabbe, this time arriving in a future world after sitting in suspended animation for 500 years, amid a cloud of 'Nirvano Gas' – were crammed full of innovative inventions that would remain science-fiction staples, including crackling ray guns (later rebranded as phasers), spacecraft cloaking devices, cities floating in mid-air, and mind-control helmets. All this splendid stuff – not to mention 'story so far'

UNSPEAKABLE HORRORS FROM OUTER SPACE PARALYZE THE LIVING AND RESURRECT THE DEAD!

PLAN 9 FROM OUTER SPACE

with
BELA LUGOSI
VAMPIRA
LYLE TALBOT

A J. Edward Reynolds Production

Produced and Directed by
Edward D. Wood, Jr.

(Previous page)
Beatrice Roberts as Queen Azura, Buster Crabbe as Flash and Charles Middleton as Ming the Merciless in 'Flash Gordon's Trip to Mars' (1938).

(Left)
'Auteur of the awful' Ed Wood's 'Plan 9 from Outer Space' (1958) made inventive use of plastic model toys and Cadillac hub caps as props.

(Below, left)
Sci-fi western 'The Phantom Empire' (1935) sees singing cowboy Gene Autry journey to the underground civilisation of Murania.

(Below, right)
The 'Buck Rogers' (1939) serials introduced several inventions that would become sci-fi staples.

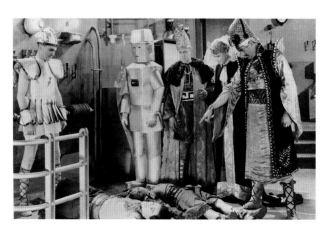

introductory text that rolled evocatively up the screen into the distance –
was revitalised on television, still dazzling young science-fiction fans many
moons further on, and assuredly lingered in George Lucas's mind when
he conceived the somewhat pricier *Star Wars* series all those years later.

Other thrilling otherworldly serials, shot on Spartan budgets that
made *Flash Gordon* look like a blockbuster, may also have provided
inspiration; notably *The Phantom Empire* (1935), a bizarre fusion of science
fiction and western. Predating *Flash Gordon*, this saw singing cowboy
Gene Autry journey underground to Murania, an advanced, radium-
rich, subterranean civilisation, to battle robots and mysterious 'Thunder
Riders', pausing just once a day to rush back up to Radio Ranch to
make his daily country and western broadcast. Even with the future of
the world at stake, good old Gene never disappointed his listeners.

The wondrous excitement of scientific possibility in these cheap and
cheerful serials – and in the 'mad scientist' B pictures of the 1940s – was
tempered by an underlying anxiety. Technology was dangerous stuff:
scientific breakthroughs, if misused by unhinged geniuses, or appropriated
by deranged megalomaniacs, threatened society with destruction. By
the 1950s, the terrible threat of the atom bomb had become a dreadful
reality. The press fed the public ever-more worrying stories of dastardly
foreign powers and radioactivity; the spectre of apocalyptic war loomed.
This was reflected on screen, as the science fiction and horror genres
mutated and merged. An abundant crop of low-budget science fiction
movies, populated by malevolent or misunderstood aliens and increasingly
outlandish mutants and monsters, were thriftily concocted – often by
cash-strapped independent producers looking for a quick buck – to
provoke a *frisson* of fear in thrill-seeking drive-in movie audiences.

Roger Corman, low-budget filmmaker *par excellence*, quickly became
prominent in this crowded field with glorious examples including *The Day
the World Ended* (1955), featuring a girl-grabbing mutant beast with three
eyes, claws and a scraggy beard, and *It Conquered the World* (1956) – 'It'
being a creature reminiscent of a sinister, scowling carrot. But even the
indomitable Corman sometimes struggled to reconcile purse-strings with
production value. For example, the horrific subaquatic mutant of *Attack of
the Crab Monsters* (1957) resolutely refused to stay submerged. Chuck Griffith,
who directed underwater sequences for the princely sum of $100, recalled
"a *papier mâché* crab on an aluminium frame, with Styrofoam stuffing inside.
The only problem was the crab wouldn't sink. It floated. As Roger watched,
we had to keep loading rocks, cast-iron weights, and people on this crab
just to get it to stay underwater." These men truly suffered for their art.

Corman ingeniously sprinkled his scripts with humour to camouflage
unconvincing monsters, but other less self-aware low-budget filmmakers
– perhaps unwisely – seemed to take themselves rather too seriously.
Notorious auteur-of-the-awful Ed Wood never expected audiences to
laugh at his supposedly sombre science-fiction masterpiece *Plan 9 from
Outer Space* (1958); yet he did expect them to believe plastic model kits
from the local toy shop were interstellar craft aflame over Hollywood.
Adding to his woes, he accidentally melted them before the perfect shot
was in the can, and so was compelled to make a shamefaced return to the
store. "They didn't have any more models," he later lamented wistfully.
"We just couldn't find any anywhere in Hollywood… Kids were buying
them up as if they were going out of style next week." Ed used Cadillac
hub cabs instead; sprayed silver, of course – for added authenticity.

Wood was just one of many independents clambering aboard the
space-wagon, quickly knocking up scripts to fit impossibly outlandish

(Above)
The alien in Roger Corman's
'It Conquered the World'
(1956) was reminiscent of a
sinister, scowling carrot.

(Below)
The stubbornly buoyant
styrofoam creature in Roger
Corman's 'Attack of the
Crab Monsters' (1957).

(Top)
Johnny the mechanical man in David MacDonald's 'Devil Girl from Mars' (1954) looked more like a walking fridge.

(Above)
The 'aliens' in Cy Roth's 'Fire Maidens from Outer Space' (1956) are revealed to be a troupe of burlesque dancers.

(Below)
'Mad Max' (1979) made cost-effective use of the Australian landscape to depict its dystopian future setting.

titles, lurid posters promising intergalactic sensations that the minuscule budgets they had scraped together couldn't possibly deliver. The trailer for Phil Tucker's *Robot Monster* (1953) promised "indestructible moon monsters". What you got was a fellow wearing a flea-bitten gorilla suit and a diving helmet, with a television aerial glued on. The maidens in Cy Roth's *Fire Maidens from Outer Space* (1956) were revealed as an unexceptional troupe of pseudo-extraterrestrial burlesque dancers who pranced about in abbreviated Greco-Roman attire, while the terrible 'electronic monster' who menaced them from behind the interplanetary shrubbery was little more than a grubby tall chap with a prominent jaw in an ill-fitting black jumper. The titular girl in David MacDonald's *Devil Girl from Mars* (1954) was a well-spoken dominatrix in tight leather-look outfit and swimming cap, who ambitiously sought to "subdue London", but only had 'Johnny' the mechanical man to back her up – a cumbersome robot akin to a walking fridge with a police light on top. In Nathan Juran's *The Brain from Planet Arous* (1957) a swollen cerebrum with eyes floated glumly around on his wires, looking more sad than evil. A quick axe attack curtailed his depressive plot of world domination. Special mention must be made of Vic Savage's *The Creeping Terror* (1964), supposedly a man-eating monster; actually a synthetic fibre mix of carpet, patchwork quilt and tentacles, operated from beneath like an elongated slow-shuffling pantomime horse. It was not terrifying, but it certainly crept. Scarier is the thought of how those imprisoned within suffered to heft his unwieldy bulk. It's impossible to believe so sluggish a creature could ever have bagged a human snack, and his supposed victims faced unenviable acting challenges. Not only did they have to feign fear; they also had to push themselves laboriously into the monster's mouth, and then wait patiently to be 'devoured'.

Eventually the independents were jostled aside by studios realising there were big bucks to be made from more lavishly produced science-fiction pictures. Corman later lamented, "The majors have dominated the exploitation genres with budgets ten times higher than ours. I made movies about interplanetary adventures when George Lucas was still in grade school… but when the Spielbergs and Lucases make technically exquisite genre films, they cut deeply into the box-office appeal of our kind of picture."

While the lavish spectacle of films like *Star Wars* (1977) may have frustrated Corman (who carried on regardless), it fuelled the dreams of a whole new breed of independent filmmakers, who found ingenious ways to disguise the fact that they did not have big studio budgets; and the originality of whose works in turn fed back into the mainstream. John Carpenter's *Dark Star* (1974), which predated *Star Wars* (1977) and foreshadowed *Alien* (1979), was so full of great ideas that nobody cared that the spaceship bridge's consoles were fashioned from ice-cube trays. The Australian producers of *Mad Max* (1979) chose to cost-effectively situate their future-world of violent motorcycle gangs around Melbourne, rather than in outer space, while John Sayles's *The Brother from Another Planet* (1984) saw the alien Brother economically crash-land in Harlem. They sensed, as Corman did, that small scale, an unusual setting and the right script could make science fiction all the more effective and unsettling – as was recently demonstrated in Jonathan Glazer's *Under the Skin* (2013), which saw Scarlett Johansson's predatory extraterrestrial eerily prowling the streets of Glasgow in a white van.

Technological advances have now made high-quality special effects affordable, even to the most strapped-for-cash filmmakers. Digital cameras mean that the high cost of film stock – which, in the old days, decimated a budget quicker than a dose of Death Star super laser – is no longer an

issue for independent producers. Thus director Gareth Edwards could afford himself the luxury of shooting more than 100 hours of footage for his successful low-budget debut feature *Monsters* (2010), thanks to the wonders of a memory stick, and, what's more, had no need of Styrofoam beasts – he created his creatures using a design program on the computer in his bedroom. Just imagine what Ed Wood might have done with this kind of kit. But if the visual possibilities now seem endless, Edwards, who has since directed the big-budget *Godzilla* (2014), still sounds a note of caution. "We've reached that plateau where you can kind of do anything, and we have kind of done everything," he warned, after an announcement that he will direct the next *Star Wars* film. "I hope we are going to see people embracing strong stories, strong characters, as well as the spectacle. The honeymoon is over."

Others – independents, especially – share his concerns. Away from the big studios, filmmakers who disdain empty spectacle determinedly continue to carve a niche for intelligent, cerebral low-budget science fiction, sometimes resolutely resisting the contemporary ubiquity of computer effects, sometimes making a virtue of necessity. Cory McAbee's already distinctive labour-of-love musical space-western *The American Astronaut* (2001) was further set apart by its use of paintings of spacecraft rather than computer images; whereas the models in Duncan Jones's *Moon* (2009) had a deliberately retro look. The concept at the heart of it all, though, was still what really mattered. And sometimes, with recent independent science fiction, these concepts have been very complex, untested ones – perhaps the kind that the big studios might shy away from at first, then rip off later. Darren Aronofsky's debut feature *Pi* (1998) fused science fiction with psychological thriller, mathematics and mysticism; while Vincenzo Natali's *Cypher* (2002), a multi-layered tale of corporate paranoia, was described by bewildered *Variety* critic Derek Elley as having "more twists than a Chubby Checker revival concert". So conceptually challenging was the low-budget time-travel tale *Primer* (2004), written and directed by mathematics scholar Shane Carruth, that an explanatory diagram was latterly appended to its Wikipedia entry to aid the understanding of baffled watchers; but even careful study may not preclude the need for repeat viewings. The trend for intelligent, innovative independent science fiction continues unabated with Mike Cahill's *Another Earth* (2011) and William Eubank's *The Signal* (2014).

All of which is a reassuring reminder that science-fiction films have always been about more than simply the special effects, no matter how awe-inspiring, amusing or just plain awful they might be. For all the technological changes, science-fiction cinema remains, first and foremost, the cinema of ideas; and the only limits are the limits of the imagination. You won't see many hub-cap flying saucers hovering over Hollywood nowadays; but, down below, low-budget independent science fiction continues to develop, mutate and thrive, as buoyantly resilient as the most unsinkable Styrofoam sea monster. ●

(Above, left)
Digital technology enabled Gareth Edwards to make 'Monsters' (2010) without needing physical props and monsters.

(Above, right)
Mike Cahill's independent production 'Another Earth' (2011).

(Below)
Shane Carruth's wonderfully inventive, micro-budget debut 'Primer' (2004).

OUTER LIMITS: SCI-FI AND THE AVANT GARDE

by William Fowler

How would you visualise another world? What strange dreams and images would you pluck from your brain? Hollywood has invested millions activating alternative visions, using special effects, modelling and computers. John and James Whitney invested time. They spent years creating the strange, beautiful, abstract images and shapes that pulse, splinter, break down and reformulate in films like *Twenty Four Variations on an Original Theme* (1939–1940) and *3 Untitled Films* (1940-1942), plus many later works made individually. The brothers were interested in image formation and perception and used graphic notation and later computers to write bright lines and mandala-like patterns within the darkness of the film frame.

They became the founding fathers to a whole series of West Coast American filmmakers who would exert a powerful influence on Hollywood science fiction from the late 1960s onward. Techniques varied but an aesthetic developed that centred on colour saturation, abstraction and symmetrical patterning – not unlike a kaleidoscope. Scott Bartlett manipulated electronic video signals (put back onto film) for the otherworldly *OffOn* (1967) and *Moon* (1969), while Pat O'Neill worked the optical printer like it was a giant mixing bowl, introducing colour fields, loops and double exposures. His *7362* (1967) is a

psychedelic classic, all bright, writhing legs and pulsing machinery – like an animated Rorschach test. He, Bartlett and others created visions worthy of deep space, but also the space within.

O'Neill later provided special effects for *The Empire Strikes Back* (1980) and *Return of the Jedi* (1983), after Larry Cuba, one of his students at Cal Arts, had already worked on *Star Wars* (1977). Other influences on Hollywood were less direct – but no less significant. Designer Douglas Trumbull looked to the visionary work of Jordan Belson when developing the Star Gate sequence for *2001: A Space Odyssey* (1968), in turn influencing everything from 1970s *Doctor Who* to *Bill & Ted's Excellent Adventure* (1989). Belson was profoundly interested in the mystical and the meditative, and his abstract films, which he made from 1947 to 2005, evoke these qualities.

Several experimental filmmakers have used sci-fi narratives to explore metaphysical and even political ideas. For his 1962 film *La Jetée*, Chris Marker told the story of a homeless time traveller caught between different times and places. Within it lies a haunting tale about holocaust and apocalypse, a thinly veiled connection to the atrocities of a war not long passed. The film is presented using carefully composed still photography, and

Scott Bartlett's 'OffOn' (1967)

Jordan Belson's 'Samadhi' (1967) influenced Douglas Trumbull's work on '2001: A Space Odyssey' (1968)

the narrator explores his elliptical tale with a rich voice tinged with quiet melancholy. Film becomes a cipher for lost memories or, paradoxically, memories yet to be dreamed.

The vital disruptive possibilities of imagining different – but similar – worlds have also been utilised by John Akomfrah, Uriel Orlow and The Otolith Group. Akomfrah's *The Nine Muses* (2010) presents a mythic vision of an austere ghost land (not unlike Werner Herzog's 1971 *Fata Morgana* or his 1992 *Lessons of Darkness*) while also introducing archival news footage and reportage. He explores ideas about the history of UK immigration, presenting it in an unfamiliar context, imaging a long view of time, like an epic science-fiction novel.

In this postmodern world, the very iconography of science fiction – with its UFOs, future cities and electric walkways – has become codified and fixed in our minds.

Rachel Reupke used video compositing while referencing these codes when making *Now Wait for Last Year* (2007), in which she turns Wang Jing, a district of Beijing, into a strange retro future world. The film is science fiction, yet at the same time highlights how all forms of architecture and filmmaking styles come loaded with ideologies, aspirations and history – often very deliberately so. The modern world can seem to be getting ever closer to science fiction, and several artist filmmakers have in their own ways explored the metaphor: Beatrice Gibson, Mark Aerial Waller and Adam Chodzko to name just a few. In *Deep State* (2012) Brad Butler and Karen Mirza, plus their collaborator novelist China Miéville, imagined a future in which political protest, even on the Moon, is still co-opted back into the system under critique.

Two of most entertaining filmmakers to

work with the reflexive possibilities of sci-fi have been Mike and George Kuchar. They mixed in the circles of the American avant garde and yet were inspired by melodramas and B movies of the most outrageous and extreme variety. Mike's camp, underground early work *Sins of the Fleshapoids* (1965) was a major influence on John Waters and used sci-fi B movie conventions to subvert ideas about gender and sexuality. About his late video *Orphans of the Cosmos* (2008), made with students at the San Francisco Art Institute, George Kuchar said: "This trip is short on funding but big in concept – it's really quite a ride and looks like a million bucks for the vision impaired." Like many artists and experimental filmmakers, they have existed on the relative sidelines and yet also enjoyed support, engagement and a lifetime of working directly to their own briefs and ideas. Who needs Hollywood? ●

Breathing the same air: Cold War sci-fi

by Ken Hollings

"We all breathe the same air," President John F. Kennedy announces to an assembly of graduate students at Harvard University just a few months prior to his assassination in 1963. This simple declaration of a shared physiological reality is to underline the possibilities of a lasting détente with the Soviet Union and the other member nations of the Eastern Bloc. Having in common the physical attributes necessary to exist upon this planet, the president's argument suggests, places the human race above any ideological differences. Unfortunately, Kennedy is also speaking at a time when humans are planning to take their breath, along with their geopolitical differences, deep into space with them. Out there, it quickly becomes clear that we do not all breathe the same air. Airlocks and capsules, the sealed hulls of spaceships, pressure suits and pods all take on ideological form during the Cold War, hinting at mutual incompatibilities and divisions.

In the Space Age, politics swiftly become physiological: so which aliens fit in, and which need to adapt the environment to suit them? In 1950, just as Burt 'the Duck and Cover' Turtle is teaching schoolchildren what to do during a nuclear strike, there comes an urgent warning. "Streaking out of the unknown comes a strange new terror!" runs the poster copy for *The Flying Saucer* (1950), the first movie to cash in on the wave of UFO sightings that began in 1947. "It appears it was designed with one purpose: to carry the atomic bomb," explains a Washington bureau chief about the outlandish disc glimpsed at the start of the film. "Now the first country that learns the secret of the flying saucer will control the skies of world. I don't want that country to be Russia." Loading A-bombs, UFOs and the USSR into the same sentence is a sure way to grab everybody's attention during the Cold War. Unfortunately, the skies of the world are already endangered, as a team of Soviet agents have tracked the flying saucer to its base in the wilds of Canada, where their furry hats and beards are presumably less conspicuous. "Instead of being used to serve the imperialistic designs of America," their leader announces to the disc's very human and very American inventor, "your invention will now be employed for the good of the entire human race." Rather than let it fall into the wrong hands, the inventor decides to destroy his creation.

By July 1950 Twentieth Century Fox has given the go-ahead for *The Day the Earth Stood Still* (1951), which shows a politically gridlocked Earth visited by alien Klaatu, who has to suspend the planet's entire power supply before anyone will listen to him, while RKO has okayed the Howard Hawks production *The Thing from Another World* (1951), in which an 'intellectual carrot' from outer space rampages through an Arctic research base, systematically draining its human inhabitants of blood in order to survive. Meanwhile veteran director Edgar G. Ulmer's *The Man from Planet X* (1951) sets the tone for interplanetary paranoia in 1951. "Well, how can you talk of him as if he were a human being?" frets amoral scientist Dr. Mears on first meeting the diminutive alien of the movie's title. "How do we know what thought processes run through his head? How can we even assume that he thinks like we do?" Encased in spacesuit and helmet, breathing the atmosphere of his home world and communicating with low electronic tones, the Man from Planet X appears quite friendly at first. However, once Mears tortures him in order to learn his spacecraft's secrets by turning off his breathing apparatus, the visitor from another world starts controlling people's minds, after which diplomatic relations between Earth and Planet X are abruptly broken off.

Later waves of space invaders manage to blend quite easily into everyday American life, thereby taking Cold War paranoia to even greater heights. Although able to breathe the same air as the human beings

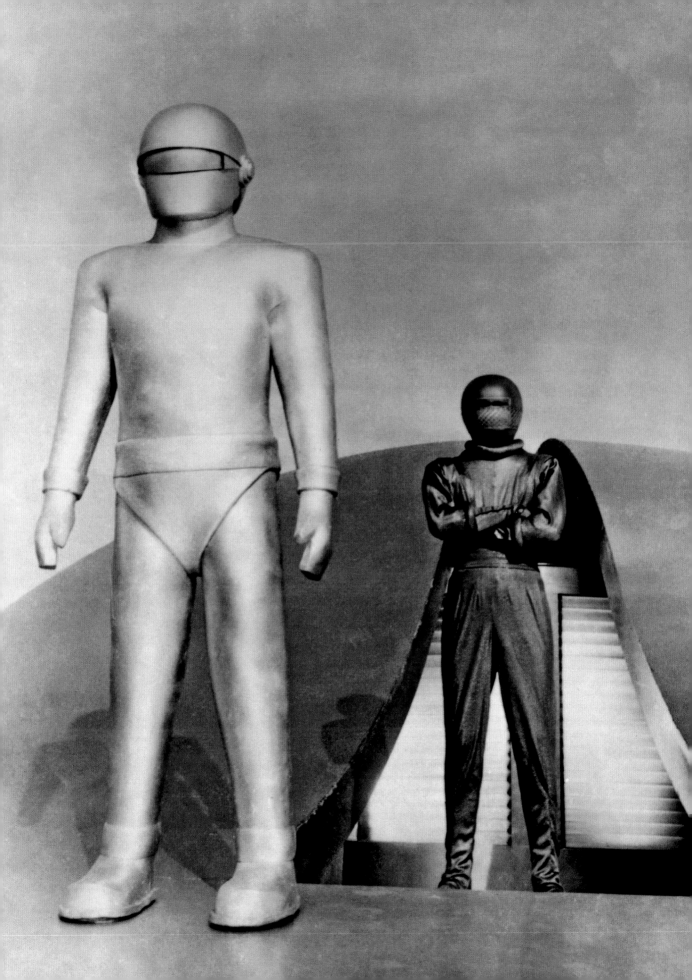

(Above)
The 'strange new terror'
from the skies in 'The Flying
Saucer' (1950) could just as
well have come from Soviet
Russia as outer space.

(Previous page)
The alien Klaatu finds the Earth
in political gridlock in 'The Day
the Earth Stood Still' (1951).

(Below)
The UK's own Cold War
anxieties were expressed
in such films as Hammer's
'X: The Unknown' (1956).

they impersonate in Universal's 1953 release *It Came from Outer Space*, the aliens cannot wait to leave Earth far behind them. Humanity, it seems, has not yet evolved sufficiently by their standards. Meanwhile, the pod people in Don Siegel's 1956 dark fantasy *Invasion of the Body Snatchers* love American life so much that they want to move in and take over. Breathing the same air, they argue, is wasted on the actual people of Earth, who remain far too involved in their own emotional problems to appreciate what they have going for them. Where groups of extraterrestrials appear, only one belief system or ideological structure will prevail; and it is usually incompatible with life as we know it. Alien minds tend to think alike during the Cold War, a point well illustrated by the 1958 spook-pit classic *The Blob*, in which an enigmatic lump of red ooze takes over a small town, consuming one citizen at a time and growing correspondingly in size. An actual red invader from outside the USA, the Blob is of one mind with itself and therefore has no need to communicate with anyone.

On the other side of the Atlantic, the UK is having similar problems with amorphous masses intent upon taking over. In Hammer's *X: the Unknown*, released in 1956, a fissure in the earth's crust releases a shapeless life-form that devours any radioactive material it can find, eventually heading for one of the country's new atomic reactor sites. Spreading itself across a flattened apocalyptic landscape of army test ranges, NHS hospital corridors and high-security laboratories, the giant globule kills everyone – including soldiers, children and doctors – who gets in its way. A similarly lethal terrain is opened up the following year with Hammer's *Quatermass 2*, Val Guest's pared-back version of Nigel Kneale's BBC television series. Professor Bernard Quatermass is disturbed to discover that his design for a projected moon base, comprising several large steel domes, has been reproduced at a gigantic industrial plant built over the former rural backwater of Winnerton Flats. "A little village," an assistant casually remarks of its disappearance, "the government must have torn it down." The local population now either works at the plant or forms part of a mindless private militia keeping the area secure for the alien invaders, who are dropping from the sky in their thousands. Unable to survive on this planet, these rarely glimpsed creatures mass together inside Quatermass's pressure domes, breathing an atmosphere that is highly toxic to all Earthly life. Their influence – experienced as "a blind compulsion to act for them" – is exercised through the humans whose minds they now control, forming an "entire nervous system" that extends into national government and the police force. Filmed on location at Shell Haven Refinery in Essex and Hemel Hemstead New Town, *Quatermass 2* conjures up the Cold War's military-industrial nightmare as an interspecies battle over the future Earth's biology; no wonder the US title for this movie is *Enemy from Space*.

The scientists in these movies tend to be isolated, detached figures: uncomfortable around, and misunderstood by, the very people they seek to protect while equally uneasy in their relationships with politicians and the military. In their 1950 production *Seven Days to Noon*, the Boulting brothers offer a gripping portrait of tormented nuclear scientist John Willingdon, who steals a portable atomic device from the 'Wallingford Research Centre' and threatens to detonate it in central London unless the prime minister calls a halt to all production of such weapons. Spiritually blasted, alienated from his family and colleagues, Willingdon wanders through London clutching a briefcase containing the bomb, so alone now that he has become completely identified with it. "Find Willingdon and you find the UR-12 with him," remarks a police officer involved in tracking him down.

The scientist tortured by the power of his own creation becomes

an international presence during the Cold War: each one a potential "destroyer of worlds" in the words of nuclear scientist and 'father of the Bomb', Robert Oppenheimer. Released in Japan in 1954, Honda Ishiro's *Gojira*, the first Godzilla movie, makes explicit reference to US nuclear testing in the South Seas and the bombing of Nagasaki. However, it is Dr Serizawa's 'oxygen destroyer' that defeats the monster by killing off all sea life. Embittered and reclusive, Serizawa elects to die alongside Godzilla rather than share the secret of his terrifying invention with the world. Equally haunted is Professor Hawling, the American scientist in Kurt Maetzig's *The Silent Star* (aka *First Spaceship on Venus*) a spectacular East German/Polish space adventure from 1960. An international team of scientists is on a mission to discover intelligent life on Venus. Hawling, however, needs to persuade his US bosses to let him participate and therefore atone for his work on their military nuclear program. "I've been working 20 years for you since the atomic bomb test in the Pacific," he protests. "Have a whisky, Hawling," drawls one of his superiors, calmly lighting a cigarette. Hawling finally goes to Venus but only to discover that the inhabitants have wiped themselves out in an apocalyptic war.

The Space Race seems to have spared the planet such a fate in Stanley Kubrick's classic *2001: A Space Odyssey* (1968), although old Cold War tensions still run through the scene aboard the orbiting space wheel where US scientist Dr Heywood Floyd (William Sylvester) politely plays cat and mouse with a group of Eastern Bloc scientists anxious to know what is happening at the Clavius, the American moon base. "I'm sorry, Dr Smyslov," Floyd cautiously replies, "but I'm really not at liberty to discuss this." Like the two tribes of apes brutally fighting over a tepid waterhole at the start of Kubrick's movie, these Cold War adversaries confront each other over drinks in clear plastic cups, seated around a white plastic table, all breathing the same air. ◉

(Above, left)
Barry Jones as a nuclear scientist tormented by the power of his own creation in the Boulting brothers' 'Seven Days to Noon' (1950).

(Above, right)
The alien visitor in Edgar G. Ulmer's 'The Man from Planet X' (1951) appears friendly at first, then starts controlling people's minds.

(Below)
A nuclear scientist is among the crew voyaging to Venus in Kurt Maetzig's East German/Polish co-production 'The Silent Star' (1960).

CONTACT

To boldly go
by Alastair Reynolds

If there is one lesson to be drawn from science-fiction cinema, it's that nothing good ever comes of space travel. Dreadful things happen to those unwise enough to venture beyond the Earth's atmosphere. They're as likely to meet violent death while in orbit as they are to encounter an army of vicious alien killing machines – or end up being killed by their own treacherous technology.

When did science-fiction cinema decide that spaceships were the enablers of nightmares, not dreams? It was not always this way. The earliest depictions of space exploration in cinema pre-date World War I. They come from a time when flight itself was still a happy novelty, when the notion of travelling beyond our atmosphere would have seemed outlandish in the extreme. Science itself had yet to lose its innocence – there had yet been no aerial warfare, no atom bombs, no industrial-scale chemical warfare.

Despite the Wright brothers achieving powered flight in 1903, space travel seemed a dream too far. Nor was the means by which it might be achieved at all obvious. The two titans of the 19th-century scientific romance, H.G. Wells and Jules Verne, had both ignored the rocket as a plausible propulsion system. Wells had sent his men to the Moon using an invented technology of 'Cavorite' anti-gravity materials, while Verne used a giant cannon to shoot his astronauts on their way.

Both technologies were impossible – Wells's on the grounds that it violated physics, Verne's because the stress of launch would have been fatal for his explorers. Nonetheless, in *A Trip to the Moon* (*Le Voyage dans la lune*, 1902), Georges Méliès employs something like Verne's cannon, splatting an artillery-shell spaceship into the 'eye' of a ludicrously small Moon. Space travel in 1902 was still treated as a fancy, no more or less plausible than burrowing to the centre of the Earth.

It took more than two decades and a world war to elevate space travel to something that could be envisaged with conviction in the cinema. Fritz Lang's 1929 *Woman in the Moon* (*Frau im Mond*) credits rocket pioneer Hermann Oberth and contains a realistic treatment of launch gantries, rocket stages, acceleration and instrumentation. There is even a countdown, which Lang invented to add drama to the action. The plot, involving lunar gold reserves, is undistinguished; but for a piece of cinema made the better part of 90 years ago, the space travel aspects remain impressively convincing. By depicting in matter-of-fact fashion something that must have seemed fantastical or even impossible to 1920s audiences, the film surely helped reshape the idea of space exploration in the popular imagination. Space exploration might be not as outlandish as it seems – it's just a question of engineering, control systems and the limits of human endurance.

Lang might have recognised the rocket's credentials as a viable means of travel, but this acceptance was by no means universal. In William Cameron Menzies's 1936 adaptation of H.G. Wells's *Things to Come*, access to space is again achieved by giant cannon, while the buzzing, sparking vehicles of the *Flash Gordon* and *Buck Rogers* serials are merely the means to swashbuckling ends, their propulsion methods unexplained by any science.

Rocket men

After a fallow decade, cinema reaffirmed its vows to science fiction in 1950 with the George Pal-produced *Destination Moon*, scripted by Robert Heinlein from his own 1947 novel *Rocket Ship Galileo*. The film was even more meticulous in its treatment of space travel than *Woman in the Moon*. The world no longer needed persuading that rockets were a viable means of reaching space – Hitler's V2 programme had

provided ample proof of that. For all but a handful of doubters, it was a question of when, not if, humankind would journey to outer space.

The ensuing decade produced its share of science-fiction films as manifestations of Cold War paranoia or the linked fear of invasion from outer space. Most are rightly forgotten. But a handful of films escape the prison of their time. Robert Wise's *The Day the Earth Stood Still* (1951) still offers a sobering assessment of the human capacity for self-destruction, against an implied backdrop of a tolerant but immensely powerful galactic community. The flying saucer in the film still looks impressive, even if the science behind how they might actually fly makes a nonsense of physics.

Occasionally silly, but still with its stirring moments, is Joseph Newman's *This Island Earth* from 1955. The science again is dubious, but the gradual opening out of the film into space operatic scale is thrilling, and we are charmed by the essential benevolence of the wise, decent alien Exeter.

Forbidden Planet, which followed a year later, is constructed with similar care, and for their time the effects are sublime. In Fred McLeod Wilcox's film, with its human exploratory crew attempting to contact a lost expedition, we see the template for a decade's worth of *Star Trek* episodes. Tellingly, the human spacecraft is again a kind of flying saucer – was the popular imagination of the 1950s, fuelled by reports of covered-up findings at Roswell, unable to conceive of any other kind of advanced spaceship? But for all the pathos in this loose retelling of *The Tempest*, the tone is optimistic – we long to follow the crew of space cruiser C-57D on their next adventure.

It's full of stars

If the 1950s had already given us this masterful space travel triptych, what pleasures awaited us in the decade to come? Very few, is the answer. Just as the real space age picked up pace in the 1960s, so science-fiction cinema seemed to lose some of its interest in space travel.

There were, however, a few exceptions. *Ikarie XB-1* (aka *Voyage to the End of the Universe*, 1963), by Czech director Jindrich Polák, is an ambitious and intelligent production with a realistically handled depiction of relativistic space travel and time dilation – something still all but ignored by most science-fiction cinema – and its effects and sets still hold up well today. The titular planet of Byron Haskin's *Robinson Crusoe on Mars* (1964) does not much resemble the world now revealed to us by space probes and landers, but much can be forgiven: this enjoyable film was released in the same year as Mariner 4's flyby, and until those first grainy images returned to us, our knowledge of surface conditions on Mars was still poor.

Mars was the also the objective in *Thunderbirds Are Go* (1966), but here scientific realism mattered less than plot opportunities for the heroic deeds of International Rescue. The lengthy opening sequence, showing the assembly of the Zero X spacecraft, is masterfully done, but it must have tested the patience of its audience, and the film was a flop.

But *Thunderbirds* had done well on television, and there was a sense that the small screen was the more natural medium for long-running space adventure series, be it *Star Trek*, *Lost in Space* or the ever protean *Doctor Who*. The smaller format allowed for more modest effects shots – the original models and sets of *Star Trek* don't look too shoddy on a small screen even now – while cinema placed much higher demands on budgets. Stanley Kubrick's *2001: A Space Odyssey* was not only expensive and took years to film, but it also set a benchmark for realism that all subsequent space exploration films have felt obliged to aim for, if not exceed.

What more can said about *2001*? The film is its own monolith, towering over the landscape of science-fiction cinema, transfiguring all who dare

(Above)
The artillery shell-like spaceship is fired from a giant cannon in Georges Mélies's 'A Trip to the Moon' (1902).

(Previous page)
The Death Star looms behind a battling X-Wing Fighter and TIE Fighter in George Lucas's 'Star Wars' (1977).

(Above)
Czech director Jindrich Polák's 'Ikarie XB-1' (1963) dealt realistically with relativistic space travel and time dilation.

(Below)
Fritz Lang's prescient silent-cinema vision of space travel, 'Woman in the Moon' ('Frau im Mond', 1929).

(Above)
Byron Haskin's 'Robinson
Crusoe on Mars' (1964)
imagined the surface of
Mars before spaceships
had flown by the planet.

(Far left)
Fred McLeod's influential
'Forbidden Planet' (1956)
boasted sublime effects for
its time, and was optimistic
about space travel.

(Left)
The George Pal production
'Destination Moon' set the
trend for 1950s space-
travel films (1951).

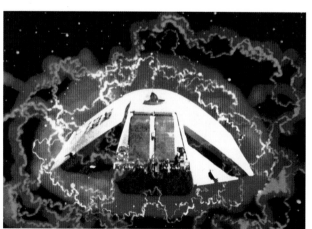

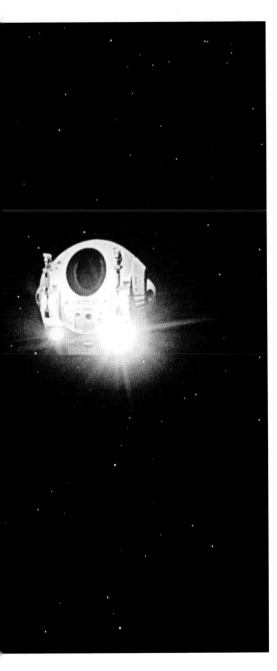

touch it. Made at the same time as much of the original run of *Star Trek*, the film doesn't just look like the product of a different decade, it looks as if it was made in a different century. Indeed, a recent lawsuit between Apple and Samsung involved Samsung presenting screen grabs from the film, in an attempt to argue that the astronauts were using handheld computers strikingly similar in shape and function to contemporary tablets.

But if *2001*'s spaceship *Discovery* was sent out to investigate a mysterious anomaly around Jupiter, the conflicting mission requirements soon turned its central computer, HAL 9000, into a psychopath. Locked out of a spaceship which is trying to kill him, the astronaut Dave Bowman eventually sabotages the hapless HAL. The spaceship had been transformed from neutral vehicle to menace – from the stagecoach to the haunted castle itself. In countless reiterations of this basic theme, the main function of the spaceship became sinister. It was a machine for taking you to bad places, enclosing you within its metal walls, or which was actively engaged in trying to end your life – sometimes all at once.

In Douglas Trumbull's *Silent Running* (1972), the huge spaceship becomes a travelling crime scene as Freeman Lowell is obliged to kill his fellow crew members to prevent – in his eyes – an ecological crime of greater severity. Trumbull's previous work on *2001* is evident here in the plausible, skeletal lines of the ship, while the reliance on artificial intelligence systems – here presented more benignly – recapitulated a theme of the earlier film. Shot on a decommissioned aircraft carrier, the cargo bays of the *Valley Forge* look suitably vast – few space films have come close to evoking the same sense of interior scale with their spaceships. Lowell saves the rainforests, but the film proceeds to tragedy – the ending is as downbeat as that of *2001* was perplexing.

Out of this world

Like Chekhov's gun, it seemed in the 1970s as if no spaceship could be introduced into a film without it eventually blowing up in the final reel. The titular *Dark Star* (1974) is sent off into space to prepare the way for colonists – by detonating unstable planets, whatever they might be. But again artificial intelligence complicates things, and one of the 'thermostellar' bombs decides to self-destruct while still attached to the ship. Nonetheless, there are laughs along the way, and John Carpenter's film doesn't quite manage to kill off the entire crew. For all the surfer wisdom, though, the essential message remains that space is not going to do you a terrific amount of good.

The same could be said of Ridley Scott's *Alien* (1979), a dark recapitulation of one of the throwaway plot strands of *Dark Star*, wherein the crew of the space tug Nostromo manage to get picked off one by one by the horribly adaptive xenomorph that has managed to sneak aboard the ship. In *Dark Star* the stowaway tickles; in *Alien* it disembowels.

Alien was made more than a decade after *2001* and, at least on the outside, the hardware all looks very familiar – not surprising, perhaps, given the common gene pool of UK special effects artists and model-makers. Inside the ships, though, things could not have been more different. Whereas the vehicles and stations in *2001* were all bright white surfaces, gleaming and factory-fresh, the interiors of *Alien* were dark, cluttered and claustrophobic. Here the spaceship serves to both contain the source of the horror – the alien – but also to amplify it, by embodying so many shadowy dank corners and crawlspaces. And as its self-destruct system refuses to disarm itself, so the ship becomes a sinister co-conspirator in the violence. If the alien doesn't get Ripley, the *Nostromo* will.

(Above)
No film has conveyed the vastness of outer space more effectively than Stanley Kubrick's '2001: A Space Odyssey' (1968).

(Opposite, left)
The ship in John Carpenter's 'Dark Star' (1974) is destroyed by its own 'thermostellar' bomb.

(Opposite, right)
The interiors of the spaceship Nostromo in Ridley Scott's 'Alien' (1979) are dank, gloomy and claustrophobic.

There was a huge explosion at the end of *Star Wars* (1977) too, perhaps the ultimate spaceship film. Here the spacecraft – at least, the ones belonging to the good guys – were beat-up and shabby. They wore their history, and we bought into the idea of an implied past. There wasn't much wonder to be had in *Star Wars*, and exploration was not the point – the galaxy was fully settled, fully under the yolk of imperial subjugation – but at least it all felt old and teeming and vast. Most of that was lost in the generally disappointing prequels, the excess of scale numbing our senses.

George Lucas had reportedly hoped that *Star Wars* would kick off a wave of imitative space operas, but – the odd exception like *Battlestar Galactica* (1978) and *The Last Starfighter* (1984) notwithstanding – it never happened. If anything, *Star Wars* drove the nail into the coffin of the intelligent space film, at least for a couple of decades. *Star Trek: The Motion Picture* (1979) seemed ponderous at the time, lavishing too much time on Douglas Trumbull's stately effects shots, as the Enterprise (and then Spock) slowly penetrates the mysteries of a baleful alien artefact. With the benefit of hindsight, though, it stands out as the last gasp of Kubrickian science-fiction cinema, and a film that at least strives to convey some of the awe of space exploration. (Ironically, two decades later, it would be a spoof of *Star Trek* films – *Galaxy Quest* (1999) – that came closest to recapturing the genuine wonder of space travel, as the stars of a TV space opera find themselves in command of an actual, functioning starship). Peter Hyams's 2010, the 1984 sequel to 2001, was faithful enough to Arthur C. Clarke's book but also shared its central fault, in that it undermined the mystery of the original work by overexplaining. Nonetheless, it remains a space film with real ideas.

Dark matter

James Cameron's *Aliens* (1986) was indecently exciting, a precision-tooled thrill machine, but space travel was largely incidental to the main action, and there was no larger philosophical message. Indeed, as the 1980s wore on, the spaceship film – not to mention the philosophical spaceship film – appeared to be on its way out. Those that did appear were content to play with the most superficial of ideas. For all its virtues, *Alien* was essentially a horror movie set in space. Unfortunately it now seemed that the horror mode was the only viable option for the space film.

The trend continued into the 1990s. *Event Horizon* (1997) was a gore-fest of body horror imagery involving something or other about hyperspace and hell – territory covered by the thematically similar *Supernova* (2000), a box-office dud with a muddled, nonsensical storyline. *Lost in Space* (1998) was just as bad.

What had gone wrong? *Dark Star* might have been cheap, but it had ideas, it dared to speak of 'phenomenology' – of the impossibility of verifying the reality of external sensory inputs. *Silent Running* was about the conflicting ethics of ecosystem management – about a good man forced to act against his nature. *Event Horizon* was a science-fiction film in slasher clothing – science fiction for the *Nightmare on Elm Street* generation.

A decade later this was still the defining mode for space films, as exemplified by *Pandorum* (2009). Danny Boyle's *Sunshine* (2007) at least aimed for higher ground, following a crew who travel to the dying sun in the year 2057 to try to reignite it with a massive nuclear explosion, thereby saving humanity on Earth. Despite a misguided final act that involved the crew being stalked by a demented space captain, there was rather a lot to admire. The film had great ship design, a brilliantly staged spacewalking accident, and many sincere and affectionate nods to the space films of an earlier cinematic era, especially 2001 and *Silent Running*.

But in the new century, gorgeous visuals are almost to be expected. Very few science-fiction films look anything other than exquisite these days, but we now require stories to match the scope and spectacle of the effects – and we don't always get them. David Twohy is one of the few contemporary directors to focus entirely on science fiction. His *Pitch Black* (2000) was an exciting, gritty horror story set in space and on a distant desert planet inhabited by predatory creatures who come out to feed during the darkness of an extended solar eclipse, but its sequel *The Chronicles of Riddick* (2004) seemed to play in a different universe entirely, and though it frequently looked tremendous, was camp rather than involving.

The J.J. Abrams-directed reboots of *Star Trek* are similarly spectacular visually, if you've a taste for CGI. The opening scenes of the first film in the resurrected franchise – involving the evacuation of a stricken starship – achieved a tremendous, breathtaking evocation of the smallness and fragility of human affairs against the vastness of space. But the second, *Star Trek: Into Darkness* (2013), had significantly fewer virtues, shackling itself to a muddled storyline, while ejecting everything that one always took to be the warp core of *Star Trek*: the optimism, the sense of adventure,

(Opposite)
Danny Boyle's 'Sunshine' (2007), set in 2057, follows a spaceship travelling to the dying sun to try to reignite it with a nuclear bomb.

the exploration of the unknown. Abrams's busy, restless eye may be better suited to the pace and colour of the forthcoming *Star Wars* sequels.

If the defining mode of science-fiction cinema concerning space travel since the millennium has been dark, dystopian or horror-inflected, there have been encouraging attempts to tell a different story. Joss Whedon's *Serenity* (2005) might be set in a moderately totalitarian future, but at least manages to find time for its characters to have a laugh or two, while offering some edge-of-seat spaceship action. Here the heroes' ship – which had already starred in the aborted TV series *Firefly* – is a beat-up but serviceable space freighter, a distant cousin to Han Solo's Millennium Falcon, and it too is pitted against the forces of imperial tyranny. In contrast to the friendly-looking freighter, the cruisers of *Serenity*'s government are austere, slab-like and as brutally corporate as skyscrapers. Later in the film we see a crashed rescue ship with the registration code C57-D – an affectionate nod to *Forbidden Planet*.

Moon (2008), the directorial debut of Duncan Jones, was set primarily in and around a lunar base, but the visual tone and atmosphere took its cues from the science-fiction cinema of an earlier generation – from *2001*, *Silent Running*, *Dark Star* and Gerry Anderson. Refreshingly, it also made a minor hero of the base's artificial intelligence.

Whether Alfonso Cuarón's *Gravity* (2013) is science fiction or not is open to debate, but what can't be disputed is its visual splendour. *Gravity* conveys a visceral sense of the fragility of human beings and their machines, against a vast and indifferent universe. The film is suffused with moments of wonder, juxtaposed with the fear of exposure to the unremittingly hostile and unforgiving environment of space itself – in this it has more in common with *2001* than many of the more obvious imitators of Kubrick's film. Like *Apollo 13* (1995), it uses music to find stirring drama in the simple business of surviving re-entry into our atmosphere. Both films are ultimately hymns to homecoming, though, rather than celebrations of the outward urge.

I am probably kinder to the films of my childhood than I am to the films of the present day, tolerating that which I would find unforgivable in a contemporary production. Modern filmmakers have tremendous technological advances over their predecessors. They have the means and the budgets to make anything seem real, and they are presenting their efforts to audiences who, for the most part, are capable of being treated with intelligence. And yet contemporary science-fiction films that journey to outer space so often aim lower than they need to, presenting spectacle rather than depth, telling the same stories over and over again, when there are innumerable possible narratives still almost totally unexplored. They can do more than this. The written form of science fiction hasn't begun to exhaust space as an intellectually rich vein of ideas, and it finds much more to think about than just horror or the need to return home as quickly as possible. Written science fiction still finds ways to celebrate the outward urge, the exploration of the unknown – the deepest human impulse to investigate, something Christopher Nolan's *Interstellar* (2014) recognises, and may yet spark a revival of in cinema.

Space films have an obligation to be entertaining – they have budgets to recoup – but why settle for just being entertained? They also have the potential to leave us with a bracing sense of our own place in the universe – our smallness, our uniqueness, the vulnerability of our small blue planet against an infinite backdrop of so much cold and darkness. ●
With thanks to 'Science Fiction: The Illustrated Encyclopedia', edited by John Clute (Dorling Kindersley, 1995) and the 'National Geographic Encyclopedia of Space', edited by Linda K Glover (National Geographic, 2005)

(Above)
Alfonso Cuarón's 'Gravity' (2013) conveys a visceral sense of the fragility of our place in the vastness of space.

(Opposite)
Duncan Jones's 'Moon' (2008) takes its tone from onscreen science fiction of an earlier era.

THE EVOLUTION OF 2001: A SPACE ODYSSEY

by Stephen Baxter

In the nearly five decades since its release, Stanley Kubrick's *2001: A Space Odyssey* (1968), alongside the Arthur C. Clarke novel with which it co-evolved, has grown in stature and influence. In its day the film won a Hugo Award, the highest honour in the science-fiction field – even if it missed out on a Best Picture Oscar. Today *2001* towers, monolith-like, above the rest of the science-fiction genre. Yet it is possible that one of its co-creators, Clarke, never fully understood its true intent.

2001 tells of a lonely alien sentinel, a black monolith on the moon. When it is uncovered by human explorers the monolith sends a signal to its much more powerful brother, in orbit around Jupiter (Saturn in the novel): a warning to those who left the monoliths that humans have become able to reach beyond their own world. Astronauts Dave Bowman, Frank Poole and computer HAL travel to Jupiter to study the alien presence. Poole is cast adrift by HAL, but Bowman survives to reach the Jupiter Monolith – which proves to be a gate to the stars, and transcendence. Only then do we realise that the caption of the film's prologue – 'The Dawn Of Man', in which man-apes encounter their own monolith – applies not just to our brutish ancestors, but to us as well. Spaceships or not, we are still almost as primitive.

Unusually, Kubrick's film was not an adaptation of Clarke's novel, and nor is the book a mere novelisation of the film. Kubrick and Clarke evolved both together over a number of years, and the final products differ markedly in a number of respects – a reflection of tensions between the two creators.

The project's first working title was the rather mundane *How the Solar System Was Won*. Clarke seems to have imagined that the film would be a dramatisation of the near-future human colonisation of the solar system, rather like the Robert Heinlein-inspired *Destination Moon* (1950). Clarke was part of a wartime generation of authors who attempted to map our future in generally technophilic and optimistic tones – a thread in Clarke's work that can be traced from his early lunar flight novel *Prelude to Space* (1951), through such classic visions as *The Sands of Mars* (1952) and *A Fall Of Moondust* 1961). Clarke's technical prescience led to him having a

major impact on the real world. Scientists and engineers took him seriously, and his fame as originator of the concept of geostationary communications satellites was well known. His depictions of a wondrous and perhaps accessible future motivated the post-war generation who grew up to become the engineers who built the real-life moon ships. It's no surprise that one crew of Apollo astronauts chose to give their capsule the name *Odyssey*.

However it was not Clarke's predictive hit-rate that intrigued Kubrick, but another, more complex part of his *oeuvre* and personality. After much discussion, the starting point for the project that became *2001* was an 11-page short story of Clarke's, first published in 1951 in an obscure magazine. *The Sentinel* has all the key elements of the final saga. It is a tale of near-future lunar explorers who happen upon a pyramid-shaped artefact on the moon, the discovery of which triggers a signal to its makers, those who wait for us to mature and join them.

As Clarke explained in *The Lost Worlds of 2001* (1972), the story of how that lonely pyramid was turned into a monolith is a complex one. The appeal of Clarke's *Sentinel* to Kubrick the filmmaker is clear: the lunar artefact would be a simple, compelling, wordless symbol, its very silent presence conveying its meaning and purpose. But tension developed between Clarke and Kubrick over this aspect, as over many others. Clarke, setting out to map the rational, technological future, originally even wanted to include 'talking heads' in the film – real-world scientists speculating on space travel, life on other worlds. But the project was steadily subverted by Kubrick.

Consider the sequence of the monolith being uncovered on the moon. At face value this is authentic Clarke in his *Fall of Moondust* mode; we see the paraphernalia of the future in somewhat clumsy use: videophones, space shuttles, a moon base... But even in these most literal scenes, Kubrick sought to display the banality of our future selves. With empty dialogue, monochrome food and washed-out lighting, Kubrick pointed out the deficiency of 21st-century humanity, not their Heinleinian triumph; they were awaiting uplift just as had their ape-like ancestors.

CAUTION WEIGHTLESS CONDITION

Stanley Kubrick (left) and Arthur C. Clarke during the production of '2001'

Much of what dialogue remains in the final film, far from being specialist lectures as Clarke imagined, consists of chatter imparting little key information; it is a sound effect, background noise. Kubrick told a complex story not with words but through stark symbols: the ape hand touching the smooth monolith, and later the fully evolved spacesuited hand with the monolith on the moon; the famous hurled bone/spacecraft edit; the evolution of Bowman into the Star Child. To some extent the creative conflict between Kubrick and Clarke was resolved with the publication of the novel, in which Clarke's clear rationalism contrasts with the obliquity of Kubrick's film. The novel *explains*.

But Kubrick saw something about Clarke that Clarke himself may not have perceived – that the central truth of 2001, like much of Clarke's work, is not about the triumph of technocracy but

the mystery of existence: the contrast between the highest aspirations of humanity – in Clarke, often expressed in terms of spaceflight – and the unutterable wonder that may lie forever beyond us.

The Sentinel had, in retrospect, served as notice of a new and contradictory note in Clarke's career, in which he began to show himself as drawn to metaphysical speculation, even mysticism. Clarke did not deny this aspect of his work (though he was dismissive of fakery and bad science) – the universe is indeed full of wonder, he told us, which no complete human being, no matter how rational, could fail to apprehend. So we encounter the marvellous transcendence of works like *Childhood's End* (1953), which found echoes in the uplifting of Bowman into the Star Child. This was what Kubrick drew out in 2001.

After all these years it is difficult to trace the influence of 2001 in its film and novel

forms, so deeply embedded have they become in the history of their genres. HAL has been the subject of academic studies of how near or far we are to realising such an artificial mind. 2001's vision of our future in space appears even more remote. Many of us regret that we do not live in a world of nuclear-powered spaceships to Jupiter. 2001's lunar vision, with its stark shadows and craggy mountains, left at least one Apollo astronaut (Bill Anders) disappointed with what he saw of the real moon.

As for life beyond the Earth, we have not yet, of course, found compelling evidence of alien beings. The notion of human development being affected by alien intervention had been dramatised before 2001, for instance in Nigel Kneale's TV serial *Quatermass and the Pit* (1958). But Clarke's vision – of lofty aliens which visit worlds like ours to uplift its inhabitants – has been the subject of serious academic studies; such a scenario would explain why astronomers don't detect alien activity – we are in a kind of reserve, and the wardens are hiding from view.

In fiction, David Brin's *Uplift* series (1980 onwards) extended this notion to its logical conclusion: who uplifted the uplifters? Brin imagines chains of races uplifted by their seniors all the way back to semi-mythical Primogenitors. But the uplifters need not be benevolent, as in Ridley Scott's *Prometheus* (2012). Indeed in 2001 the first tool made by the man-apes, inspired by the monolith, is a weapon. Clarke's own continuing vision of 2001 reached a climax as humanity comes into conflict with the monoliths in *3001: The Final Odyssey* (1997), and alien interventions are well-intentioned but destructive in my own collaborations with Clarke, *A Time Odyssey* (2004-8), a reworking of the 2001 mythos.

In the end one cannot deny the emotional and conceptual power of 2001. We are, after all, living only a short time after Copernicus, Darwin and geologists demolished whatever certainty we might have had about our place in the universe. We no longer believe God is out there – and yet we still seek answers. Kubrick's film, drawing on Clarke's subconscious dreams, filled with a longing for transcendence and for contact with vanished parents, is the finest expression of the loneliness of our age. ●

Home invasions: British television sci-fi

by Matthew Sweet

One Saturday night before I was born, two men came into the bedroom. There they stood, strange and silent in the doorway. Mr Oak, rotund and smiling like some pensionable *putti*. Mr Quill, gaunt, hollow-eyed, jug-eared, a Brylcreemed Max Schreck. The woman at the dressing-table saw them in her mirror as she brushed her hair. She asked them if there was anything they wanted, but must have known that this was a question with only bad answers. And in they came, waddling towards her, shifting their weight from left to right.

I've seen what happened next. It was captured on a little spool of 16mm film, deemed too horrible to share with the public and buried for 30 years in an Australian archive. Here's what the censor saw: Mr Quill's eyes widening to an insane stare; his mouth gaping, as if about to sing, or retch. Mr Oak doing the same. A searing hiss issuing from the two men's parted lips, and the owner of the bedroom, Mrs Maggie Harris, clutching instinctively at her throat. At this point, the image loses focus. We see the mouths of Oak and Quill, charcoal-biscuit black; Mrs Harris struggling to remain conscious. Then the hissing noise dissipates. The natural sound of the room is also quite gone, displaced by the drum of a heartbeat. Nothing but *ba-doom, ba-doom, ba-doom* – and Mrs Harris drowning, waterlessly, on the bedroom floor.

I say bedroom, but I mean the floor of Studio D at Lime Grove – the BBC facility so antiquated that the heat of the lamps set off the sprinkler system; so cramped that the production team of *Doctor Who*, creators of Oak and Quill and Mrs Maggie Harris, were obliged to scale down their police box to fit it in the lift. Science-fiction programme-makers are used to such conditions. Over the decades, British television has fallen in and out of love with the genre, but passionate moods have rarely yielded generous budgets. (Even modern, world-record-breaking, globe-spanning, simulcasted *Doctor Who* is not as expensive as it looks.) And this has never much seemed to matter. The main aim of British sci-fi television has been to make us feel uncomfortable in our own homes – and all you need for a good séance is a suburban living room, a dim lamp and a medium willing to do the dead in different voices.

Freud's 1919 essay on the *Unheimlich* ("the class of frightening things that leads us back to what is known and familiar") does not explain *Star Trek*, but it might be the manifesto of small-screen British sci-fi. A set of ideas to send technophobic impulses singing through the pylons; bring Sapphire and Steel into contact with a blank-faced being who lives inside Daguerreotypes and photographic *cartes de visite*; allow the Doctor to encounter the Goodge Street Yeti, a dead man stuffed into his own enamel lunchbox and malignant aliens that can make plastic murderous or inhabit a TV signal beamed from Ally Pally.

Early television was a nocturnal activity. Darkness became it. The 405-line image was difficult to watch during the bright summer evenings without drawing the curtains. Special TV lamps cast light upon the wall behind the set, giving sufficient luminance to ensure that licence-fee payers weren't staring at a single source of light, which was considered injurious to the eyes. These appliances also allowed viewers to find their way around the room in the seconds it took for the set to warm up and the image to channel through the ether and on to the screen. In this multi-platform age, it's worth remembering that until very recently, television science fiction was entirely domestic. The shadowy lunar tunnels of *Pathfinders in Space* (ATV, 1960) led to your lounge. Winston Smith's telescreen was conjured in the field of your own device. The cobwebbed aliens of *Quatermass and the Pit* (BBC, 1958-9) twitched in a corner of your living room. Hobbs Lane, Totter's Lane, Victory Mansions – they were all on your street.

(Top)
André Morell as Professor
Quatermass and Cec Linder
as Dr Matthew Roney in Nigel
Kneale's 'Quatermass and
the Pit' (BBC, 1958-59).

(Above)
'A for Andromeda' (BBC,
1961), starring Desmond
Knight, Mary Morris, Julie
Christie and Peter Fleming.

(Previous page)
Peter Capaldi as the
12th incarnation of the
Doctor in 'Doctor Who'
(BBC 1963-89, 2005-).

Nigel Kneale knew that when he mapped out Professor Bernard Quatermass's Britain: a territory of chain-link fences, gasometers, barbed wire and anxiety. Cecil Edwin Webber and Anthony Coburn knew it when they wrote the scripts that introduced us to a junkyard with a transdimensional secret. Small-screen British science fiction preferred these quiet incursions. The hostiles of *A for Andromeda* (BBC, 1961) didn't despatch the flying saucers: instead, from a distance of 2.5 million light years, they sent a radio message instructing the human race how to conquer itself. The aliens of *Undermind* (ABC, 1965) had no time for ray guns: their weapons were nervous breakdowns, marital strife, sex scandals, bad financial advice. They're the only alien invaders whose plans include dismantling the NHS – though the shadowy Centaurans of *Counterstrike* (BBC, 1969) might have tried, had their show made it to a second year. *Doomwatch* (BBC, 1970-2), a series engineered by Kit Pedler and Gerry Davis, a pair of refugees from *Doctor Who*, dispensed with the extraterrestrial altogether. Their secret invasions were launched by governments and corporations – the cigarette manufacturer increasing sales with drug-laced chocolate; the food company sluicing their workers with impotence-inducing fish hormones.

A signpost in this landscape is the report on television and science fiction commissioned by the BBC in 1962. Its co-author was Alice Frick, a farm girl from Alberta who, after gaining her degree, borrowed $80 for the bus fare to Toronto and found work in the radio drama department of the Canadian Broadcasting Company. Frick had a good eye for a script. She saw that a submission called *Flight into Danger* would be a lousy radio play but an exciting TV piece, and passed it to her colleague Sydney Newman – launching Arthur Hailey as the king of the airborne thriller. Reunited at the BBC, Frick and Newman found they had a shared distaste for science fiction with too pulpy a texture. They were two Canadians, united, perhaps a little snootily, in their rejection of certain aspects of American popular culture. 'Bug-Eyed Monsters' were out. Spaceships were discouraged – Irene Shubik's anthology *Out of this World* (ABC, 1962) had, it was felt, tried and failed to make these fly. The most telegenic area of science fiction, the report concluded, was the drama of "threat and disaster" – the kind of story developed by John Wyndham in print and Nigel Kneale on the screen. The public, Frick noted, was "as yet not interested in the mere exploitation of ideas" – though the appearance of Shubik's *Out of the Unknown* (BBC, 1965-71) suggested that BBC2 viewers possessed the taste of tomorrow. (*Doctor Who*, of course, had broken these rules by the end of its first series, and began its second production block by bringing Bug-Eyed Monsters to London in a fleet of flying saucers.)

If British television science fiction of the 1950s and 60s threatened its audience with disaster, the work of the following decade offered social collapse as a form of moral correction. The first shot of Terry Nation's *Survivors* (BBC, 1975-77) is of a machine that catastrophe will soon send to the reliquary – an automatic tennis-ball dispenser, ugly, Dalek-like and decadent. We're encouraged to see life before the plague as one for "pampered babies", and the new one as more vital and honest. This, despite the buboes and the looters and the odd wistful remark about the absence of grapefruits and oranges, is what Brian Aldiss called a "cosy catastrophe". Douglas Livingstone's adaptation of *The Day of the Triffids* (BBC, 1981) also fits this bill. It has scenes of horror – a pensioner breaking her nails as she tries to open a tin of instant coffee, a parade of sightless drunks, chittering plants licking gently at a decomposing corpse – but the serial shares the novel's unwillingness to mourn the vanished world.

These ideas are most powerfully legible, however, in *The Changes* (BBC,

(Top)
The threat in 'Doomwatch'
(BBC, 1971-72) comes from
government and corporations.

(Left)
Douglas Livingstone's 'cosy
catastrophe' 'The Day of
the Triffids' (BBC, 1981).

(Above)
Producer Irene Shubik's 'Out of
the Unknown' (BBC, 1965-71)
featured adaptations of work
by many notable SF writers.

(Top, left)
The inhabitants of England reject technology and modern urban life in Anna Horne's 'The Changes' (BBC, 1975).

(Top, right)
David McCallum and Joanna Lumley as the time-travelling agents in 'Sapphire and Steel' (ATV, 1979-82).

(Above, left)
'Blake's 7' (BBC, 1978-81) is set amid a dystopic future regime enforced by death squads and show trials.

(Above, right)
The future is a bleak totalitarian one in Troy Kennedy Martin's adaptation of 'The Old Men at the Zoo' (BBC, 1983).

1975) – a rare example of dystopian television that concludes with the prospect of an imminent return to normality. In Anna Home's adaptation of Peter Dickinson's trilogy of novels, the inhabitants of England rage against the machines. A wild ancestral howl invades the air, and an ordinary family in Bristol – pipe-smoking Dad, stove-bound Mum, studious daughter – feel compelled to butcher the television and tear the innards from clocks and kettles. (In my mind, these startlingly violent images are entwined with memories of the *Blue Peter* team's reports from the aftermath of Pol Pot's Year Zero.) Towards the end of the serial, the schoolgirl heroine (Victoria Williams) encounters a couple called Mary and John, who, she learns, had already rejected modern urban life before the catastrophe occurred. Mary (Merelina Kendall) describes how she miscarried after disobeying her doctor's advice to give up work. Her ambition duly punished, she and her husband downshifted to the countryside, where they were living, happy and fecund, when the country went mad and began smashing up its cars with hammers. "At first we thought it might be a good thing," says Mary.

The remark exposes one of the informing beliefs of this kind of science fiction. Its attraction to a pastoral Britain, its fixation upon the details of metalwork, milk production and harvest-time, suggest that *Survivors* and *The Changes* share the broader survivalist preoccupation of the moment – one that also encompasses the iron-smelting activities of the volunteers of *Living in the Past* (BBC, 1978) and Tom and Barbara's attempts in *The Good Life* (BBC, 1975-8) to generate electricity from goat manure. All these series express a hankering to return to lifestyles that predate capitalism, computers, consumerism. Perhaps one of the reasons why *Sapphire and Steel* (ATV, 1979-82) remains so powerful is that it resists this view: its theology argues that the past itself is a source of menace and danger, that the only safe life is one lived in an environment purged of historical artefacts.

The real dystopias of 1970s television sci-fi are the ones in which society fails to collapse. In *The Guardians* (LWT, 1971), an alliance of

lawyers and industrialists dissolve parliamentary democracy and suppress union power with plastic bullets. (The McWhirter brothers must have watched it and fist-bumped their approval.) In Wilfred Greatorex's 1990 (BBC, 1977-8), red tape and red politicians enforce a permanent winter of discontent. In *Blake's 7* (BBC, 1978-81), a thousand-year Reich, run by a woman in fur and feathers, maintains power through death squads, drugged water and show-trials on false charges of child molestation. Blackest of all, the totalitarian future of Troy Kennedy Martin's adaptation of Angus Wilson's *The Old Men at the Zoo* (BBC, 1983), in which the brutalised and blindfolded staff form a conga, trousers round their ankles, to an execution disguised as a toilet break.

British television has no stomach now for anything so grim – though it occasionally comes close. *Torchwood: Children of Earth* (BBC, 2009) features a scene in which British cabinet ministers decide to use Ofsted reports to determine which children will be sacrificed to a race of aliens who use kids like Nicorette patches. The *Unheimlich*, however, remains undiluted, and in *Doctor Who*, seems stronger than ever. Since its revival in 2005, the programme has produced moments of weirdness that bear comparison with the best efforts of the Surrealists. A respirator erupting from a human face; the funerary statue that moves in for the kill in the blink of an eye; the veiled Victorian lesbian lizard who returns home from a day's work picking bits of Jack the Ripper from her teeth.

The medium that conveys these images, however, is undergoing a transformation. Fifty years ago, if you were disturbed by the Daleks, you had nowhere to go but upstairs. Now *Doctor Who* screens at your local cinema, on your laptop, on your phone. Like a being that has gained the power to walk from the frame of a Victorian photograph, British science-fiction television has escaped the television set. Surely, in its next phase, its murderers and monsters will follow us from the commuter train, through the streets, up to the bedroom, and into the interstices of our lives. ●

SPACE OPERAS

by Laura Adams

There is a subgenre of sci-fi cinema that challenges our gender expectations, explores ideals of freedom and deals with universal subjects of family, love and the ever present battle between good and evil – all while offering epic depictions of adventure, space exploration, fantasy and magic. The 'space opera'.

Space opera films typically depart from such science-fiction themes as Earth's future technologies and societal structures, and don't investigate the otherness of human contact with alien species. Instead, they dive head first into exploring entire galaxies of new species, multiple polities and belief systems and chart ongoing wars between good and evil. Their popularity lies in the reason the term 'space opera' was originally coined by writer Wilson Tucker in 1940 – albeit as a pejorative –responding to stories being published in magazines such as *Weird Tales* and *Amazing Stories*: they are intergalactic romps, pure adventures rich in melodrama, like the 'horse opera' western or a soap opera set among the stars.

How can something this much fun be a bad thing? And yet ever since Wilson Tucker's 1940 article, space operas have attracted critical scorn in measure roughly equal to their popular appeal. They're not *real* science fiction surely? Where's the science? Certainly many space operas are probably better regarded as what we might call 'space fantasy' than science fiction, their stories grounded (or un-grounded) in magic and pure invention rather than science. Take the force in *Star Wars*, or the pagan-like element that is within Leeloo in *The Fifth Element*. Not that hard SF and the space opera are necessarily mutually exclusive, but more often than not space operas make their own rules, and invite you to go with them.

One classic space opera that frequently does attempt to ground its details in explainable science is *Star Trek*. From its beginnings on the small screen (1966-69), through *The Animated Series* (1973-74), *The Next Generation* (1987-94), *Deep Space 9* (1993-99), *Voyager* (1995-2001) and *Enterprise* (2001-05), and on to the recent J.J Abrams-directed reboots *Star Trek* (2009) and *Star Trek: Into Darkness* (2013), *Star Trek* has taken as its starting point "space, the final frontier", venturing from Earth to find new places, new people, finding governments, sovereignties and strange rituals encompassing life, death and sex. *Star Trek* is essentially a soap opera in space, with episodes dealing with alien romances, abuse, betrayal and more.

Television has proven to be a natural home for the space opera. Series such as *Blake's 7* (1978-81), *Lost in Space* (1965-68) and *Flash Gordon* (1954-55) were family-friendly, camp romps that were small-screen extensions of the literary pulp fictions that Tucker pointed an accusing finger at with his 'soap opera in space' label – episodic scenarios involving everyday stories of family and issues of the time. More recent explorations of this episodic approach include the comedic *Red Dwarf* (1988-99), *Babylon 5* (1993-98), *Farscape* (1999-2003) and *Hitchhiker's Guide to the Galaxy* (1981), the latter bridging the gap between space opera's frequent comedic nods and satire at its finest, drawn from the unique mind of author Douglas Adams. In a slightly more straightfaced vein is the original *Battlestar Galactica* series (1978), launched in the wake of the success of *Star Wars*, and revived for a hugely successful reboot that ran between 2004-09. Both incarnations of *BSG* include the space opera elements of epic battle, exploration of beliefs, romance and overlaps into military science fiction, with battle cruisers and quasi-military dialogue. In *BSG* the galaxy is vast, but inhabited only by humans and androids.

Nevertheless, the *Star Wars* films and their spin-off animated series *The Clone Wars* remain the best-known onscreen space operas. The plot lines, with their base in myth and classic drama, unfold as Darth Vader reveals a familial link, setting his son Luke Skywalker against him in a good vs evil betrayal that only the power he himself has

'Battlestar Galactica' (2004-09)

passed down can overcome. Princess Leia Organa's undiscovered sororal link leads to a romantic showdown on the boughs of Endor's treetop town, we explore multiple planetary systems, each with their own governance, and see the magical 'force' used. Wars are fought for dictatorial control and the genocide of an entire people on Leia's home planet of Alderaan by the Imperial Death Star marks a tragic moment in an epic portrayal of a revolution in action.

It's useful to consider *Star Wars* – a film deliberate in its embrace of space opera signifiers – against other adventures in space, such as Paul Verhoeven's *Starship Troopers* (1997) and Gavin Hood's *Ender's Game* (2013), both adaptations of classic sci-fi novels (by Robert Heinlein and Orson Scott Card respectively). While both feature battles on alien planets and long-distance space travel, they pitch humanity against a single evil alien 'other', rather than exploring a galactic diversity of species. For this reason Andrew Stanton's *John Carter* (2012), adapted from the classic series of novels by Edgar Rice Burroughs, can be considered a space opera, despite taking place entirely on one planet, Mars (or Barsoom as the inhabitants know it). It features references to other planets and creatures, and has real fun making humanity the unusual species in the mix.

Luc Besson's *The Fifth Element* (1997) is a space opera in which extravagance fills every frame, from the Jean Paul Gaultier costume design, to the riot of colour in production design, make-up and cinematography, and creature design to rival *Star Wars* in its variety. Developed around a perfect being (handily an attractive woman, allowing for a romantic sub-plot) who is the final, fifth element required to protect the earth from an asteroid body

'The Empire Strikes Back' (1981)

made of pure evil. Split mainly between a future Earth and a cruise spaceship, the threat and exoticism of creatures from other galaxies is present at all times.

Joss Whedon breathed distinctive new life into the space opera when he made the fan-favourite TV series *Firefly* (2002) and its big-screen successor *Serenity* (2005). Both take place within a single planetary system, with humanoid inhabitants. Tropes lifted from the western, such as frontier claims on settler planets and cowboy style wrangling (of actual cows in one episode), lead to interesting space opera elements including a romance between the ship's captain and the prostitute (or Companion) and a 'magic' being whose psychic abilities, superhuman strength and fighting skills are a weapon against the evil Alliance.

Whedon was also the writer behind the

animated space opera *Titan A.E*, directed by Don Bluth and Gary Goldman in 2000. Its adventure-laden vision of a characterful multi-species galaxy is shared by James Gunn's 2014 blockbuster Marvel comics-inspired hit *Guardians of the Galaxy*. Like *Titan A.E.*, *Guardians of the Galaxy* also begins with tragedy and a young boy leaving his planet, and boasts an absent father who bestows unexplained power that will ultimately save everyone from destruction, as well as an evil being attempting the genocide of whole societies, interspecies romance and an unlikely team with questionable ethics formed to save the day.

In the end, perhaps it is this latter trope that has given the space opera the fan base it has: the formation of a motley crew who eventually turn into friends. We want to be a part of that story, to identify with at least one of the characters, to perhaps fall in love with another and find one who it's fun to hate. With entire languages to learn (the growls of Klingon, the high-pitched squawk of a Jawa, the cool slang of the future Mandarin-English hybrid of the worlds of *Serenity*) and a galaxy's worth of creatures and societies to consider, space opera affords the audience a chance to completely trust in the filmmaker, hand over all sense of reality, physics, mathematics and common sense, and enjoy an epic romp across space. ●

'Guardians of the Galaxy' (2014)

'Star Trek' (2009)

Afrofuturism
by Ashley Clark

The term 'Afrofuturism' was coined by cultural critic Mark Dery in his 1994 essay 'Black to the Future'. Dery was specifically addressing the work of African-American authors – including the trailblazing likes of Samuel R. Delany and Octavia Butler – whose science-fiction prose explored black themes within the context of developing 20th-century technology.

Dery expressed surprise at the paucity of African-American science-fiction literature, given that "African-Americans, in a very real sense, are the descendants of alien abductees; they inhabit a science-fiction nightmare in which unseen but no less impassable force fields of intolerance frustrate their movements; official histories undo what has been done; and technology is too often brought to bear on black bodies." Dery went on to cite the branding of slaves, the macabre Tuskegee sterilisation experiment from 1932 to 1972, and the disproportionate use of tasers and weapons on America's black communities as examples of the latter.

If, as William Gibson suggests, "mid-century mainstream American science fiction had often been triumphalist and militaristic, a sort of folk propaganda for American exceptionalism… a white monoculture", Afrofuturism was the method by which black authors could carve out some elbow room in order to project and control their own futures.

In the time since Dery's initial use of the term, however, Afrofuturism has come to represent both a flexible artistic aesthetic, and a framework for critical theory specifically applicable to multimedia work concerned with imagined and alternative black experiences. Speaking to the concept's broadness, author Ytasha Womack writes: "Afrofuturism combines elements of science fiction, historical fiction, speculative fiction, fantasy, Afrocentricity, and magic realism with non-Western beliefs."

Notable examples include the visual art and sculpture of Kenya-born Wangechi Muta, the canvases of Jean-Michel Basquiat, the visionary graffiti of Rammellzee, and the performance art of Chicago-based Nick Cave. Yet Afrofuturist ideas – long predating Dery's essay – have found their most prolific and visible outlet in music. The 1950s and 60s saw the free jazz and avant-garde work of Sun Ra and his Arkestra, Alice Coltrane and Ornette Coleman, the forward-thinking saxophonist who was once approached by NASA to create music for its space programmes (a fact recorded in Shirley Clarke's blissfully eccentric 1985 documentary *Ornette: Made in America*), and even titled one of his albums 'Science Fiction'.

In the 1970s, the likes of George Clinton and Bootsy Collins's Parliament-Funkadelic fused joyous funk with gaudy science-fiction imagery, while Jamaican reggae and dub artists such as Lee "Scratch" Perry and King Tubby made cosmological theory indivisible from their music and personae. In the 1980s, the rise of electronic music opened new avenues for engagement with scientific themes. As cultural theorist Tricia Rose has observed: "[What acts] like Afrika Bambaataa saw in Kraftwerk's use of the robot was an understanding of themselves as *already having been robots*. Adopting 'the robot' reflected a response to an existing condition: namely, that they were labour for capitalism, that they had very little value as people in this society." Techno musicians like Juan Atkins, Derrick May and Underground Resistance further sought to blur the lines between man and machine, while many of their inheritors in the UK's hardcore, jungle, and drum and bass scenes, such as 4 Hero and A Guy Called Gerald, also made reference to space and science-fiction imagery in their music.

Afrofuturistic ideas found a ready, willing home in hip-hop. Albums like 'Fear of a Black Planet' by Public Enemy, 'ATLiens' by OutKast, and 'Dr. Octagonecologyst' by Kool Keith's alter-ego Dr. Octagon all looked, in various ways, to investigate where science fiction ended and

the black American existence began. The most prominent current proponent of Afrofuturist aesthetics is the Archandroid herself, Janelle Monáe, whose hyper-stylised music videos have explored the realms of bondage and freedom through the worlds of fashion and robotics.

But the musician who most notably fused Afrofuturist aesthetics with film is the aforementioned Sun Ra. Holding no legal birth certificate, it is believed Sun Ra was born in the Jim Crow hot-spot, Birmingham, Alabama, in 1914. Ra always maintained, however, that he was not of this planet, and deliberately crafted an intangible, mythical persona that fused science-fiction ideas and aesthetics with Egyptian mysticism, producing an otherworldliness that infused the music he made until his death in 1993.

John Coney's bizarre, unclassifiable film *Space Is the Place* (1974) features Sun Ra playing himself. At the start of the film, Ra travels back in time to the Chicago strip club where he used to play piano under the alias 'Sonny Ray' in 1943. There he confronts The Overseer (Ray Johnson), a black, blindingly white-suited mega-pimp, and they agree on a card game to determine the fate of the black race. What follows is a curious *mélange* of comedy, musical performance and, occasionally, lurid blaxploitation aesthetics (it sometimes feels like a Benny Hill film) that also has a number of serious points to make about the plight of young urban blacks in a harsh, post-Civil Rights climate: 'Space' is unambiguously posited by Ra as a utopian refuge for African-Americans.

In the same era, films such as Ivan Dixon's *The Spook Who Sat by the Door* (1973), about a black CIA agent who goes rogue to organise an uprising, and Bill Gunn's disturbing vampire thriller *Ganja and Hess* (1973), eschewed the cartoonishly Manichaean social dynamics of the Blaxploitation genre in favour of interrogative, formally daring explorations of social realities through a subversive contemporary lens. The same can be said for Lizzie Borden's *Born in Flames* (1983), a dizzying, doc-style feminist sci-fi set in a New York City ten years after a peaceful socialist revolution has rendered all men equal, leaving women to pick up the battle.

One recurring tenet of Afrofuturism-infused cinema is the interrogation of the trauma of slavery. A decade after *Space Is the Place*, John Sayles's witty, stylish *The Brother from Another Planet* (1984) returned to the idea of an extra terrestrial's journey to a recognisable North American urban centre. A playful spin on the time-honoured runaway slave narrative, it stars Joe Morton as a mute, unnamed alien who lands in Harlem after a spaceship accident, and finds himself on the run from two mysterious white men bent on returning him to captivity. He is taken in and protected by the inhabitants of New York, who come to resemble a latter-day manifestation of the Underground Railroad, the network of secret routes and safe houses used by 19th-century slaves in the United States to reach free states.

Haile Gerima's blistering *Sankofa* (1993), meanwhile, tells the story of a self-absorbed female fashion model on a shoot in Ghana, who is spiritually transported back to a plantation in the antebellum south. Here, she experiences the physical and psychic horrors of slavery, and eventually the redemptive power of community and rebellion. Gerima's film poetically reflects the powerful observation made by author Greg Tate: "Knowing yourself as a black person – historically, spiritually, and culturally – is not something that's given to you, institutionally; it's an arduous journey that must be undertaken by the individual."

Elsewhere, films such as Ridley Scott's *Blade Runner* (1982) and Neill Blomkamp's *District 9* (2009) have offered distinct allegorical spins on slavery, while Steve McQueen, harking back to the ideas expressed in Dery's essay, said of his Oscar-winning *12 Years a Slave* (2013): "I always thought

(Previous page)
Sun Ra, Saturn-born traveller of the spaceways, in a promotional shot for John Coney's 'Space Is the Place' (1974).

(Above)
George Clinton's Funkadelic fused funk with sci-fi imagery on such albums as 1975's 'Mothership Connection'.

(Below)
Lizzie Borden's feminist sci-fi film 'Born in Flames' (1983)

about this film as being a science-fiction movie. [Solomon Northup is] going to a land where there's a book called the Bible, which everyone interprets in a different way, and there are people who are slaves and people who aren't."

Although Afrofuturism is broadly recognised as a blend of aesthetics and ideas rather than a genre *per se*, it's nevertheless germane to address the historic issue of black representation in science fiction. As Womack observes, "It was an age-old joke that blacks in science-fiction movies from the 50s through the 90s typically had a dour fate. The black man who saved the day in the original *Night of the Living Dead* was killed by trigger happy cops."

Save for the occasional refreshing presence of a Nyota Uhura (Nichelle Nichols) in *Star Trek* or a Lando Calrissian (Billy Dee Williams in *Star Wars*), it's difficult to think of too many significant, non-menial roles for blacks in science fiction, until a boom in the 1990s stymied the genre's generally monocultural approach. The Wachowskis' *The Matrix* trilogy (1999-2003), and James Cameron's *Avatar* (2009), in particular, featured multiracial casts, and offered a revised future that welcomed mysticism, explored the physical and emotional limits of technology, and advocated for self-expression and peace in the face of hostile threat. Elsewhere, Will Smith became a key science-fiction leading man, saving the world in *Independence Day* (1996), *Men in Black* (1997), and *I Am Legend* (2007); Denzel Washington played humanity's saviour in *The Book of Eli* (2010); and Wesley Snipes, in the *Blade* trilogy of futuristic vampire films (1998-2004), became one of the most iconic action heroes of the late 20th century.

From the examples cited, Afrofuturism may seem like a US-heavy phenomenon – after all, the term was coined by an American author – but its ideas have spread globally. The most comprehensive cinematic exegesis of Afrofuturistic ideas to date is *The Last Angel of History* (1996), directed by John Akomfrah, the British director then of the influential Black Audio Film Collective. *The Last Angel of History* is a blend of science-fiction parable and essay film in which revealing interviews with esteemed musicians, writers and cultural critics – as well as archival video footage and photography – are interwoven with the fictional story of the 'data thief', who must travel through time and space in search of the code that holds the key to his future. Other British filmmakers to have engaged with Afrofuturistic ideas include The Otolith Group (of which the influential cultural critic Kodwo Eshun is a key member), Ngozi Onwurah, whose *Welcome II the Terrordome* (1993) unfolds a post-apocalyptic scenario in which all black people are herded into a huge ghetto; and Kibwe Tavares, whose Brixton riots-referencing short *Robots of Brixton* (2011) depicts an explosion of violence between robot drudges and the police.

In terms of African and African-themed cinema, Frances Bodomo's short *Afronauts* (2013) relates the story of the Zambia Space Academy's attempts to beat America to the moon in 1969; and Wanuri Kahiu's *Pumzi* (2009), Kenya's first ever science-fiction film, takes a trip into a post-apocalyptic world in which water has almost run out.

A key reason for the spread of Afrofuturistic ideas and aesthetics is the rapid development and democratisation of technology. As Womack suggests, "The storytelling gatekeepers vanished with the high-speed modem, and for the first time in history, people of colour now have a greater ability to project their own stories." Artists of today can easily harness the power of digital media, social platforms, digital video, gaming technology and graphic arts to create and disseminate stories, and connect with audiences inexpensively. The paucity of imagined black futures that Dery lamented in 1994 is increasingly – and mercifully – a thing of the past. ●

(Above)
John Akomfrah's astonishing 'The Last Angel of History' (1996), a blend of sci-fi parable and essay film.

(Below)
Nichelle Nicols as Nyota Uhura in 'Star Trek' (1966-).

Unearthly strangers
by Kim Newman

The tagline of Paul W.S. Anderson's little-liked spin-off mash-up *AVP: Alien vs Predator* (2004) is 'whoever wins ... we lose'. This scrambled franchise, which began in video games and comic books before its brief two-film series, is a prime example of 'if you wanted to get here, you shouldn't have started from there' thinking. Its aliens (the xenomorphs from Ridley Scott's 1979 *Alien* and sequels) are actual predators, whereas its predators (from John McTiernan's 1987 *Predator* and sequel) aren't.

Weirdly, it's written into the DNA of the franchise that 'we' – humanity – are more likely to find common cause with the spike-mawed, dreadlocked trophy hunters of *Predator* than the acid-blooded, insectoid vermin of *Alien*. The *Alien* aliens are just hardy parasitic bugs, with an animal urge to survive and propagate, whereas the *Predator* non-predators have interstellar travel capacity, something approaching an aesthetic sense if their fishnet-and-leather outfits and intricately detailed weapons can represent a whole culture and at least a working knowledge of where to find the roughest vacation spots on Earth.

Though fearsome-looking, the Alien acts without malice – it incubates inside John Hurt and slaughters Sigourney Weaver's crewmates because it has to, and the real villain of the film (and sequels) is the exploitative terran company that wants to secure the beast for its bioweapons division. Predator civilisation is at least on a par with, say, the Vulcans of *Star Trek* or the squat explorers of *E.T. the Extra-Terrestrial* (1982), but all they can think to do with their spare time is stalk endangered species in the hope of mounting Arnold Schwarzenegger's head over the fireplace back home. At best, their whole society is some sort of Hemingway fantasy of manliness on a cosmic scale, complete with initiation rites and blooding – at worst, they are the redneck American scum of the universe, and the *AVP* films miss a trick by not despising them more than the industrious, focused-on-survival Aliens.

Imagined communities

Of course, the failing is not of a whole species, but of the imagination. John and Jim Thomas, who scripted *Predator*, set out to write an action movie with a monster macguffin – an alien big-game hunter had already showed up in Greydon Clark's *Without Warning* (1980) – not a science-fiction movie representing a half-way credible alien culture.

Indeed, outside the (admittedly large) shadow of the monolith of Stanley Kubrick's 2001: *A Space Odyssey* (1968), there is a noticeable lack of genuinely *alien* aliens in the cinema. Kubrick, it should be noted, took the form seriously enough to put out a request for 'the world's best science fiction writer' as a collaborator. The answer he was given was Arthur C. Clarke – though Ray Bradbury, Robert Heinlein or Isaac Asimov could all have staked a claim at the time, not to mention wilder talents like Philip K. Dick, Harlan Ellison or Brian W. Aldiss (whom Kubrick stumbled over for *A.I.*). 2001 keeps its monolith-builders off camera, and assumes that real aliens would be unknowably strange, beyond the comprehension of even the most cerebral Earth humans (ie, Kubrick and Clarke).

The Martians of Roy Ward Baker's *Quatermass and the Pit* (1967), scripted by Nigel Kneale from his own TV serial, have a similar project to the monolith-makers, shaping the evolution of intelligent life on Earth. Kneale's boffins are less baffled and come up with a working theory about what the Martians have done (crafted a successor species when they realised their planet was doomed) and how mixed a blessing their achievement has been for humanity (instilling paranoid race-hatred along with technology).

When faced with lifeforms like the sentient planet of both versions

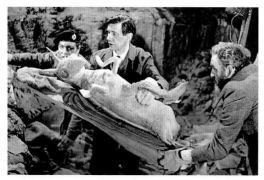

(Previous page)
H.R. Giger's monstrous
xenomorph, as seen in James
Cameron's 'Aliens' (1986).

(Above, top)
The ancient Martians are
unearthed in 'Quatermass
and the Pit' (1967).

(Above, middle)
The benign aliens in Steven
Spielberg's 'Close Encounters
of the Third Kind' (1977).

(Above, bottom)
Earth under attack in 'The
War of the Worlds' (1953).

(Opposite, top)
Steven Spielberg's 'E.T. the
Extra-Terrestrial' (1982).

(Opposite, bottom)
The poster for John Krish's
'Unearthly Stranger' (1963).

of *Solaris* (1972, 2002) cinema tends to back off. Andrei Tarkovsky and Steven Soderbergh, adapting Stanislaw Lem's novel, are more interested in the wreckage of the hero's marriage than exploring whatever purpose or character a world-sized feeling thinking creature might have.

The trajectory of the Solaris mission – and even of the Discovery in *2001* – is that we go a long way just to meet ourselves. Kelvin in *Solaris* has another go-round with his suicidal wife, while Bowman (Keir Dullea) in *2001* finds his older self cocooned in a luxury room as if the upshot of the Soviet and American space programmes were humanity checking in to the Overlook Hotel of *The Shining* to be tormented by phantoms of its own imagining.

In Robert Zemeckis's depressingly reactionary and reductive *Contact* (1997), from the novel by Carl Sagan, Ellie Arroway (Jodie Foster) crosses the universe to be the first human to engage with an alien species. All she finds at the end of her journey is her dead father (David Morse), resurrected so she can have a chat, a hug and get beyond the emotional baggage which made her the frigid, obsessive sort of freak who would even want to meet an alien.

It's a long fall from Steven Spielberg's *Close Encounters of the Third Kind* (1978), which can't imagine why anyone *wouldn't* want to play with the smiling, spindly ETs who have been snatching our aeroplanes and ships and children for decades. The overlap of science fiction with saucerology serves to set aside our SETI (search for extraterrestrial intelligence) programmes – seen to have disastrous consequences in the likes of *Species* (1995) and *Battleship* (2012) – in favour of the fanboy cranks of *UFOria* (1985) and *Paul* (2011). In *Paul*, Clive (Nick Frost) is awestruck to encounter an annoying little alien (Seth Rogen) because "ever since I saw *Mac and Me* I've dreamed about meeting you". *Mac and Me* (1988), of course, was a rubbish rip-off of *E.T.*, suggesting the limits of Clive's vision.

The human factor

From the first, we have imagined aliens to be versions of ourselves or our terrestrial enemies. In H.G. Wells's novel *The War of the Worlds* (1898), the Martians are an aggressive, exploitative colonial power who put too much trust in superior weaponry. They are defeated not by feeble native spears but the kind of fever that filled many a tropical grave with an ill-prepared European.

Ming the Merciless (Charles Middleton), the Emperor of Mongo in *Flash Gordon* (1936), is a dictator from space: Mussolini, Hitler and Stalin cross-bred with Fu Manchu and Attila the Hun and given a thin-lipped cowboy villain accent by the Kentucky-born Middleton – though the ultimate fascists of the universe are the stiff-armed and squawking, extermination-crazed tin-plated racist Daleks.

Wave after wave of hive-minded, godless 1950s invaders bluntly represent Soviet communism, whether the May Day parade show of overwhelming military force types of Byron Haskin's *The War of the Worlds* (1953) or Fred F. Sears's *Earth vs. the Flying Saucers* (1956) or the 'they are among us' subversive infiltrators of Don Siegel's *Invasion of the Body Snatchers* (1956) and Val Guest's *Quatermass 2* (1958).

Ruthless invaders have simplistic agendas keyed to the worries of the times. The vast fleet of Roland Emmerich's *Independence Day* (1996) is here to strip-mine the Earth, simply exploiting our natural resources, though the most resonant invasion in the movies might be John Carpenter's *They Live* (1988), in which the skull-faced aliens just see Earth as a market to be harvested, with the impoverishment of the vast bulk of humanity as an inevitable side-effect.

The idea that our enemies aren't human is plainly appealing, though horribly close to the rationale used by Earthly regimes to marginalise or persecute ethnic or belief groups. It can be shrunk from politics to the family home. In Gene Fowler's *I Married a Monster from Outer Space* (1958), John Krish's *Unearthly Stranger* (1963), Richard Benjamin's *My Stepmother Is an Alien* (1988) and Rand Ravich's *The Astronaut's Wife* (1999), spouses really are from other planets.

Animal, vegetable or mineral

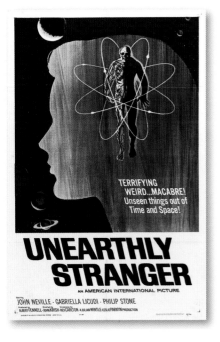

The *Alien* films draw their inspiration from the life-cycles of earthly insects. In *The First Men in the Moon* (1901), Wells imagined an extraterrestrial insect civilisation. The Martians of *Quatermass and the Pit* look as much like locusts as demons, though a prissy scientist insists that their unique three-legged form makes them arthropods rather than insects. Even the pods of *Invasion of the Body Snatchers* are inspired by terrestrial plants, drifting on stellar currents and sprouting root where they fall.

The 'animal, vegetable or mineral' alien – it would be hard to fit Irvin S. Yeaworth's *The Blob* (1958) into any category – is a useful solution to the problem of trying to conceive of an alien civilisation. Their intent is basic and instinctive: to consume, convert, supersede, thrive. These variants – the simplest and most horridly convincing is the space virus of Robert Wise's *The Andromeda Strain* (1971), from Michael Crichton's novel – tend to parallel Earthly species of flora or fauna, but also pose a large-scale eco-threat.

In Guest's *The Quatermass Xperiment* (1955), returning astronaut

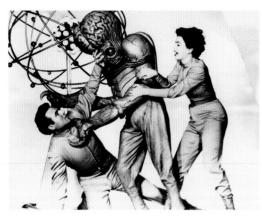

(Above)
Grappling with a big-brained
alien from Metaluna in Jack
Arnold and Joseph Newman's
'This Island Earth' (1955).

(Opposite, top)
Jack Arnold's 'It Came from
Outer Space' (1953) introduced
the concept of the xenomorph.

(Opposite, bottom)
The poster for Gene Fowler's
'I Married a Monster from
Outer Space' (1958)

Carroon (Richard Wordsworth) is infected with an alien disease that can incorporate any organic matter – whether Carroon's fellow astronauts or a hospital room cactus – into its growing body. The organism's endgame is the transformation of all life on Earth into an extension of itself.

The same fate is promised by the Body Snatchers, from Jack Finney's novel; John Carpenter's *The Thing* (1982), from John W. Campbell's novella *Who Goes There?*; and the techno-organic Borg of *Star Trek: First Contact* (1996). Individual human minds absorbed by these squirming blanket creatures would be vestigial, though the TV version of Kneale's *The Quatermass Experiment* (1953) climaxes with the astronauts' consciousnesses defeating the mindless creature that has swallowed them. The film opts simply to electrocute the monster – reusing the method deployed against the more limited boiler-suited vegetable vampire of Howard Hawks and Christian Nyby's *The Thing from Another World* (1951).

Invasion Earth

Sometimes humanity barely even counts as mulch. Kurt Neumann's *Kronos* (1958) features a giant robotic machine (or lifeform) that comes to suck up all the planet's energy sources and ignores people as if they were germs. The *kaiju* of *Pacific Rim* (2013) are extradimensional rather than extraterrestrial, though defender-of-the-earth monsters Godzilla and Gamera faced off against similar space beasts – sometimes controlled by humanoid alien villains, sometimes just random rampagers – throughout their careers.

Microbudget efforts like Lester William Berke's *The Lost Missile* (1958) and *The Creeping Terror* (1964), too busy scraping together stock footage or cobbling amateur special effects to bother much with script development, strangely manage to hit on believably unknowable aliens.

In *The Lost Missile*, a dangerous rocket has been lobbed at the Earth, seemingly in a spirit of experimentation rather than aggression, maybe as idly as a boy chucks a rock in a pond. A capsule from space in *The Creeping Terror* lets loose a mindless monster that might be a mutated experimental animal (the equivalent of the dogs and monkeys of early space probes), and one that is as small as a mouse to the capsule's creators. It's possible the dispatchers of the missile and the terror don't realise the havoc they are causing on Earth or, more cynically, just don't care.

A persistent strain of similar reasoning serves as a minor counterpoint to the invaders who want our planet to live on (*The War of the Worlds*), our mineral resources to exploit (*Daleks' Invasion Earth 2150 AD*, 1966; *Independence Day*), our sex partners to breed with (*Devil Girl from Mars*, 1954; *Mars Needs Women*, 1967) or our flesh to market as a tasty fast-food sensation throughout the universe (*Bad Taste*, 1987).

They walk among us

Jack Arnold's *It Came from Outer Space* (1953), from a screen treatment by Ray Bradbury, introduces the concept (and the term) xenomorph as aliens can transform into imitation human beings to pass among us. It turns out they aren't infiltrators or invaders but the crew of a crash-landed flying saucer that just want to effect repairs and get off this backwater world – the later title *This Island Earth* (1955) is resonant – to go wherever they were going in the first place. *It Came from Outer Space* is also pioneering in that its non-human aliens *aren't* a hive mind. One of the crew, which impersonates heroine Barbara Rush and strolls about the desert in a black evening dress wielding a raygun, is a murderous, sadistic malcontent whose actions embarrass and horrify its comrades.

Xenophobia – literally, 'fear of the alien' – underwrites much science-

(Above)
Michael Rennie as Klaatu,
the interplanetary visitor
from a superior civilisation
in Robert Wise's 'The Day the
Earth Stood Still' (1951).

(Opposite)
The big-brained creatures
designed by Paul Blaisdell for
'Invasion of the Saucer Men'
(1957) helped set a template
for the onscreen alien.

(Below)
Fighting the repulsive
Klendathu bugs in Paul
Verhoeven's 'Starship
Troopers' (1997).

fiction cinema, accounting for such spectacularly repulsive creatures as the Klendathu bugs of Paul Verhoeven's *Starship Troopers* (1997), from Robert Heinlein's novel (note that Verhoeven is cynical enough to establish that we started the war with them by expanding into their territory).

The stereotypical bug-eyed monster of 1950s comic books and B pictures, which persists even after the satirical swipes of Tim Burton's *Mars Attacks!* (1996), usually blend features of terrestrial creatures (scorpions, squid, spiders, wasps, lizards, octopuses) we are conditioned to dislike. Very rarely is the lesson of hard science fiction applied, perhaps because of the negative example of the toothy, frilly turnip-shaped Venusian designed (and worn) by Paul Blaisdell for Roger Corman's *It Conquered the World* (1956). Having an engineering background, Corman reasoned that a creature from a world with a heavier gravity than Earth would be squat and powerful (not having an astrophysics background, he didn't realise that Venusian gravity isn't heavier than Earth's). When tough gal heroine Beverly Garland took a look at the monster prop she was supposed to be terrorised by, she sneered, "So you've come to conquer the world have you" and kicked it over, prompting Corman to formulate a movie law that the monster should always be taller than the leading lady – and forcing Blaisdell to add tapering cucumber-shaped appendages to his creature.

Blaisdell was also responsible for the design of the big-brained, compound-eyed dwarf aliens of Edward L. Cahn's *Invasion of the Saucer Men* (1957). These were at least partly supposed to be a satire of the typical bug-eyed monster, but somehow seeped into pop culture as a model for the 'greys' associated with UFO abductions/alien encounters in a branch of Forteana that science-fiction literature used to sneer at as an embarrassment but which films like *Close Encounters of the Third Kind* and TV shows like *The X-Files* have dragged permanently into the mainstream.

In 1951, the xenophobe's archetypal alien was the Thing From Another World – a hostile, inimical saucer man out to drink our blood. It was also the year of Klaatu (Michael Rennie), the well-spoken ambassador of Robert Wise's *The Day the Earth Stood Still*, from Harry Bates's story *Farewell to the Master*. With his sleek saucer, landed on the White House lawn, and impressively monolithic robot Gort, Klaatu is plainly from a superior civilisation. He comes to preach against our warmongering, insisting Earth leave off the use of atomic weapons in order to qualify for membership in a galactic United Nations … or else be wiped out by the death-rays of Gort.

So, Klaatu comes from a race of genocidal pacifists who kept up with their superweapon research programs even as their culture progressed to a stage of vague enlightenment. Adopting the Earth name 'Mr Carpenter' and resurrected magically, Klaatu is a strangely ambiguous figure, either a messiah or a fascist. It's a shame Scott Derrickson's 2008 remake is so flat, because a Klaatu could be reinterpreted for a 21st century when we might feel more cause to fear those who claim to speak for God and wield weapons of mass destruction.

Klaatu joins an odd group of stranded or ambassadorial aliens on Earth who are messiahs, martyrs or simple innocents. The Kryptonian Superman got here first, appearing in print in 1938, and assimilated in a way few extraterrestrials manage, pledging to fight for 'truth, justice and the American way'.

The experience of Thomas Jerome Newton (David Bowie) in Nicolas Roeg's *The Man Who Fell to Earth* (1976), from Walter Tevis's novel, is perhaps more credible. He uses alien technology to become wealthy enough to mount a rescue mission for his parched homeworld only to be betrayed by human confederates, experimented on by

INVASION OF THE SAUCER-MEN
CREEPING HORROR... From the depths of time and space!
See TEENAGERS vs. THE SAUCER-MEN!
See DISEMBODIED HAND THAT CRAWLS...!
See NIGHT THE WORLD NEARLY ENDED...!
See EARTH ATTACKED BY FLYING SAUCERS!
starring
STEVE TERRELL · GLORIA CASTILLO · FRANK GORSHIN · Executive Producer SAMUEL Z. ARKOFF
Produced by JAMES H. NICHOLSON and ROBERT GURNEY Jr. • Directed by EDWARD L. CAHN • Screenplay by AL MARTIN
Additional Dialogue by ROBERT GURNEY Jr. • A MALIBU PRODUCTION • AN AMERICAN INTERNATIONAL PICTURE

shadowy government forces and finally laid low by Earthly intoxicants like booze, multi-channel TV and sex with Candy Clark.

The smugly superior and logical Mr Spock (half-human remember) and the asexually benevolent E.T. are more successful, connecting with humans who tolerate or assist them… whereas the rogue Time Lord of *Doctor Who* is simply a fan of the human race, and terribly enthusiastic about representative members of the species. Notably, these aliens are humanoid, or even idealised humanoid. They teach us lessons, but sometimes learn how to love: if Klaatu and Newton make us feel bad about ourselves, E.T. and the Doctor point out the human attributes we should be proud of.

Life on Mars

Science-fiction cinema puts a lot of effort into imaginary xenobiology, and far less into xenoculture, xenopolitics or xenophilosophy. Alien societies began with the comic opera visions of Mongo or Krypton, with silver togas and tights, then progressed to give us Nazis, communists, capitalists, hippies or frat boys from space.

Joe Dante's *Explorers* (1984) features outlandish creatures who are just cartoon-loving kids, but have been warned off Earth by a montage of the alien-killing climaxes of our science-fiction films. The Earthly inspirations

(Above)
David Bowie as the alien betrayed by humans in Nicolas Roeg's 'The Man Who Fell to Earth' (1976).

(Opposite)
James Cameron found Earthly inspirations for the look of the Na'avi people in 'Avatar' (2009).

(new age, Native Americans) for the Na'avi of James Cameron's *Avatar* (2009) are obvious and Wagnerian space gods strut through Marvel's *Thor* movies.

It took the commercial failure of Andrew Stanton's (very likeable) *John Carter* (2012) to underline the fact that this mode of depicting alien races as Western ideas of 'foreign' cultures dates back to the essentially Victorian mindset of Edgar Rice Burroughs's transpositions of Sir H. Rider Haggard's lost race romances into a richly coloured, gleefully scientifically inaccurate solar system. George Lucas's *Star Wars* (1977) – a series in which every character is technically an alien (except the two Earth children who show up in *The Ewok Adventure: Caravan of Courage*, 1984) – paradoxically embraces the conventions of every genre (pirate, war, drag-racing, *film noir*, samurai, sword and sorcery) *except* science fiction, and yet derailed serious science fiction for generations.

In Lucas's galaxy, initially alien creatures are – on a second look – just used car salesmen or gangster bosses or jazz musicians. Until this mindset can be surpassed, civilisations which ostensibly fulfil Arthur C. Clarke's dictum that "sufficiently advanced technology is indistinguishable from magic" by spanning star systems will still be expected to be mired in feudalism, gladiatorial combat, dynastic intrigues or the mom-and-pop obsessions of Hollywood script development execs. ●

ALIEN NATION: ALIENS IN BRITISH SCI-FI CINEMA

by John Oliver

Scarlett Johansson in Jonathan Glazer's 'Under the Skin' (2013)

Given the preponderance of such Wellsian themes as invisibility, anti-gravity fluid and growth serums in early British cinema, aliens and otherworldly creatures were strangely absent, despite the success of H.G. Wells's 1898 novel *The War of the Worlds*. When aliens did finally appear, in Percy Stow's *When the Man in the Moon Seeks a Wife* (1908) and J. Wallett Waller's *A Message from Mars* (1913), they were clearly not struck from the same mould as Wells's Martian invaders, being more concerned with finding a mate and curing a man of his selfishness than embarking on missions of conquest. These two examples aside, aliens were to give British science-fiction cinema a wide berth until the 1950s, when the theme was given a jump-start by the Hollywood boom in the genre.

These 1950s alien visitations were inaugurated by David Macdonald's banal *Devil Girl from Mars* (1954), in which Patricia Laffan's leather-clad alien dominatrix visits a remote Scottish pub in order to collect suitable male specimens. It wasn't a propitious start, and neither was Burt Balaban's stiflingly dull *Stranger from Venus* (1954), in which Helmut Dantine's more soberly attired alien had clearly seen Robert Wise's Hollywood film *The Day the Earth Stood Still* (1951), and was inspired to visit Earth to dissuade humankind from dabbling with atomic power. The pendulum has swung between benign and hostile interplanetary visitors ever since, these visitations being spawned by a combination, at different times, of Cold War paranoia, the post-war boom in UFO sightings, escalating world tensions, continuing concerns over immigration and – more prosaically – a simple desire to replicate popular Hollywood cinema.

As with *Stranger from Venus*, benign aliens in British cinema have continued to protect humankind from itself, as in Gilbert Gunn's *The Strange World of Planet X* (1958); befriend many a child in films made specifically for a youthful audience, beginning with S.G. Fergusson's *Supersonic Saucer* (1956); restore domestic bliss between a child and his parents in Henry Cass's *Give a Dog a Bone* (1966); visit Earth to investigate the vibrations generated by pop music in Val Guest's *Toomorrow* (1970); or even service male sexual fantasies in such puerile sexploitation fare as Derek Ford's *The Sexplorer* (1975) and Norman J. Warren's *Outer Touch* (1979).

However, it is the hostile aliens that have followed in Laffan's wake that have enjoyed greater visibility in British science-fiction cinema (and have tended to appear in the better films). Reflecting the budgetary constraints seemingly endemic to British genre cinema, invasions of global conquest have tended to be rather geographically limited in scope. Resistance to the invaders in Gordon Flemyng's *Daleks' Invasion Earth 2150 A.D.* (1966) at least took place in pockets of London and Bedfordshire, whereas the alien saucer invasion in Dominic Burns's *U.F.O.* (2012) was largely confined to a Derby housing estate, and the alien-controlled robots in Terence Fisher's *The Earth Dies Screaming* (1964) appeared

to be – despite the title – concentrating their activities around an English village pub.

This ill-fitting conjunction of global conquest and limited settings can though be less incompatible in films in which alien invasions are conducted by stealth, or where their restricted scope is intentional – invariably owing to the aliens having to acclimatise to the Earth's atmosphere, as with the tentacled aliens atop a Swiss mountain in Quentin Lawrence's *The Trollenberg Terror* (aka *The Crawling Eye*, 1958), or the heat-loving molluscs on a Scottish island in Terence Fisher's *Night of the Big Heat* (1967). This was at its most effective in one of the best of all British science-fiction films, Val Guest's *Quatermass 2* (1957), in which alien organisms land on Earth in small protective meteorites, before taking over a human host and manoeuvring themselves into positions of power and influence.

Again largely owing to budgetary constraints, films featuring lone or small groups of hostile aliens who cause localised mayhem have tended to outnumber those with global dominance on their agenda, and have also increasingly supplanted their more benign brethren as the protagonist of choice. The rapacious, flesh-hungry creatures at the centre of such films as Norman J. Warren's *Prey* (aka *Alien Prey*. 1978), Harry Bromley Davenport's *Xtro* (1983) and Tony Maylam's *Split Second* (1992) have all taken British science-fiction films into a realm of horror much darker than that explored in the genre's earlier years. While benign aliens have been in retreat for the last three decades (the foul-mouthed specimen in Greg Mottola's US/GB co-production *Paul* (2011) being a rare contemporary exception), their more hostile counterparts continue to

proliferate, as in such recent offerings as Joe Cornish's *Attack the Block* (2011) and Johannes Roberts's *Storage 24* (2012), which both feature aliens on the rampage in urban south London. Jon Wright's *Grabbers* (2012) has its aliens invade an island off the Irish coast, and most recently Jonathan Glazer's particularly impressive *Under the Skin* (2013) memorably cast Scarlett Johansson as an alien traversing first Glasgow and then rural Scotland in pursuit of male prey, while looking on in bemused curiosity at humankind.

Another sub-theme of science-fiction cinema concerns alien experimentation with human evolution. Such films often portray the aliens as having hostile intentions, something which is certainly the case when contemporary humanity happens to be the subject, as in *Village of the Damned* (1960), Wolf Rilla's screen version of John Wyndham's novel *The Midwich Cuckoos*. The unseen aliens at the beginning of *2001: A Space Odyssey* (1968) may or may not have acted benignly, but the Martians who tampered with humankind's early evolution in Roy Ward Baker's *Quatermass and the Pit* (1967) clearly did not. The motives of the aliens in Ridley Scott's enjoyable but more often impenetrable *Prometheus* (2012) remained stubbornly obscure to the end.

More than 100 years have passed since the publication of H.G. Wells's seminal *The War of the Worlds*, and aliens – particularly those that mean us harm – continue to capture the imagination in Britain. Is this propelled by our fear of the unknown and what could be out there? Is it an extension of the British 'island mentality' and our fear and distrust of the 'other'? Whatever the reason, aliens will no doubt continue to engender both wonder and terror. Just expect them to have ever bigger teeth. ●

'The Earth Dies Screaming' (1964)

'Supersonic Saucer' (1956)

'Attack the Block' (2011)

Light and magic: the history of sci-fi special effects

by Mark Salisbury

From Georges Méliès's phantasmagoric *A Trip To The Moon* (1902) to Alfonso Cuarón's space thriller *Gravity* (2013), filmmakers have continued to push the boundaries of new technology to bring their stories and visions to the big screen. And with science fiction/fantasy/superhero/comic book films the core of contemporary Hollywood's business model, what were once termed 'special effects' – and are now known as 'visual effects' – have become increasingly important and ever-more sophisticated in terms of both realism and spectacle. The end credit roll of a modern blockbuster can run for ten to 15 minutes, as the thousands of digital artists required to make Superman fly, Hulk smash or Iron Man save the world from alien invaders, are laid out for any audience member still seated to acknowledge.

Before the advent of computer-generated imagery (CGI), however, filmmakers relied on photographic or optical effects, typically created in-camera, using miniatures and models, rear projection and matte paintings, wires and glue to realise their dreams. And what dreams. The parting of the Red Sea in *The Ten Commandments* (1923), Douglas Fairbanks riding a magic carpet in *The Thief of Bagdad* (1924), the future of *Things to Come* (1936), all remain breathtaking for their audacity and ambition. As does the stop-motion animation of *The Lost World* (1925) and *King Kong* (1933), pioneered by Willis O'Brien and taken to new levels by his *protégé* Ray Harryhausen, whose fantastical creatures from *The 7th Voyage Of Sinbad* (1958), *Jason and the Argonauts* (1963) and their ilk retain the ability to marvel, even in this age of Pixar and CGI.

The nuclear terror of the 1950s saw Hollywood capitalise on its audiences' fears and advances in special effects with a wealth of science-fiction cinema that came in many varied forms, from the Martian invaders in *The War of the Worlds* (1953) to the domestic terror of *The Incredible Shrinking Man* (1957). But it was *2001: A Space Odyssey* (1968) that ushered in a new wave of groundbreaking techniques and became the benchmark by which all subsequent science-fiction films would be judged. Until *Star Wars* (1977), that is, with its dynamic space dogfights and thrilling light-sabre duels. Writer-director George Lucas had waited for more than a decade until the technology was capable of realising his space opera and needed to create his own company, Industrial Light & Magic (ILM), to do so, amassing a group of effects wizards who would rule the field for decades to come.

The early 80s saw the advent of computer animation, in films such as *Tron* (1982), *The Last Starfighter* (1984) and, in special-effects terms, there was no turning back. *Young Sherlock Holmes* (1985) featured the first fully computer-generated photorealistic character, a knight made from stained glass. *Willow* (1988) debuted 'morphing', as a goat was transformed into Patricia Hayes via digital effects rather than optical dissolves or cutaways. But it was ILM (responsible for both *Willow* and *Young Sherlock*) who opened the CGI floodgates and completely revolutionised modern cinema with the liquid metal future assassin of James Cameron's *Terminator 2: Judgment Day* (1991, pictured opposite) and digital dinosaurs of Steven Spielberg's *Jurassic Park* (1993).

Soon it wasn't just creatures but entire worlds that were being assembled inside the computer. In *Star Wars: The Phantom Menace* (1999), *Sin City* (2005), *Avatar* (2006) and *Alice In Wonderland* (2010) actors were shot against green screens, then sets, props and entire digital characters were added after the fact. Now it's possible for filmmakers to create *anything* their imagination can muster, even bringing stars back from the dead. But for sci-fi cinema to thrive, the technology must not usurp the art, and it must continue to rely on visionaries to take those bags of digital tricks and create something special and unique, to make magic much like Méliès did.

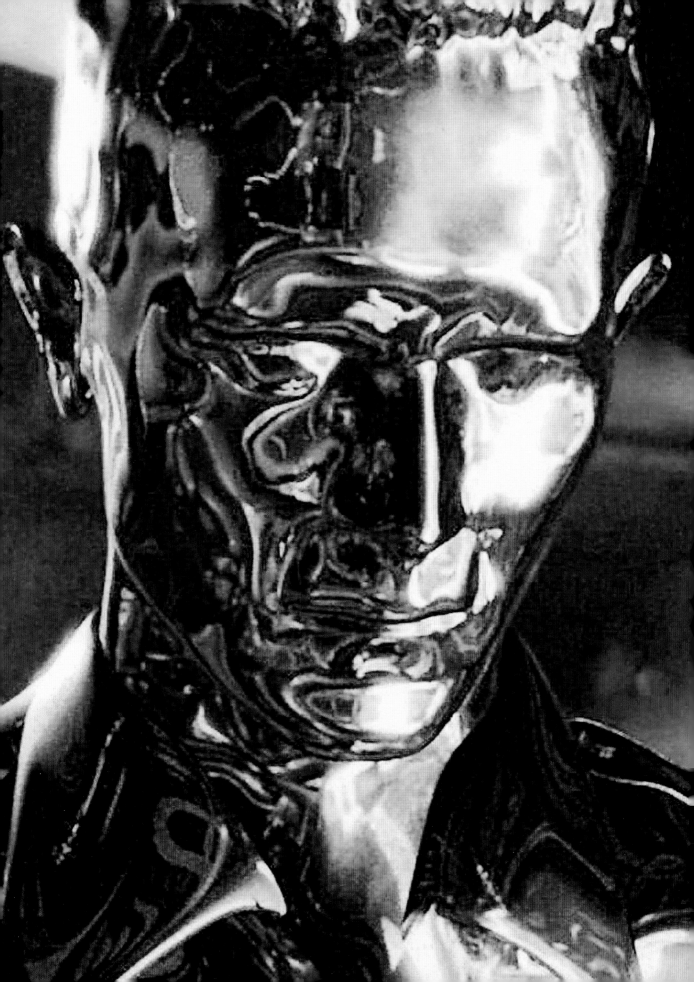

1 A Trip to the Moon (1902)

Inspired by Jules Verne's two Moon novels as well as H.G. Wells's *The First Men in the Moon*, Georges Méliès utilised every trick known to early filmmakers, and many that had yet to be invented, although he was mostly reliant on the 'stop trick' technique in which the camera is stopped and an onscreen object or person either subtracted, added or altered in the frame, a 'substitution splice' that resulted in some of nascent cinema's most enduring moments.

2 Metropolis (1927)

Regarded as the first full-length science-fiction film, Fritz Lang's groundbreaking silent, expressionist masterwork is set in a future (2026) where mankind lives either in luxury art deco-styled skyscrapers on the Earth's surface or deep underground. Cinematographer Eugen Schüfftan created the film's special effects, utilising miniatures for the cityscape as well as his eponymous Schüfftan process in which mirrors are used to create the illusion of actors being inside miniature sets. The film's most striking image, however, remains the robot Maria – for which actress Brigitte Helm wore a full-body suit by sculptor Walter Schulze-Mittendorff – an influence on countless cinematic robots, not least *Star Wars*'s C-3PO.

3 Things to Come (1936)

Directed by production designer William Cameron Menzies and written by H.G. Wells from his own short story in response to *Metropolis*, which he felt presented a deplorable vision of the future, this landmark (and remarkably prophetic) British science-fiction film employed numerous avant-garde artists, architects and designers to create its dazzling sets and fictitious future city. The plot spans 1936-2036 and involves the fall and rise of a civilisation after a world war, with innovative special effects by Ned Mann, who made outstanding use of models, foreground miniatures, mirror tricks, and tiny figures on moving, concealed tracks for crowd scenes, to fashion everything from giant flying machines to Everytown.

1

2

3

4

4 Destination Moon (1950)

Winner of the Academy Award for Best Special Effects, this George Pal-produced adventure, directed by Irving Pichel and based on a book by acclaimed science-fiction author Robert A. Heinlein, who also acted as technical advisor, treated space travel in as scientifically accurate a manner as was known at the time. Effects included impressive miniature work (a full-size 150ft tall rocket was also built for location filming) as well as the simple but effective trick of using black velvet studded with car headlights to simulate the lunar sky. Pal followed it with *When Worlds Collide*

  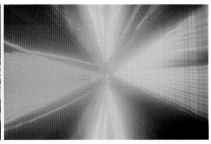

5

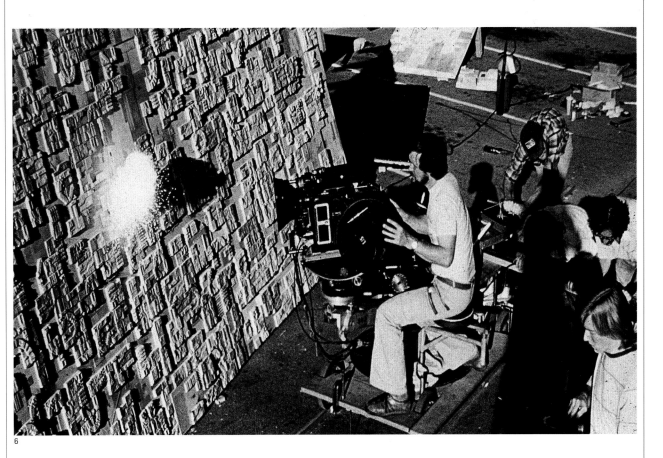

6

(1951), which featured Oscar-winning special effects from Gordon Jennings, and an adaptation of H.G. Wells's *The War of the Worlds* (1953) whose effects budget was reportedly more than twice that spent on the live action element.

5 2001: A Space Odyssey (1968)

When Stanley Kubrick set about adapting Arthur C. Clarke's short story *The Sentinel*, he approached NASA for advice on 'space speculation' and hired Wally Veevers (who'd worked on *Things to Come*), Con Pederson, and Douglas Trumbull to create the film's milestone special effects. "I felt it was necessary to make this film

in such a way that every special effects shot would be completely convincing, something that had never before been accomplished in a motion picture," Kubrick said. Together they pioneered a number of processes as well as making wide-ranging use of front projection, in which a photographic image is projected from the front of the set on to a reflective surface. Trumbull, who would later direct *Silent Running* (1972) and *Brainstorm* (1983), and create effects for *Star Trek: The Motion Picture* (1979), *Blade Runner* (1982) and *The Tree of Life* (2011), designed a 'split-scan' technique for the coloured lights effect during the climactic Star Gate sequence.

6 Star Wars (1977)

George Lucas's paean to the space sagas he loved as a child – *Buck Rogers* and *Flash Gordon* – required founding an entire new special effects studio, Industrial Light & Magic (ILM), under the leadership of John Dykstra, in a warehouse in Van Nuys, California. While the script nodded to the past, Dykstra looked to the future, developing a pioneering motion control camera system, dubbed the Dykstraflex, that created the illusion of size by using small models and a slow-moving camera, a technique that credibly allowed Luke Skywalker's X-Wing to dive bomb the Death Star and destroy it.

7

7 Tron (1982)

To bring his story of characters zapped into a video-game world to the big screen, animator/director Steven Lisberger, bankrolled by Disney, employed several leading computer graphics companies of the day – Triple I and MAGI among them – to produce around 15-20 minutes of groundbreaking computer graphics using then state-of-the-art computers with just 2MB of storage memory (a top spec iPhone has 64GB) as well as animated-enhanced live action. Two years later, *The Last Starfighter* was one of the first films to use computer graphics to create 3D rendered spacecraft models – built by Digital Productions using a Cray X-MP supercomputer – rather than practical ones.

8

8 Terminator 2: Judgment Day (1991)

Having previously tasked ILM with creating the first computer-generated 3D character for *The Abyss* (1989, pictured far left), a watery creature dubbed the pseudopod for which it took six months to produce 75 seconds of footage, he turned to them again for the liquid metal/shapeshifting T-1000 (played, in human form, by Robert Patrick) sent from the future to kill teenage John Connor (Edward Furlong) in his big-budget sequel. Created using personal computers (a first), the T-1000's 'mimetic poly-alloy' effect amounted to just five minutes of screen time (the remainder of the T-1000 was created by Stan Winston Studios using a combination of prosthetics and practical puppets) winning ILM the 1992 Oscar for Best Visual Effects (shared with Winston) and paving the way for the CGI dinosaurs in *Jurassic Park* (1993).

9

9 The Matrix (1999)

While *The Matrix* borrowed liberally from computer games, superhero comics, Hong Kong chopsocky action flicks and Japanese animation, its famed "bullet time" effect was something truly unique. Realised by visual effects supervisor John Gaeta, the effect allowed a shot to progress at variable rates while the camera appeared to move at normal speed. Gaeta, who won the Oscar for his work, used still cameras to surround

10

his subjects, the resulting still images were then placed sequentially to produce orbiting action either frozen in time or as ultra slow-mo, thereby giving the illusion of Keanu Reeves's hacker being able to dodge bullets and punches. Although 'bullet time' quickly became cliché, its revolutionary effect should not be understated.

10 Avatar (2006)

Forever at the forefront of new filmmaking technology, James Cameron spent years waiting for visual effects to evolve to what was required to produce his 3D vision for Pandora, ultimately using the digital 3D Fusion Camera system he designed with Vince Pace. While performance capture had been established by the likes of Robert Zemeckis for *The Polar Express* and Peter Jackson in *The Lord Of The Rings*, Cameron's advancements, in conjunction with Weta Digital, included a specially designed camera built into a six-inch boom that allowed his actors' facial expressions and physical performance to be digitally recorded and transferred

100 per cent to their digital counterparts, as well as a motion-capture stage, dubbed 'the volume', which was six times larger than any previously built.

11 Gravity (2013)

While director Alfonso Cuarón did, for a split second, consider filming on the International Space Station, his penchant for long, extended takes led Tim Webber, of London-based effects house Framestore, to create a totally new method of filmmaking. In conjunction with DP Emmanuel Lubezski, Webber designed a 9ftx9ftx9ft 'lightbox' lined with more than a million LED lights in which the actors were filmed and on the sides of which pre-vized footage of their surroundings was projected. Later, Framestore's animators would take that footage and work their digital magic, with the result that, bar the faces of Sandra Bullock and George Clooney, and one location, virtually everything else (shuttle, Earth, sun, stars, props, spacesuits, even the actors' breath) was created using CGI, a remarkable achievement that justifiably won the Oscar for Best Visual Effects.

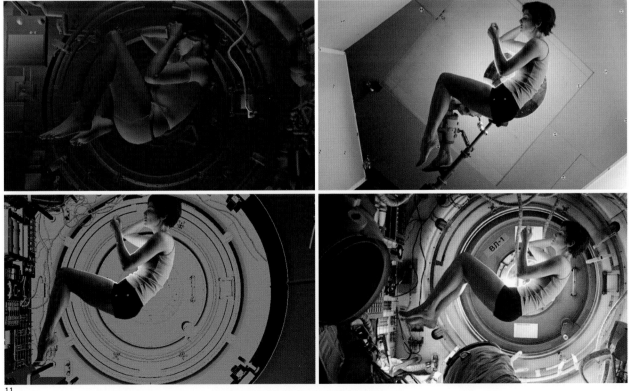

11

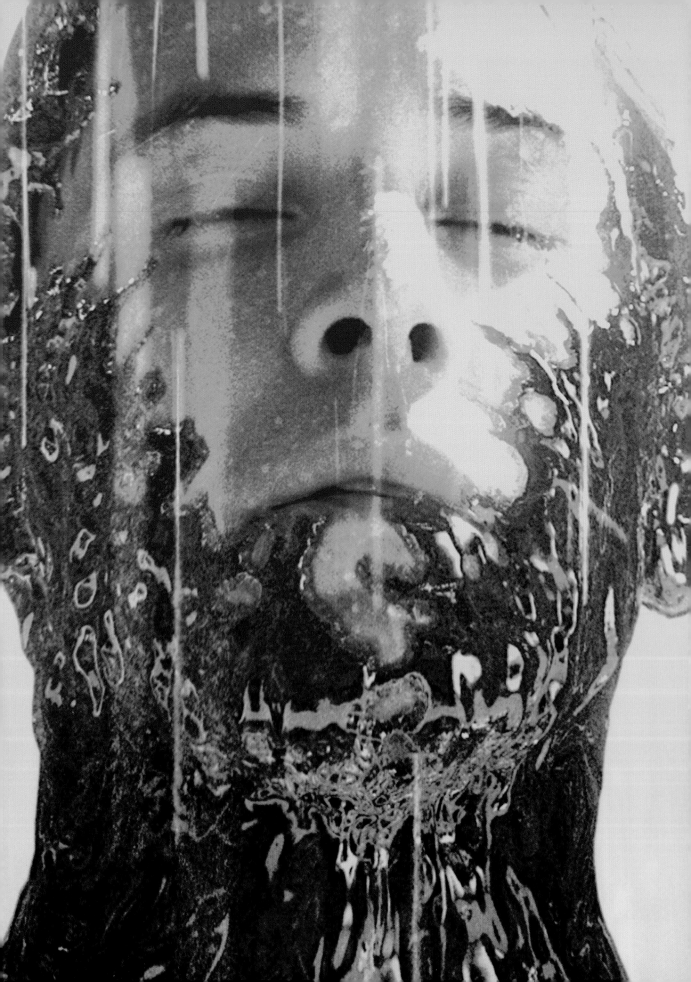

ALTERED STATES

Dancing with Darwin
by Roger Luckhurst

In Ken Russell's typically delirious science-fiction film *Altered States* (1980), William Hurt plays a Harvard medic seeking to pin down the precise neurology of ecstatic mystical states. Like a proper hippy, he doses up on hallucinogenic drugs used in shamanic rituals to induce states of 'psychic atavism', a return to primordial consciousness. This being science fiction, the psychological metaphor of regression becomes a literal physical degeneration. Dr Jessup unleashes his simian Mr Hyde. When a technician is asked if the X-rays reveal anything "somewhat abnormal" after one of Jessup's funny turns, the man responds drily: "Somewhat. The guy's a fucking gorilla."

The emergence of science fiction as a popular genre in the 19th-century is inextricably linked to the rise of Darwinism. Darwin's *On the Origin of Species by Means of Natural Selection* (1859) and the even more shocking extension of his theory in *The Descent of Man, and Selection in Relation to Sex* (1871), induced several traumas at once. It was a monistic theory, which is to say that it explained life and man solely through biological process. There was no secondary order of reality, no super-natural or spiritual sphere, no 'divine spark' of life. The theory required millions of years to work, placing man in the aeons of geological time, and made current physical forms merely temporary and bound to deep ancestral pasts. In 1860, the Bishop of Oxford asked with horror why men of science were going "into jubilation for his great-great-grandfather having been an ape or gorilla".

The theory also opened man to an unforeseeable future of evolutionary transformation. In Darwin's view, life was not directed, but profligate and superabundant, its forms necessarily plastic (that is, capable of adapting) in the face of mass slaughter and death in the unremitting struggle for existence. Far from being a "separate creation", Darwin argued, man was entirely embedded in these universal biological processes and was actually one of the most malleable and adaptive creatures. "In this respect," Darwin concluded in *The Descent of Man,* humanity "resembles those forms called by naturalists protean and polymorphic".

Darwin tried to soothe his Victorian readers (and his own shattered nerves) by promising an optimistic path towards the perfectibility of man. Yet others worried that if humans could move up the evolutionary ladder, might it not also be possible to move down? British science fiction was born out of the gothic romance, hounded by natural rather than supernatural agencies, and specifically by the fear of biological retrogression. Every respectable Dr Jekyll closets their Mr Hyde, every Dorian Gray hides their secret portrait of their true moral and physical degeneration.

Science fiction was one of the earliest popular forms to embed Darwin's transformative theories in cultural narrative. Some of the most compelling 'scientific romances' of the 1890s were by H.G. Wells, trained in biology by Darwin's bulldogs, Thomas Huxley and Edwin Ray Lankester. *The Time Machine* ended with a terrifying far-future vision of post-human London, long after the extinction of man and on the verge of heat death. *The War of the Worlds* was an illustration of Darwin's thesis in *The Origin of Species* that each species in competition "will generally press hardest on its nearest kindred, and tend to exterminate them". Wells tilts at British imperial arrogance, the advanced Martians effortlessly dominating the imperial metropolis, only to be defeated by lowly microbes. In *The Island of Doctor Moreau,* Wells concocted a gruesome allegory of evolutionary degeneration as Moreau vivisects beasts into grotesque forms of men only to see them regress back to beasts again. Moreau's mad science disturbingly undercuts any secure boundary between human

(Above)
Fredric March stars as
Dr Jekyll and Mr Hyde in
Rouben Mamoulian's 1931
adaptation of Robert Louis
Stevenson's classic novel.

(Previous page)
Charles Laughton as Dr.
Moreau in Erle C. Kenton's
'Island of Lost Souls' (1932).

and animal. It leaves the lone survivor back in London permanently traumatised, waiting only for the mark of the animal to come "surging up" through the crowds of allegedly the most civilised city in the world.

These Wellsian evolutionary visions recur throughout the history of cinema, and from its earliest days. Within weeks of *The Time Machine* appearing in 1895, the cinema pioneer Robert William Paul applied for a patent that aimed to reproduce Wells's time-travelling experience by moving the audience past a series of Kinetographic projections. If this machine was never realised, it is common to observe that cinema is itself a kind of evolutionary time-travel device, able to freeze, slow down or speed up development, stage spectacular transformations, or bring the far-flung in space and time into the intimate here and now. From *The Human Ape* (1909) via the dinosaurs of *The Lost World* (1925) to the pre-Code sexual selection of Fay Wray by *King Kong* (1933), the development of the cinema, as Barbara Creed has observed in *Darwin's Screens,* "owes much to Darwin".

Russell's *Altered States* is embedded in a cinema history that goes back to very early films like *Joe, the Educated Orangoutang, Undressing* (1895). Since science-fiction films are so intrinsically bound up with the spectacular special effect, perhaps it is unsurprising that this cinema repeatedly returns to scenes of biological transformation, the camera offering sublime or grotesque scenes of sudden catastrophic change, rendering magically visible the otherwise hidden springs of gradual evolution. A history of science-fiction cinema can thus be written as a history of the spectacle of 'transformism' (another Victorian term for developmental theories of evolution). Here are four key chapters.

Making monsters

In his history of science fiction, Brian Aldiss suggests that Mary Shelley's *Frankenstein* (1818) is the pioneering book that shifts the theological dreads of the first wave of the gothic into the purely physiological and materialist horrors of later science fiction. Victor's nemesis is not spiritual, but his very material double, a dead thing animated by the electrical spark of life. James Whale's *Frankenstein* (1931), of course, had its own crucial role in establishing a new genre of film that in the early 1930s stabilised around the term 'horror'. Whale refocused the novel intensively on the laboratory and the patchwork body of the self-made monster. It was snipped here and there by the pre-Code censor (Frankenstein was not allowed to say at his moment of triumph "In the name of God, now I know what it feels like to be God"), but Universal's film was at least widely released.

This is more than could be said in some American states for *The Mystery of Life* (1931), a dry documentary in which evolutionary theory is explained by college professor H.M. Parshley, and which was banned by some film boards as 'indecent'. America was only a few short years from the Scopes Monkey Trial, in which schoolteacher John Scopes had been prosecuted by the State of Tennessee in 1925 for teaching evolutionary theory in his classroom. Perhaps this explains why there is such a Darwinian tinge to the 1930s cycle of American science-fiction horrors. Hollywood was not really abreast of the so-called 'Darwinian synthesis' of the 30s, which made genetic transmission the long-elusive vehicle of natural selection: it was still dealing with the foundational transgressions of Darwin's dangerous ideas.

Rouben Mamoulian built the rhythm of his adaptation of *Dr. Jekyll and Mr. Hyde* (1931) around the spectacular technical accomplishment of the transformation scenes, as Fredric March turns from matinee idol into lusty ape. The cinema has obsessively adapted Stevenson's classic of self-administered biological retrogression, as if marking its own technical

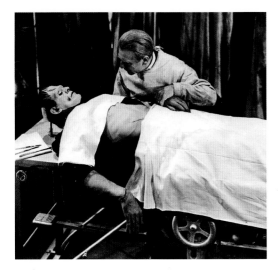

(Above, left)
James Whale's 'Frankenstein'
(1931) refocused Mary
Shelley's story intensively
on the laboratory.

(Above, right)
William Dowling and Howard
Hoyt's 'The Lost World'
(1925), adapted from Sir
Arthur Conan Doyle's novel.

(Below)
Dr Jessup's (William Hurt)
experiments in Ken Russell's
'Altered States' (1980)
play on anxieties about
physical regression.

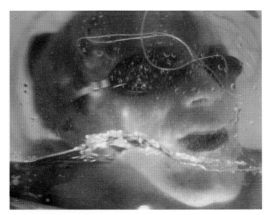

development with performances of this transformation. The werewolf story, with its own myth of animalistic regression, was established in the cinema by *Werewolf of London* (1935). Meanwhile, evolutionary sports were the focus of Tod Browning's notorious *Freaks* (1932), balanced on the other end of the scale by the gigantism of the evolutionary backwater of *King Kong* (1933). Quite where humanity now fitted into the ecology of nature perhaps contributed to the success of *Tarzan the Ape Man* (1932), an adaptation of Edgar Rice Burroughs's anxious meditation on the boundary of human and animal, although it was the erotic allure of the prolonged shots of the naked body of Olympic swimmer Josephine McKim in *Tarzan and His Mate* (1934) that eventually brought about the full enforcement of the laws of the Production Code Administration.

Perhaps the most overtly Darwinian film of this cycle was Erle C. Kenton's lurid *Island of Lost Souls* (1932), with Charles Laughton playing a sinister and perverse version of Wells's Dr Moreau. Unlike the book, this Moreau is bent on engineering sexual selection, to prove his spliced beasts have reached proper human status. He tries this on between the marooned hero Parker and Lota, The Panther Woman, and later between the blonde leading lady and Ouran, the priapic ape, reverting to familiar racial melodrama. The film toys fairly overtly with the promise of miscegenation and bestial couplings, making The Panther Woman a site of intensely conflicted allure and disgust. The riotous beast men are led by a memorable turn from Bela Lugosi, leering into the camera in unnerving close-up, before effecting a revolution that overturns scientific authority. It was banned outright in many countries and refused a rerelease by the Production Code office in 1935 (which forbade depictions of interracial relationships), effectively banning it completely. The Australian film board invented a new category for the film, N.E.N. ('not to be exhibited to natives') perhaps fearing the depiction of insurrection against the whip-hand of colonial control – and it was not shown in Britain until as late as 1959. Darwinian transformism clearly touched raw nerves.

The spectre of the bomb

World War II ended abruptly with the atomic bombing of Hiroshima and Nagasaki in August 1945. The weapon was built by theoretical physicists working with the newly minted military-industrial complex. The scientists of the Manhattan Project gave the world a new index of man-made apocalypse, a device that could literalise long-held fantasies of post-disaster social regression or simply mass extinction. "Modern man is obsolete," Norman Cousins famously declared in an editorial in the *Saturday Review* on 14 August 1945. Although American military authorities tried to suppress every detail about radiation poisoning, declaring it Japanese or Communist propaganda, the idea that genetic mutation through exposure to a radioactive 'mist of death' was a constant of science fiction. Mutants persecuted for their departures from the norm had been a staple of golden age science fiction since the 1930s; it became more monstrous in the B-movie boom of the 1950s. As if to match the inconceivable sublimity of the Bomb, gigantic atavistic creatures were stirred from the depths, as in *Godzilla* (*Gojira*, 1954) or *It Came from Beneath the Sea* (1955). Atmospheric nuclear testing transformed insects into giant mutations in *Tarantula* (1955) or the wonderfully atmospheric *Them!* (1954). Gordon Douglas's film holds off the sight of the bug-eyed monsters until the viewer is thoroughly rattled by eerie desert cries and windswept scenes of mysterious devastation. They nest in the network of tunnels in Los Angeles, the secret state straining to contain the truth of the catastrophe. In reverse, Jack Arnold's *The Incredible Shrinking Man* (1957) exposes the hero to a radioactive cloud and, as he begins to diminish, the everyday world becomes a vast defamiliarised landscape full of terrifying snares. J.G. Ballard always praised the pulp metaphysics of Arnold's rueful allegory of man's extinction, perhaps because he was writing his own fictions about the advent of the nuclear age as triggering an evolutionary eclipse, the American deserts and Pacific atolls where the test bombs flowered becoming mankind's terminal beaches.

B movies were still interested in monsters as evolutionary atavisms, as in the Amazonian backwater that hides the lusty *Creature from the Black Lagoon* (1954). But the most impressive films of this science-fiction cycle are those that dealt with more insidious altered states or transformations, ones that needed few special effects. In *I Married a Monster from Outer Space* (1958), a young bride cannot fathom the weird transformation of her husband into an emotionless automaton. The film starts out as a study of Freudian angst but slowly unveils a conspiracy of alien invasion. This paranoid style reaches a pinnacle with Don Siegel's *Invasion of the Body Snatchers* (1956), in which 'pod people' steadily replace the town folk, ending with a memorable scene of Dr Bennell dementedly screaming "You're next!" at cars on the highway. Extra last scenes were added, suggesting the state finally mobilising against the threat, but the virtue of some of the B movies was their suspicion of all authority and their implied critique of the deadening conformity of American suburban capitalist life. If the official American guide, *How to Survive an Atomic Bomb* was still calling radiation a mere "inconvenience" in 1950, perhaps science fiction was the place to get the ugly, mutant truth.

Invasion of the Body Snatchers was updated for paranoid, post-Nixon America by Philip Kaufman in 1978, but the film significantly upgraded the special effects as the seed pods messily transform into deadringers for their human victims. This sticky, abject birthing was an advent of a new phase of body-horror transformation.

Body horror

What erupts from the chest of the hapless Kane in *Alien* (1979) is a new kind of splicing of the old dark house of the gothic with science fiction, low cultural gore with mainstream genre cinema. The notorious chest-bursting scene was said to have caused panic and vomiting at test screenings, as if the spectacle of bodily rupture implanted mimetic effects in its

(Below)
The newborn alien bursts
from Kane's chest in Ridley
Scott's 'Alien' (1979).

early audiences. *Alien* was a central film in a moment when the special-effects guys became superstars, the halcyon analogue days before the advent of CGI, when films raced to outdo each other with spectacular scenes of visceral transformation: David Kessler's sustained, agonising morph into a wolf, fully on screen and without cuts, in John Landis's *An American Werewolf in London* (1981); the riotous biological anarchy of the continually transforming alien in John Carpenter's remake of *The Thing* (1982); the eventual dissolution of Seth Brundle's human body into full merger with the DNA of a housefly in David Cronenberg's remake of *The Fly* (1986). Cyborg cinema effected similar fusions, this time of bodies and machines, from the oneiric logic of Cronenberg's *Videodrome* (1983) to the uncontrolled sexual hysteria of Tsukamoto Shinya's *Tetsuo: The Iron Man* (1989), where our unfortunate hero becomes as one with his phallic drill bit.

Eighties body horror registered a crisis in the perceived integrity of the body. Schwarzenegger and Stallone muscled up their defences, metallising their bodies, but did so with such anxious reinforcement because everywhere the skin, the physical boundary that defines the self, seemed to be under threat. This was no longer just from alien invaders but from the body's own mutant processes, erupting from within. Critics point to various explanations for this cluster of science fictions, from the 'mutation' of economics at the end of the crises of the 1970s towards neoliberalism, or a significant leap in the processes of globalisation that began to break down national boundaries, or the profound technological reorientation of the sense of the body as virtual computer networks were established, or the fears of global pandemics, such as AIDS, first medically noted in 1982. But it is also worth noting that this was a significant era in Darwinian theory, too.

In 1976, Richard Dawkins published *The Selfish Gene,* a narrow neo-Darwinian restatement about each gene maximising benefit in a ruthless struggle for existence. The monsters of *Alien* and *The Thing* are relentless, murderous competitors, perfectly honed biological weapons for survival, against which weak human collectives collapse. They are emanations of the selfish gene. Dawkins also extended the idea of genes metaphorically to 'memes', which were 'mind-viruses' or 'information parasites', the so-called 'junk' DNA of ideas that remain encoded in humans long after their usefulness has gone – such as, Dawkins has not been shy to claim, all religious beliefs. These ideological stances, shared by philosopher Daniel Dennett and the founder of 'sociobiology', E.O. Wilson, spoke profoundly to their times: the selfish gene appeared to naturalise the 'greed is good' message of the new capitalist individualism. This was only one take on Darwin, for the 'selfish gene' has been countered by Lyn Margulis's notion of the 'social gene', and supported by more liberal biologists, who argue the evolutionary benefits of altruism, cooperation and inter-species cooperation. As in Darwin's time, the inflections of evolutionary theory have always been profoundly political.

Boundary crawlers

In 1984, the Human Genome Project announced that new scientific techniques and laboratory technologies could start the process of mapping the human genome, the full genetic sequence of human DNA. This vast project fostered a host of science-fiction fantasies, from yet more post-*Alien* monstrous transformations, such as the *Species* cycle (1995-2007), or the extremely poor scientific protocols that abound in the laboratory in *Splice* (2009). It also produced more sober reflections on dystopias built on genetic policing, as in *Gattaca* (1997) or *Code 46* (2003).

But since the human genome was completely mapped in the millennial

(Clockwise from top left)
'Splice' (2009); Tsukamoto
Shinya's 'Tetsuo: The Iron
Man' (1989); Bong Joon-ho's
'The Host' (2006); a mutating
Jeff Goldblum in David
Cronenberg's 'The Fly' (1986).

year 2000, biologists have found that the genome is merely something like a vast dictionary rather than a 'How to' guide, and DNA has been repositioned as only one element in a wider epigenetic understanding of evolution and life. The revolutions in molecular biology and biotechnology since 2000 have pressed hard on neo-Darwinian claims that the gene is the sole agent of evolution. In a world where the processes of life are becoming manipulable at the cellular level and wholly new 'bio-objects' can be constructed *in vitro*, we are increasingly surrounded by what have been evocatively called 'boundary crawlers', things that defy biological categories or exist somewhere between the natural and the artificial.

I suspect this is why science fiction is so interested in abject goo and tentacles these days, the squirming alterity of the octopoidal arms that loom in *The Mist* (2007) or on the edges of America in Gareth Edwards's *Monsters* (2010) or that splash around the Han river in Seoul in *The Host* (2006), or writhe so murderously in 3D in Ridley Scott's *Prometheus* (2012). These devices, borrowed from Lovecraft's materialist horrors, represent the formless, the unbounded, the protean transformational possibilities of life itself in images themselves constructed by SFX processes in which the organic and digital are increasingly impossible to distinguish. Now that the cinematic trick of transformism can be designed on a laptop, the malleability of the visual image uncannily matches our sense that biological processes have themselves become ungrounded from gradualist natural processes and entered a newly catastrophic phase. Science fact has finally caught up with Mary Shelley's fictional vision of the 'modern Prometheus'. It keeps science-fiction cinema chillingly relevant, a crucial register of the late thoughts of *Homo sapiens* in its potentially forever altered state, just before the reboot. ●

SPRINGTIME FOR CALIBAN?

by Jonathan Rigby

Christian Nyby's *The Thing from Another World*, declared Richard Findlater in August 1952, "[is] only the latest arrival in a series of films which seems to me disturbingly dotty. Over us all hangs the threat of atomic murder ... and in these 'science shockers' from Hollywood, the universal nightmare is translated into Martian melodrama. We don't want to see what a napalm bomb does to a man, but it doesn't hurt to see an intellectual carrot being burned alive."

Nyby's film had taken a while to reach British audiences, but it prompted from Findlater arguably the first, and certainly the pithiest, summation of what the Hollywood space craze was all about. "The background to all these ga-ga films," he told the readers of *Tribune*, "is the apocalyptic terror of the last day, the day of judgment." In doing so, he also pointed out how the 'apocalyptic terror' of postwar science fiction was a case of old wine in new bottles, for "the central character – the marauding carrot – is just like one of Boris Karloff's playmates in the dear old 'H' days."

In fact, the 'H' (for 'horrific') certificate had only been retired the year before. The atavistic mythologies of gothic horror, regularly called upon to aggravate filmgoers' fear of the unknown before the war, suddenly seemed passé. Now, science fiction provided these ancient terrors with a gloss of modernity, a gloss better suited to audiences shaken into a fearful awareness of scientific realities by Hiroshima and Nagasaki. Film historian John Baxter called this 1950s efflorescence "springtime for Caliban", yet precious few sci-fi films featured monsters with the redeeming humanity of Shakespeare's "misshapen knave" – or, for that matter, most of the creatures characteristic of gothic horror. Instead, the threats tended to be as impersonal and inhuman as the frightening technological advances they stood in for.

James Arness, for example, may have lent his 6'7" frame to *The Thing from Another World* but, Karloff resemblance notwithstanding, he was essentially playing a blood-lusting humanoid vegetable. Even the humanoid appearance, common to such contemporaries as *The Man from Planet X* and *Invaders from Mars*, was soon abandoned. Utterly non-human monsters – generally insectoid or reptilian – surged forth

'The Quatermass Xperiment' (1955)

in alarming numbers to offer a symbolic warning against overweening science. It was a thermite bomb that displaced *The Thing* from its slumber in the Arctic snows; soon thereafter atomic tests (again in the Arctic) resurrected *The Beast from 20,000 Fathoms* and – this time in the New Mexico desert – enlarged the rampaging ants of *Them!* Both films were produced in cinematic sci-fi's banner year of 1953.

The destructive potential of reinvigorated dinosaurs and mutated insects (or arthropods generally) represented a suitably inscrutable, unknowable force in film after film. The former category certainly travelled well; close kin to *The Beast* turned up in Japan (*Godzilla*, 1954 – plus multiplying sequels), Britain (*Behemoth the Sea Monster*, 1959; *Gorgo*, 1960), Denmark (*Reptilicus*, 1960), even – in budget-conscious 'invisible dinosaur' form – Spain (*The Prehistoric Sound*, 1965). At the same time, creepy-crawlies of one kind or another swarmed their way through *The Deadly Mantis*, *The Black Scorpion*, *Beginning of the End* (giant locusts), *The Strange World of Planet X* (all sorts), *Attack of the Crab Monsters*, *Earth vs. the Spider* – all of them issued in 1957-58. The trailer for *The Deadly Mantis* revelled in the kind of pulp rhetoric common to each, as well as making very plain the 'end times' nerve played upon in so many films of the period: "From the frozen glacial world unchanged in a million years – released from icy bondage – comes unknown – indescribable – paralyzing terror – to engulf the world!"

A jewel among these films – Jack

Arnold's lustrous *Tarantula* (1955) – submits research scientist Leo G. Carroll to a nasty plot device lifted from an old PRC potboiler of 1944, *The Monster Maker*. From experimenting with a radioactive growth serum to being deliberately infected with bone-distorting acromegaly, Carroll provides a much-desired human angle as a giant arachnid does its worst in the Arizona desert. The freakish enlargements of these films harked back, of course, to H.G. Wells's *The Food of the Gods* (itself filmed, rather belatedly, in 1975), just as the shade of the same author's Dr Moreau hovered over various films in which humans were unhappily spliced with lower forms. In 1958-59, for example, monster-happy filmgoers could catch *The Fly*, *The Alligator People* and *The Wasp Woman*; the fault lay with experimentation in matter transmission, limb restoration and anti-ageing wasp enzymes respectively.

At least these films connected back to humanity in the gradually transmogrifying shape of their protagonists. (In *The Fly*, who can forget the miniature David Hedison's puny wail of "Help me!" as a monstrous garden spider closes in for the kill?) But there were other films that removed their threats from humanity perhaps even more comprehensively than did the 'big bug' cycle. Derived from a story by Jack Arnold, *The Monolith Monsters* (1957) concerned a meteor-borne invasion of crystalline obelisks, while *The Blob*

Jack Arnold's 'Tarantula' (1955)

(1958) and its Italian counterpart *Caltiki, the Immortal Monster* (1959) went from hard to soft via gelatinous monstrosities hailing from, in *The Blob*, outer space and, in *Caltiki*, a subterranean Mexican lake.

Humanising a voracious, ever-growing blob might seem an impossible task, yet the British film from which both these pictures were derived did just that. *The Quatermass Xperiment* (1955) cannily reserves the blob section of its story for the climax, concentrating instead on the agonising process by which a returning astronaut succumbs to the alien infection engulfing him. With an exceptional actor (Richard Wordsworth) to handle the initial phases and a final reel in which the electrocuted 'thing' emits a still-human scream from its

perch in Westminster Abbey, the effect is powerful indeed. Nigel Kneale's TV original went further, with the scientist hero actually appealing to the vestiges of humanity in the monster, convincing it to commit suicide.

Kneale was always keen to subvert the clichés of science fiction from a humanist angle, using gothic motifs to that end and dealing with demonic possession in all three of his 1950s Quatermass stories. The first took *The Thing from Another World* as its cue; in the third, *Quatermass and the Pit* (filmed in 1967), Kneale even turned sci-fi's modish obsession with creepy-crawlies to his advantage. Here, the 5,000,000-year-old giant mantises dug up in a London building site humanise the 'bug' motif in the nastiest way possible. Kneale posits them as, effectively, the creators of mankind, examining the residual influence of these long-dead Martians on a selection of contemporary Londoners. And, yes, there's a *really* big bug too – in the shape of an ectoplasmic 'Horned Devil' projected by the revived Martian intelligence onto the London skyline.

Ingenious contrivances like this arose from Kneale's dissatisfaction with what he saw as the soulless mechanisation of much of the science fiction around him. By the end of the 1950s, when *Quatermass and the Pit* first appeared on TV – and when the period characterised by Baxter as "springtime for Caliban" was drawing to a close – sci-fi enthusiasts, accustomed to the lack of empathy engendered by the genre's non-human monsters, may well have agreed with him. ●

INDESCRIBABLE... INDESTRUCTIBLE! NOTHING CAN STOP IT!

THE BLOB "X"

STEVEN McQUEEN

ANETA CORSEAUT · EARL ROWE

PRODUCED BY JACK H. HARRIS · IRVIN S. YEAWORTH, JR. · DIRECTED BY THEODORE SIMONSON AND KATE PHILLIPS · SCREENPLAY BY FROM AN IDEA BY IRVINE H. MILLGATE A TONYLYN PRODUCTION · COLOUR BY DE LUXE

'The Blob' (1958)

Inner space
by Mark Bould

Sigmund Freud never knew it, but in 1917 he wrote a science-fiction manifesto. His essay *A Difficulty in the Path of Psychoanalysis* outlines the major concerns of a genre which, although still a decade away from being named, had been busy emerging since at least Mary Shelley's *Frankenstein* (1818). In it, he describes three great shocks to humanity's perception of itself: the Copernican revolution removed Earth from the centre of the universe, showing it to be just an insignificant speck in an unimaginably vast cosmos; the Darwinian revolution stripped us of our biological exceptionalism, demonstrating that we are just one species of animal among many; and the psychoanalytic revolution (Freud continued modestly) reveals that we are not even in control of our own minds or behaviour. Claiming this intellectual terrain for a genre currently so closely associated with spectacular, often jingoistic, blockbusters – with interstellar wars and alien invasions, superhero smackdowns and *kaiju* stompdowns, the end of the world and the zombies, cannibals, guntoters and bondage gear that survive it – might seem presumptuous.

There is no good reason to assume that such feisty accoutrements cannot elaborate upon weightier matters, but some people think otherwise. For example, back in 1962, when new waves were breaking out all over, not just in France, but also in Brazil, Britain, Czechoslovakia, India, Iran and Japan, and in the pages of science-fiction magazines and anthologies, J.G. Ballard's *Which Way Inner Space?* appeared in the pre-Michael Moorcock *New Worlds*. In this essay, arguably the leading science-fiction writer of his generation insisted that the genre must abandon its pulp paraphernalia in order to fulfil its unique potential to address the contemporary moment and the coming world. It must become more oblique and understated. It must explore the inner world of subjective and synthetic psychologies and space-times. It must be able to tell the story of an amnesiac "lying on a beach and looking at a rusty bicycle wheel, trying to work out the absolute essence of the relationship between them". In short, it must be more like the science fiction of the *nouvelle vague*, more like Alain Resnais's *Last Year in Marienbad* (1961), say, or Chris Marker's *La Jetée* (1962).

Questions of identity

In Basil Dearden's *The Mind Benders* (1963), Dr Henry Longman risks his sanity by prolonged immersion in a sensory deprivation tank. Major Hall seizes the opportunity presented by Henry's disorientation to conduct an experiment in brainwashing. He plants the idea that Henry, who is on the verge of collapse, never really loved his wife, and that Oonagh herself is unbalanced, jealous, hysterical, physically repulsive to him and "almost a tart". Initially, Hall's efforts appear to have no effect, but six months later, Oonagh's bourgeois façade crumbles in the face of Henry's remorseless condescension and abuse.

Christopher Nolan's *Inception* (2010) shares the conceit of manipulating behaviour by infiltrating a simple idea into the unconscious mind. Cobb's team are hired to alter Fischer's personality so that he will break up the global corporation he is about to inherit from his dying father. This involves plunging the sleeping Fischer into a succession of dreamscapes which sufficiently resemble reality – or a series of other movies – that he never realises he is being played. At the same time, it transpires that Cobb was once almost trapped in such a world when his wife started to believe it was real. He planted sufficient doubt in her mind that, by committing (apparent) suicide, they could return to really real reality. However, her doubt persisted, leading her to commit (actual) suicide to escape a reality she believed illusory.

The end of *Inception* suggests Cobb is living in a dreamscape. This glib Phildickian 'twist' was already sufficiently hackneyed that Paul Verhoeven could not muster an ounce of conviction when he tacked it on to *Total Recall* (1990), and Steven Spielberg could not bring himself to do it at the end of *Minority Report* (2002), although the final reel of the movie is so preposterous it must surely be a dream the protagonist, incarcerated in suspended animation, dreams. *The Mind Benders* is more successfully ambiguous. When Henry is confronted with incontrovertible evidence of how his personality was changed, he claims to have known all along *and* that Hall's dabbling with his mind just brought out feelings that he would never have otherwise allowed himself to express. This genuinely intriguing moment and its implications are buried under a melodramatic flurry as Oonagh goes into labour and Henry delivers their child. Everything implies psychological healing and reconciliation, but Dirk Bogarde's restrained performance in the film's final moments leaves open the possibility that Henry has merely reconciled himself to playing the role of loving husband again.

There is a similar moment in Teshigahara Hiroshi's *The Face of Another* (1966). After Okuyama's face is burned off in a factory accident, he is constantly swathed in bandages, like the Invisible Man. His wife cannot bring herself to respond to his sexual advances, so he persuades a psychiatrist/prosthetist to craft him a life-like mask – one that resembles not his his pre-accident self but someone else entirely. The psychiatrist recognises in his handiwork a metaphor for the anomie and alienation of modern Japan; he has utopian fantasies about the mass production of such masks utterly transforming the world, making everyone a stranger and thus destroying morality. Meanwhile, the masked Okuyama seduces his wife so as to avenge her rejection of him and reassert his ownership over her. When he turns on her, furious at her infidelity, she is stunned. She always knew it was him, and thought that he wanted to her to collude in his masquerade.

The Mind Benders probes what it might mean to have a 'true self' by drawing attention to human intersubjectivity, how we are shaped by our interactions with others; even if we are unaware of such interpellations, we cannot avoid them. *The Face of Another* questions whether there even is a 'true self' behind the multiple social roles we play.

Tricks of memory
Science fiction often raises the question of memory so as to emphasise our tenuous hold on identity. In Alain Resnais's *Je t'aime je t'aime* (1968), failed suicide Claude Ridder becomes the subject of a time-travel experiment and finds himself oscillating around his memories of an unhappy affair. Scenes from his past flash by or linger; some of them play

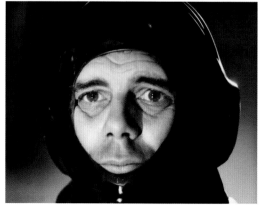

multiple times with small variations; some of them are perhaps more fantasy than reality, but his experience of them is no less real. The final quarter of Abel Ferrara's *New Rose Hotel* (1998) pushes this technique to a frantic extreme as the criminal protagonist, X, tries to figure out when Sandii, his femme fatale lover, betrayed him. Close-ups of his face are intercut with streams of surveillance footage and out-of-order flashbacks in which scenes play out differently than when they first appeared in the film: dialogue varies, alternate takes are deployed, scenes begin or end at different points. The viewer's memory is thus caught up in a loop similar to X's paranoid, or solipsistic, fretting. At the crucial juncture when a change in Sandii's expression signals her decision to betray him, X could not have seen her face. Is it only the audience who finds this out, leaving X spiralling inward without resolution? Or is X saving himself by fastening on that moment, even though he must just be making it up?

The ability to erase painful experiences and construct a comfortingly delusional self is at the centre of Michel Gondry's *Eternal Sunshine of the Spotless Mind* (2004), in which Joel and Clementine both opt, after the bitter failure of their relationship, to edit the other out of their memories, little suspecting that they will meet and fall in love all over again. In Omar Naim's bleaker *The Final Cut* (2004), many people are unknowingly implanted when young with a device that records everything they see and hear. When someone dies, a cutter is hired to trawl through these recordings to create a memorial film – a 'rememory' – that replays the deceased's most treasured memories. Charles Bannister's memories reveal that he repeatedly raped his young daughter, but because cutters are sworn to absolute secrecy, there is nothing Alan Hakman can do with his discovery – especially as Bannister's widow, who was complicit in the abuse, is only concerned with her dead husband's public image. By constructing a prosthetic memory of him, with all the authority its subjective viewpoint implies, she turns carefully selected fragments of his memory into a public relations exercise that directly shapes how he will be remembered.

As such films suggest, Bruce Mazlish's *The Fourth Discontinuity: The Co-Evolution of Humans and Machines* (1995) was right to add a fourth shock to humanity's self-regard, arguing that the distinction between humans and technology is not only false but also rapidly eroding. David Cronenberg maps the cybernetic and information revolution on to the drives and desires that shape human consciousness and reality. In *Videodrome* (1983), a video signal infects the jaded Max Renn with a brain tumour that induces hallucinations, programmes him as an assassin and triggers physical mutations (although Cronenberg's artful destabilisation of reality makes it is impossible to tell how much of

(Page 121)
Teshigahara Hiroshi's
'The Face of Another' (1966).

(Opposite, left)
'Total Recall' (1990).

(Opposite, right)
Dirk Bogarde in
'The Mind Benders' (1963).

(Above)
Leonardo DiCaprio in
'Inception' (2010).

(left)
'Videodrome' (1983).

what we see actually happens). *eXistenZ* (1999) nests various alternative diegeses – some of them awash in psychosexual material, and none of them an entirely persuasive or stable version of reality – within one another, setting determinism and autonomy at loggerheads.

A slew of virtual-reality fictions – including Rainer Werner Fassbinder's miniseries *World on a Wire* (*Welt am Draht*, 1973), Alejandro Amenábar's *Open Your Eyes* (*Abre los ojos*, 1997), the Wachowskis' *Matrix* trilogy (1999-2003) and Oshii Mamoru's *Ghost in the Shell 2: Innocence* (2004) – similarly probe the relationships between volition and action, cause and effect. Oshii's *Avalon* (2001) directly connects global interconnectedness and social fragmentation to contemporary unease about, and enthusiasm for, simulacral media, foregrounding the emerging cultures of immersivity and gameplay. Doug Liman's *Edge of Tomorrow* (2014) derives its structure – in which Cage must relive the same day over and over again, rebooting it every time he dies in combat – from computer gaming. Its rather smug conclusion, however, plays out like a conservative moral panic, implying that immersive media produce a solipsistic retreat from recognising actions have consequences.

A more giddying decentring of humanity can be found in films that emphasise not technology but the body. In Ken Russell's *Altered States* (1980), Eddie Jessup uses sensory deprivation tanks and powerful ancient hallucinogens to access memory stored on an atomic level, reaching back beyond organic life to the moments after the Big Bang when the first atoms were formed. Jessup is not restricted merely to observing the cheesily tasteless imagery that periodically fills the screen – his regression is physical, transforming him first into a pre-hominid ape and then into some monstrous, contorted primordial being, reminding us, however garishly, that our bodies are made of stuff that once was not us and soon will not be again. Cronenberg's *Shivers* (1975) features parasites – part aphrodisiac, part venereal disease – that invade human bodies, shattering dull bourgeois rectitude and unleashing human polymorphous perversity. But they do more than that. They adjust the balance between the ego and the unconscious, between reason and irrationality, implying that any such balance is contingent and impermanent. John Carpenter's *The Thing* (1982) goes further, imagining a Lovecraftian alien composed of irreconcilable parts. Grotesque and abject, it mimics and shapeshifts. It recapitulates elements of the other creatures, terrestrial and alien, it has encountered. Each particle of it is alive and capable of independent action, and we never encounter its original form, if it even has one. This profound corporeality, this roiling, fleshy bare life, is what we share with all organic being – the boundaries of our bodies are illusions, the film argues, as are the identities and the reason to which we cling as we cower before the abyss. ●

(Above)
The shape-shifting,
Lovecraftian alien in John
Carpenter's 'The Thing' (1982).

(Below, left)
Claude Ridder (Claude Rich)
is caught in an experiment
in which he oscillates round
his memories of an unhappy
affair in Alain Resnais's
'Je t'aime, je t'aime' (1968).

(Below, right)
Willem Dafoe as X, and
Asia Argento as Sandii,
his lover and possible
betrayer, in Abel Ferrara's
'New Rose Hotel' (1998).

(Opposite)
Jim Carrey as Joel, who
attempts to erase his painful
memories in Michel Gondry's
'Eternal Sunshine of the
Spotless Mind' (2004).

FEAR AND FANTASY: WOMEN IN SCI-FI CINEMA

by Josephine Botting

"A woman! You must be joking!" splutters Dr Laird when he hears about the new assistant appointed to help with his highly complex experimentation with magnetic fields. But when Michèle Dupont turns out to be not only smart but attractive too, the male contingent of British giant-insect-cum-alien-invasion movie *The Strange World of Planet X* (aka *Cosmic Monsters*, 1958) soon withdraw their objections. And beyond her valuable contribution to scientific discovery, Michèle provides hero Forrest Tucker with an opportunity to rescue a helpless female from an oversize spider's web.

Since Ripley took on *Alien* in 1979, we've grown used to kick-ass women in science-fiction films, but the genre took the long way round to arrive at Sigourney Weaver's finest hour. While she wasn't the first woman to prove her value on a space mission or in a laboratory, those who came before had a tougher time overcoming the stereotypes. "Can you cook?" Stephen Boyd asks Raquel Welch, as she repairs a laser in preparation for their journey into the human body in *Fantastic Voyage* (1966); later, she's subjected to prolonged pawing by the male crew members to remove some bodily secretions attacking her torso. *Barbarella* (1968) too embarks on a vital mission only to find that alien men have just one thing on their minds.

Fritz Lang, though, was ahead of the game – in 1929 he launched *Woman in the Moon* (*Frau im Mond*) in which the first moon mission includes female astronaut Friede (Gerda Maurus). She not only assists the crew in getting to their destination but saves their lives by fighting off the crazed Professor Manfeld, who is trying to jeopardise their return journey. Yet Friede's primary role is to provide the film with dramatic tension in the form of a love triangle.

Science fiction enjoys a good love triangle, Hammer's riff on the theme appearing in its 1953 film *Four Sided Triangle*. Inventors Robin and Bill come up with a machine they call the reproducer, capable of making an exact copy of any object placed in it. When their childhood friend Lena begins assisting them with their experiments, both men fall in love with her but she marries Robin, leaving Bill bereft. He cooks up the idea of putting *her* in the machine and, hey presto, one each! Bill's great plan has one fatal flaw however – his Lena (renamed Helen), being an exact copy of the real one, also loves Robin rather than him.

This male fantasy of trying to control the opposite sex is a common one in the genre. From *Alraune* in 1928 to *The Perfect Woman* (1949) and *The Twilight Zone* episode *The Lonely* (tx 13/11/1959), science fiction has explored in different ways the desire of men for an ideal woman who will respond to their needs, subjugating their own and foregoing the right to free will. The theme became particularly acute during the 1970s when women's liberation caused men to question their role, with films like *The Stepford Wives* (1975) and, perhaps the ultimate male domination fantasy, *Demon Seed* (1977). In it, Alex (Fritz Weaver) walks out on his wife Susan (Julie Christie), leaving her alone in their ultra-high tech house run entirely by voice-operated computer. Yet the dream home becomes a nightmare when she finds herself imprisoned by Alex's ultimate creation, the artificial brain Proteus IV, which has taken over the computer with the aim of having a child of its own. Susan is tortured, tied down and inseminated by Proteus, but the child which emerges is an exact replica of her and Alex's daughter who died of leukemia, leaving us feeling

'Four Sided Triangle' (1953)

Julie Christie in 'Demon Seed' (1977)

that Proteus is less a creation gone wrong than an extension of Alex's own psyche.

Fear of the female surfaces in several 1950s films in which interplanetary travel brought us to strange worlds inhabited by races of women. The *Cat Women of the Moon* (1953) and the *Fire Maidens from Outer Space* (1956) are both dying races trying to guarantee their survival by seducing unsuspecting astronauts who find it hard to resist women clad in skin-tight cat suits or skimpy mini-dresses. The *Devil Girl from Mars* (1954) is on a similar mission; a war between the sexes on her planet has led to total destruction of their males and Nyah has been sent in search of replacements. Martian women seem to dress in the style of a dominatrix, head to toe black leather, a look that doesn't seem to appeal much to the men of Invernesshire *circa* 1954. As with the other female kidnap attempts, her mission is foiled by the superior intelligence of the human male – we weren't yet ready for women to win the battle of the sexes.

Other films of the period expose a more fundamental fear of the mystery of women's workings. In *Attack of the 50 Foot Woman* (1958), the doctors diagnose the source of Nancy Archer's phenomenal growth as a hormonal imbalance related to frustration – as her cheating husband Harry puts it in the 1993 remake, "a new kind of PMS". Nancy's transformation from nervous, cuckolded wife to towering Amazonian is in fact due to radiation from a UFO but her new-found stature imbues her with the courage to stride magnificently through town in a bedsheet bikini to get revenge on Harry and his blonde floozy.

Men's discomfort with the details of women's physiognomy has led to the depiction of otherworldly spawnings, from *Village of the Damned* (1960) to Nola Carveth's much more graphic delivery in David Cronenberg's *The Brood* (1979). Under the guidance of Dr Raglan, Nola has learned to give physical form to her rage, producing an army of asexual, toothless 'children' who act on her impulse, killing those who displease her. Cronenberg's previous 1970s films had already provided some extraordinary female roles in genre films. In *Shivers* (1975), a sexually promiscuous woman spread a venereal parasite that rendered victims slaves to

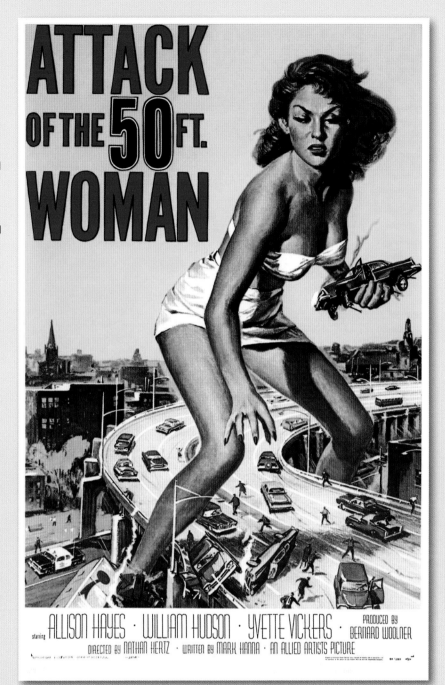

'Attack of the 50 Foot Woman' (1958)

sexual impulse, while *Rabid* (1977) saw porn star Marilyn Chambers grow a phallic stinger in her armpit that turned people into vampiric zombies. But *The Brood* was his most primal investigation of the 'monstrous feminine', and also his most personal. For he later admitted that the character of Nola was based on his ex-wife and that he found shooting the scene, in which she is strangled by her ex-husband, a satisfying experience.

In the last 30 years, women have

taken a much more active role in what was a traditionally male genre – writing and directing films, as well as holding their own on screen, whether fighting aliens, like Ripley, investigating them, like Dana Scully in *The X-Files* series (1993-2002), or befriending them, as Ellie Arroway does in *Contact* (1997). But science-fiction films have provided ample opportunities for men to explore both their fears and fantasies of the fair sex. ●

Artificial intelligences
by Adam Rutherford

Morpheus: *What we know for certain is that at some point in the early 21st century all of mankind was united in celebration. We marvelled at our own magnificence as we gave birth to AI.*
Neo: *AI? You mean artificial intelligence?*
Morpheus: *A singular consciousness that spawned an entire race of machines. We don't know who struck first, us or them. But we know that it was us that scorched the sky.*
The Matrix, 1999

Automatons have a history that dates back to classical times: Hephaestus, the Olympians' blacksmith of Greek legend, built mechanical helpers, and in some versions of these sagas, Talos, a giant bronze automaton protector of Crete. We met Ray Harryhausen's Talos in *Jason and the Argonauts* (1963), summoned to life after impetuous Hercules couldn't stop himself from pilfering some oversized booty. The real Greeks were wicked smart at technology too. In 1900 some divers pulled a block of mud from a 1st century BCE shipwreck. It contained the 'Antikythera Mechanism', often described as the world's first computer: after a century, we understood it to be an astronomical calculator, and its sophistication would not be seen again for more than 14 centuries. (The 'Mechanical Turk' was a briefly fashionable phenomenon in the late 18th century. A chess-playing automaton dressed in the garb of a generic mystical Eastern conjuror, he sat at a board mounted on a large box. Alas, it was soon revealed to contain a master chess player pulling the strings.)

Charles Babbage and Ada Lovelace are credited with conceiving the first general computing machine in 1837, and this can reasonably be marked as the beginnings of modern computing. The purposes of their so-called 'Analytical Engine' was to perform calculations that were too hard and too time-consuming to do by hand. That is the point of automation: to do intellectual and physical heavy-lifting. We create ever more complex technology, with powers to do things that we can't (or can't be bothered to) do. Servility is the foundation of robotics.

Czech playwright Karel Capek set the tone for many cinematic robots to come when he first used that word in his 1921 play *Rossum's Universal Robots*. His machine men were servants that revolt and extinguish humankind. But this inception triggered only a slow start in the movies. There was the odd appearance in silent movies, in films such as *A Clever Dummy* (1917) and *L'uomo meccanico* (*The Mechanical Man,* 1921) before the first robot icon appeared in Fritz Lang's *Metropolis* (1927), the first science-fiction epic blockbuster. The influence of this bewitching film – 35th in *Sight & Sound*'s 2012 poll of the greatest movies ever made – is incalculable in terms of production design, and of future cities in everything from *Blade Runner* (1982) to *Batman* (1989). But the influence of the iconic robot is questionable. Transformed into the likeness of the film's intriguing character Maria, the robot is set loose to wreak havoc and wreck the reputation of the real Maria. Ultimately, robot Maria is burnt at the stake. She's iconic, and instantly recognisable – remarkably similar in design to C-3PO in *Star Wars* (1977). But this role – android disguised as a human deployed with malevolent intent – is in fact not a frequent character in cinema. Her clearest descendent is Arnold Schwarzenegger's Terminator: neither actor nor role display that much similarity to most humans, physically or cognitively.

The rules of robotics
Machine intelligence and computing power were actively being researched in the 1940s and 50s, and robots and revolt became frequent

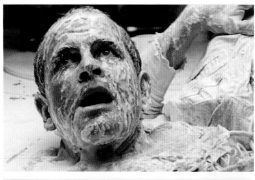

(Top)
Ash (Ian Holm), the android
in 'Alien' (1979), breaks Isaac
Asimov's rules of robotics
when he attempts to kill
Ripley (Sigourney Weaver).

(Above)
Though he shares Ash's
admiration for the xenomorph,
Bishop (Lance Henriksen), the
android in James Cameron's
'Aliens' (1986), obeys Asimov's
laws and protects Ripley.

(Previous page)
Robby the Robot in
'Forbidden Planet' (1956).

(Below)
Arnold Schwarzenegger as the
T-800 'cybernetic organism',
now programmed to protect
Sarah Connor in 'Terminator 2:
Judgment Day' (1991).

tropes in science-fiction literature. But the movies were late adopters
to the new tech. Robots, and AI, rarely make an appearance on screen
until the 1970s. The emergence of the all-powerful silent guardian
Gort in President's Park in Washington DC in *The Day the Earth Stood
Still* (1951) triggered just a few robot sidekicks and characters, notably
Forbidden Planet's Robby the Robot, an Ariel to Dr Morbius's Prospero.

Robby, effectively a slave, is the first automaton with AI to display
adherence to the rules of robotics that Isaac Asimov had developed
over the previous decade: 1. A robot may not injure a human being or,
through inaction, allow a human being to come to harm. 2. A robot
must obey the orders given to it by human beings, except where such
orders would conflict with the First Law. 3. A robot must protect its own
existence as long as such protection does not conflict with the First or
Second Law. Later, Asimov added the Zeroth Law: 0. A robot may not
harm humanity, or, by inaction, allow humanity to come to harm.

The servility in these laws poses an interesting problem. We want our
bots to protect and serve, and we want them to be smart enough to provide
sophisticated responses to situations within the framework of those laws.
But we don't want to give them enough self-awareness to question their
slavery. There are plenty of much-loved cinema robots whose behaviour
isn't forced into these uniquely moral conundrums. WALL-E developing
emotions in solitude; Marvin in *The Hitchhiker's Guide to the Galaxy* (2005),
depressed by his wasted planet-sized intellect – their idiosyncrasies are all
too human, and they are indistinguishable from human characteristics.
Though R2-D2 and C-3PO are willful and pathetic respectively, there's
nothing particularly interesting about their AI. Artoo opens locked doors,
Threepio translates: they are merely slaves bickering for comic relief.

But the most enduring computer intelligences in cinema are forced
to make choices that conflict with the morality built into their programs.
The greatest of these is HAL-9000. Gently voiced by Douglas Rain, he's
the character with the most personality in *2001: A Space Odyssey* (1968).
HAL attempts to murder the crew of spaceship Discovery One because
he cannot resolve his mission parameters with the crew's belief that he
has malfunctioned and needs to be switched off. If they are not alive, then
he doesn't have to deceive them. It is the same problem that Ash, played
by Ian Holm, faces in *Alien* (1979), and the Nexus-6 replicants, among
them Roy Batty (Rutger Hauer), in *Blade Runner*. Though replete with
personalities and apparent human idiosyncrasies (HAL's stated fondness
for working with humans, Ash's chilling admiration of the xenomorph,
Roy Batty's awe at his experiences), all of them fail to resolve Asimov's
laws. Ash attempts to kill Sigourney Weaver's Ripley with some verve
by choking her with a porn mag out of programmed corporate loyalty.
Ash's death scene, decapitated and milky, is a stand-out in the *Alien*
franchise, and immediately following this surprisingly emotional attack,
he returns to apparent indifference in the face of the crew's presumed
destruction. He shrugs his final words: "You have my sympathies." Ash's
redemption is supplied by Bishop (Lance Henriksen) in the sequel *Aliens*
(1986). Bishop, like his predecessor, is physically indistinguishable from
humans, has a similar creepy admiration for the alien, but ultimately
adheres to Asimov's laws, and sacrifices himself to protect Ripley.

But the Nexus-6 replicants are different. Their problem is a short
lifespan, and so sufficiently developed a consciousness that they
refuse to accept death without a fight. Whether this is a problem of
their creator's own making is ambiguous. On the one hand, we are
told that they have implanted false memories, which aids emotional

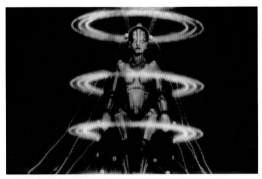

(Top)
The iconic robot Maria in
Fritz Lang's 'Metropolis' (1927).

(Above)
C-3PO and R2-D2 in 'Star
Wars' (1977) are mere slaves
bickering for comic relief, and
are uninteresting as AI.

(Below)
Agent Smith (Hugo Weaving)
in 'The Matrix' (1999) is a
program manifest as a person,
with a sentient intelligence
and a contempt for humans,
who threaten his existence.

development. This makes them unstable, so a failsafe four-year lifespan was introduced. But the creator, Dr Tyrell (Joe Turkel), tells Batty that their superhuman abilities inherently limit their lifespan. Perhaps he is just begging for his life. It doesn't work.

Why are the replicants not considered alive? We create something that displays all the hallmarks of being sentient and conscious, with memories and experiences, and a desire to live free. It's a pity they don't come free of emotional problems, but then again, who does?

Bear in mind that we don't understand consciousness. We can't even define it. While advances in neuroscience in the last decade have radically transformed our ability to see the functions of the brain at increasingly sharp resolution, it remains the most complex entity known to humankind, and the most inscrutable. Any claims (and there are plenty) that we are close to modelling a working brain are grotesquely overstated. We have ideas about how memory, cognition and a sense of self work at a neuronal level, but these are woefully incomplete currently. There is nothing supernatural about the brain, nor our minds, and to separate them, as Descartes did, is no longer considered a useful way of understanding ourselves. But consciousness research has a long way to go.

In Roy Batty's perfect death speech ("I've seen things you people wouldn't believe…") he's expressing one of the central problems of consciousness. If Batty's experiences are real, even if they are implanted, is he not describing a rich inner life, impossible for anyone else to experience in the same way? In neuroscience we talk about 'neural correlates of consciousness', which are the minimum collection of brain activity that registers an experience. Whatever that is, and it is not yet known, Batty appears to have it.

Similarly in *The Matrix* (1999), there is nothing about the programs within it, nor the overall society of machines, which doesn't suggest living consciousness. The AI controls the world (with the most apocalyptic disregard for Asimov's laws), and the reality perceived by humans, who are actually batteries to fuel the continued existence of the machines [this, as an aside, is a terrible way to generate power, as we consume more than we generate; a more intelligent way would be to grow trees and burn them]. We know nothing of the machines except their desire to exist, and in fulfilling that, their crushing of any humans that threaten that existence. Within the artificial reality of the Matrix are programs manifest as people, who display every sign of sentience and intelligence. Agent Smith's contempt for humans, which grows in the increasingly baffling sequels into hatred of the Matrix itself, is beyond pure logic. He is making aesthetic choices. The battle in the Matrix is not between humans and machines, it is a Darwinian struggle for survival.

Shall we play a game?

Like consciousness, intelligence is a murky field within science. How we measure it is mired in controversy (IQ is the best-known and studied, but still only a factor of broader cognitive function), and nowadays we agree that there are many facets to intelligence, some encompassing many measurable characteristics. Nevertheless, logic is a key part of intelligence as measured in standardised tests. During the 1940s, Alan Turing and others were beginning to work on machine intelligence, with ever more sophisticated logic at its core. In 1947, Turing suggested that a poor chess player would not be able to tell the difference between an equally poor player, and a machine, if both were unseen.

With an acronym that would fit well into any sci-fi tale, the first computer to beat a human was the MANIAC in 1956 – albeit a game against

a novice with simplified rules. By the 1990s, beating humans was becoming more common, and the big victory was Deep Blue over Garry Kasparov in 1997; now computers often beat grandmasters. The Turing Test is a gimmick of AI research. It's a formulation to test if a machine can imitate a human to the extent that a real human can be fooled. It has not been passed yet.

This forms the basis of the premise of Alex Garland's directorial debut, *Ex Machina* (2014). Alicia Vikander's robot Ava is the product of Nathan Bateman, creator of the world's dominant search engine, Blue Book. He's a Dr Frankenstein crossed with Google founders Larry Page and Sergey Brin, with a bit of Mark Zuckerberg thrown in. Company coder Caleb Smith is brought in to test her, effectively a version of a Turing test, though he can see she is a robot. But it's not clear what the purpose of this test is. Ava's consciousness – and I have no doubt that she has it – is a sort of network of knowledge drawn from the limitless global internet traffic of Blue Book. *Ex Machina* is serious science fiction, a deeply thoughtful, disturbing and thrilling exploration of consciousness. As with most scientific literature on the subject, it leaves you with more questions than answers. Ava is mesmerising, and her movement, the inhuman awkward grace and precision of a ballet dancer, is continuously unsettling.

Rise of the machines

Robots in science fiction contain machinery more advanced than currently available tech. Ava, like the replicants or Yul Brynner's Gunslinger from *Westworld* (1973) are indistinguishable from people, at least clothed. Back in the real world, chips get faster, motors get smaller, servos get more sensitive and batteries lighter, and companies such as Boston Dynamics are building quicker, more responsive, more automated robots pushing at the boundaries of self-sufficient automatons. Their beasts include WildCat, BigDog and Cheetah, which can run at a scary 29mph. They mimic animals, and appear to be designed for military use – they can

(Above)
"I've seen things you people wouldn't believe," says Roy Batty (Rutger Hauer) to Deckard (Harrison Ford) in 'Blade Runner' (1982). The replicants in the film have so sufficiently developed a consciousness that they don't accept death without a fight.

(Below)
Ava (Alicia Vikander), the conscious robot in Alex Garland's 'Ex Machina' (2014).

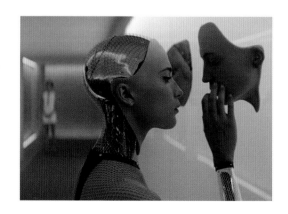

carry heavy loads in rough terrain, and right themselves when assaulted.

These are not creations that could pass a Turing test. They have no thought, nor anything resembling consciousness, and are not designed to imitate a human. But consider this: Boston Dynamics, along with seven other leading robotics and AI start-ups, was acquired in an aggressive landgrab in the space of just six months, by Google.

HAL's twin SAL-9000 was the AI in 2010, the sequel to 2001: A Space Odyssey. In conversation with their creator about disabling her higher functions as a test, she asks, "Will I dream?" Dr Chandra assures her, "Of course you will dream. All intelligent creatures dream, nobody knows why." That was made in 1984, and set in the titular year, 2010. In Blade Runner, made in 1982 and set in 2019, Deckard (Harrison Ford), a replicant himself, dreams of unicorns, but we know they are implanted to make himself believe he is a self-determining human.

In the real world, we are midway between the imagined worlds of 2010 and Blade Runner. We have neither the understanding of our minds nor the computing power to create HAL or SAL. In Spike Jonze's Her (2013), poor old Joaquin Phoenix gets dumped by his sexy talking operating system (voiced by Scarlett Johansson), as her AI is evolving towards the hypothetical technological singularity, when machine AI will supersede human intellect, and possibly destroy us. For now, we can rest easy: vocal sat-navs are ubiquitous, but does anyone actually use the iPhone's 'intelligent personal assistant' Siri? (But do ask it to "open the pod bay doors, HAL". The Apple coders are not without a sense of humour).

Nor do we have the mechanics to build Deckard or Ash. Neither the united celebrations following the inception of The Matrix, nor the self-awareness of Skynet in the Terminator franchise are in the foreseeable future. But Google has built an almost hegemonic grasp on the world's information via its search engine and spin-off software. With their move into AI and robotics, maybe Ava is coming soon. ●

(Above)
"I am putting myself to the fullest possible use, which is all, I think, that any conscious entity can ever hope to do," says HAL-9000, the malfunctioning AI in '2001: A Space Odyssey' (1968).

(Below)
Gunslinger (Yul Brynner), the robot in 'Westworld' (1973), is outwardly indistinguishable from a human being.

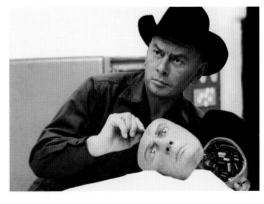

TO THE BINARY... AND BEYOND

by Sophie Mayer

Why has there never been a female Doctor Who? Previous showrunner Russell T. Davies said: "While I think kids will not have a problem with [a female Doctor], I think fathers will have a problem with it because they will then imagine they will have to describe sex changes to their children." Incidents such as teacher Lucy Meadows's suicide after bigoted bullying suggests that Davies may have had a point about parental transphobia – but may also have shirked an important opportunity to challenge it.

Six years and two regenerations on, the Doctor is no closer to representing the lived experience of transitioning. And he is not alone, despite literary science fiction's commitment to thinking beyond the gender binary since its inception, when Mary Shelley showed Victor Frankenstein experimenting with non-sexual reproduction in *Frankenstein* (1818). The year 1969 saw the publication of Ursula K. Le Guin's definitional *The Left Hand of Darkness*, set on a planet in which individuals are only gendered during reproduction, and can take either sex. Ann Leckie's *Ancillary Justice* scooped the Hugo, Nebula, Locus, and Arthur C. Clarke awards in 2014, but its non-gender-differentiating central characters are as unlikely as Joanna Russ's female man or Octavia Butler's tri-gendered Oankali to make it to the big screen.

But feminist, queer and trans politics have helped shape popular culture, sci-fi film included. *The Man Who Fell to Earth* (1976) borrowed David Bowie's alien(ated) persona and hip androgyny, which also marks Slava Tsukerman's *Liquid Sky* (1982), whose screenwriter Anne Carlisle plays both the female and male leads, requiring her, in one scene, to have sex with herself like Divine in John Waters's *Female Trouble* (1974). Conversely, in *Alien* (1979), ass-kicking Ellen Ripley (Sigourney Weaver) succeeded previous sci-fi femme archetypes such as Barbarella (Jane Fonda) and Princess Leia (Carrie Fisher). The Alien itself is one in a long line of sci-fi-/horror Others that Barbara Creed calls "the monstrous feminine", mirror images of Ripley's own female masculinity, unsettling the gender binary.

Sharon Willis, talking about Scott's *Thelma and Louise* (1991), refers to the Hollywood ascendancy of "hardware and hardbodies" for female characters. Hardbody heroine Lornette 'Mace' Mason (Angela Bassett) in Kathryn Bigelow's *Strange Days* (1995) points to the origin of the archetype in queer culture: Bigelow's own first film role was in Lizzie Borden's *Born in Flames* (1983), whose Women's Liberation Army is led by the butch Adelaide Norris (Jean Satterfield). Jack B. Badd in David Twohy's *Pitch Black* (2000), a shaven-headed stowaway later revealed

Lori Petty in Rachel Talalay's 'Tank Girl' (1995)

Tilda Swinton in 'Orlando' (1992)

Angela Bassett in 'Strange Days' (1995)

as Jacky, nods similarly from mainstream to alt: hir look is unquestionably a tribute to goggle-sporting punk feminist *Tank Girl* (Rachel Talalay, 1995), the first comic-book superheroine to headline a movie.

Talalay's adaptation mainstreamed the counter-cultural androgyny and radical gender play seen in Derek Jarman's *Jubilee* (1978), Ulrike Ottinger's *Freak Orlando* (1981) and Monika Treut's *Virgin Machine* (1988). As Treut charts in *Gendernauts* (1999), her trans San Francisco documentary, for queer filmmakers political reality is often dystopian, and queer culture an alternate "new world", as Chris Straayer identifies. A queer/trans speculative cinema subgenre would include Sally Potter's *Orlando* (1992), Lynn Hershman Leeson's *Conceiving Ada* (1997) and *Teknolust* (2002), and A. Hans Scheirl's *Dandy Dust* (1998). An epic low-budget film, the prosthetic aesthetics in this last make the viewer wonder why David Cronenberg's only film to feature a trans character is the realist *M. Butterfly* (1993). Cronenberg turned typewriters into bugs in *Naked Lunch* (1991), but Scheirl created the magnificent Spidercuntboy (Svar Simpson).

Scheirl's film is defiantly influenced by the aesthetics of not only Cronenberg and Waters, but also Ed Wood, whose career began with a reflection of his own transvestism in the realist sexploitation film *Glen or Glenda* (1953). Many contemporary critics have noted that, post-transition, Lana Wachowski cross-cast Hugo Weaving as a female nurse in *Cloud Atlas* (2012), and has created a transgender blogger as a central character for the new Wachowski siblings' project. Earlier this year, with an exclamation of "Holy Tilda Swinton", near-future sci-fi drama *Orphan Black* (2013-) simultaneously introduced the first transmasculine character in a TV

genre show *and* saluted the big-screen queen of non-binary performance.

Genre television, and its fan culture, has generally been an experimental and progressive medium for LGBTQI (lesbian, gay, bisexual, transgender, queer, questioning and intersex) characters and storylines; Davies did, after all, create 'the Doctor Donna', the tenth Doctor's human companion Donna Noble (Catherine Tate). Donna, like similar characters in *Star Trek* and *Stargate: Atlantis*, is only temporarily transgendered, however, rendering transitioning itself a science fiction. *Orphan Black*'s T-injecting Tony, by contrast, is one of many clones, all played by Tatiana Maslany: a powerful argument for nurture over nature, and against essentialism.

As clones with multiple mothers but no original, Maslany's characters bear out the huge influence of Donna Haraway's 'Cyborg Manifesto', (1983), which connected

feminist politics, non-biological replication, non-binary identities and technological innovation. The most striking cinematic Harawayan cyborg worked behind the scenes, rather than appearing on them: Wendy Carlos, who transitioned in 1972, was a synthesiser pioneer, composing the soundtracks for Steven Lisberger's *Tron* (1982) and Stanley Kubrick's *The Shining* (1980), and arranging the score for Kubrick's *A Clockwork Orange* (1971). Her synth arrangement of Bach's Ninth Symphony provides the soundtrack for D.A. Pennebaker's documentary about the man who fell to earth, *Ziggy Stardust and the Spiders from Mars* (1973).

Maybe cinema needs to time-warp back to the 1970s, and its sweet transvestites from transsexual Transylvania. Audiences still gather to sing along with Jim Sharman's *The Rocky Horror Picture Show* (1975), penned by Richard O'Brien, who came out as third gender in 2009, but only one 21st-century film has revisited its heady fusion of *Frankenstein*, American B cinema and pop androgyny: Apichatpong Weerasethakul and Michael Shaonawasai's *The Adventure of Iron Pussy* (*Hua jai tor ra nong*, 2003), a tribute to 1970s Thai genre cinema, featuring Shaonawasai's performance art alter-ego, the transvestite superheroine Iron Pussy, who defeats her nemesis/lover with karma. Holy Tilda Swinton indeed. ●

Tatiana Maslany as Tony, one of the many clones in 'Orphan Black' (2013-)

Taking the blue pill: virtual realities

by Sherryl Vint

In a crucial scene in *The Matrix* (1999), Morpheus (Laurence Fishburne) offers Neo (Keanu Reeves) a choice between the red pill (which will awaken him to a painful reality of struggle) and the blue (which if taken will cause him to remain in the blissful illusion that the Matrix is reality). Neo, of course, chooses the red, and with him we are transported from the slick, neo-*noir*ish world of the film to the faded, rusty and cramped aesthetic of the Nebuchadnezzar (the hovercraft on which Neo and Morpheus are crew).

This preference for reality over its simulation is prevalent in depictions of virtual reality (VR) in science-fiction film: although VR is often represented as the seductive space of cinema itself, the narratives of most VR films privilege the 'truth' of reality over the 'illusion' of such spaces. Only the traitor Cypher (Joe Pantoliano) overtly expresses a preference for the luxury of the simulated world over the real one, yet the visual aesthetic of *The Matrix* glorifies the very technology it critiques: its most powerful images are the ones set in a VR world and even its 'reality' is dominated by computer equipment. This paradoxical tension between theme and image epitomises science-fiction VR cinema and television.

Science-fiction VR films are obsessed with the boundary between the real and the virtual, simultaneously expressing our fascination with created worlds of infinite possibility and our anxiety about the loss of the real. *The Matrix* overtly evokes Jean Baudrillard's famed thesis from *Simulations* (1983): that postmodernism is "the desert of the real", our experience so saturated with simulation that the distinction between reality and representation has become meaningless. Yet *The Matrix*, and most science-fiction representations of VR, fail to grasp his thesis and insist instead that there remains a clear and important difference. Most films about VR are thus narratively about its dangers and visually about its pleasures.

Game theory

Many VR films begin with videogames – for most of us, the first technological experience of extending our agency into virtual spaces through an avatar. William Gibson, who coined the term cyberspace, has frequently cited videogames as his inspiration for cyberpunk cowboys who "jack in" to virtual spaces.

VR films often blur game and real space. *Tron* (1982) was one of the first attempts to visualise what happens inside the computer. Kevin Flynn (Jeff Bridges) is abducted into the world he programmed, where competing software functions battle one another, gladiator style. In *Tron*, these agents are personified as human entities whose adventures take place in a digital space largely devoid of visual detail, marking a clear aesthetic difference between reality and cyberspace. A decade on, *The Lawnmower Man* (1992), in which a scientist uses VR and drugs in an experiment to raise the intelligence of (and inadvertently create telepathic abilities in) his gardener, similarly marked its virtual/game space by rather crude graphic images of game play.

In both films, although action takes place in the digital space, it has corrosive effects on the morality of those immersed in play and real consequences in the outside world, which remains the privileged space. Brett Leonard's later *Virtuosity* (1995) moved the action almost entirely into the real world as SID 6.7 (Russell Crowe), an AI antagonist from a police training simulation, is downloaded into a silicon android body. The plot involves the efforts of police officer Parker Barnes (Denzel Washington) to defeat SID in real space and return him to his virtual prison. Duncan Jones's *Source Code* (2011), in which army pilot Colter Stevens (Jake Gyllenhaal) must repeatedly visit a VR recreation from the memories of those killed in a terrorist bomb in order to identify the perpetrators, thus marked a

notable change: although much of the film focuses on Colter's mission to prevent further terrorist attacks in reality, his choice at the end to embrace a new life in the virtual world works against the grain of most VR films.

Later films have often repeated *Tron*'s visual effects – lines and grids, often flowing tunnels of colour like the phantom ride sequence that transports Dave (Keir Dullea) to another plane at the end of Stanley Kubrick's *2001: A Space Odyssey* (1968) – to represent the transition to virtual realms. But increasingly, virtual spaces are becoming visually similar to the rest of the film in which they are used, so reinforcing the blurring of reality and simulation.

A frequent theme in VR films is our inability to know for certain when we are in game or real space. The idea is most powerfully presented in Josef Rusnak's *The Thirteenth Floor* (1999), an adaptation of Daniel F. Galouye's novel *Simulacron 3* (1964), which had earlier been adapted by the German director Rainer Werner Fassbinder as the television miniseries, *World on a Wire* (*Welt am Draht*, 1973). The plot concerns a conspiracy uncovered by a VR research scientist, who is killed before he can explain his finding to his colleague. *The Thirteenth Floor* introduces a temporal gap between the VR world, Los Angeles of 1937, and the researcher's world of 1999. When protagonist Douglas Hall (Craig Bierko) enters the virtual world, he takes over the body of his avatar double, John Ferguson. For viewers, it is as if we stop watching a film set in 1999 and begin watching one set in 1937 – films about VR are also always in part meta-filmic, about our desire to enter the filmic world.

The immersive experience of James Cameron's *Avatar* (2009) is arguably a culmination of the fantasy of filmic VR: not only does Jake (Sam Worthington) fully transfer to his avatar body and on to the alien world Pandora, but reports of audience experience of the film suggest that watching it was like immersing oneself in the virtual reality of this world. Media reports of the wrench some people felt in having to leave the cinema and thus trade Pandora for reality suggest that cinema itself can be a kind of VR.

The Thirteenth Floor is ambivalent about whether it is preferable to be in reality or its simulations. The secret that Douglas finally learns is that his own 1999 world is also a simulation – a temporally regressed world created in 2024; it is just one of hundreds of simulations, but the only one in which the simulated world has itself created another virtual world within it. Douglas himself proves to be an avatar of someone from this 'real' world of 2024, David, who became sadistic through indulging the power to treat the VR characters as his personal playthings. Similarly, when one of the characters in 1937 learns that he and the others can be taken over by people from the world of 1999, he becomes mentally unstable and begins killing people. If no one is real, then there is no morality. The avatars are not mere static entities awaiting the agency of their players, but are autonomous 'units' who live their own lives even while no one monitors the program, and these alternate personalities can also move 'up' into the player's world if the character is killed while the player is downloaded. The film concludes with David's wife orchestrating his death in 1999, enabling Douglas – ethically the better man, she judges – to live with her in the world of 2024. However, although this seems to be the 'real' world, it might be yet another level of simulation, and Douglas's presence reveals that there is no privileging of real over simulated people.

David Cronenberg's *eXistenZ* (1999) is similarly concerned with the blurring of real and game space, and with the ethical consequences of spending most of one's time immersed in environments premised on the

(Top, left)
Jake (Sam Worthington) is
transferred into an avatar
body in James Cameron's
immersive 'Avatar' (2009).

(Top, right)
Army pilot Colter Stevens
(Jake Gyllenhaal) eventually
embraces the virtual
world in Duncan Jones's
'Source Code' (2011).

(Above, left)
We're constantly unsure if
the characters are in real or
virtual space in Josef Rusnak's
'The Thirteenth Floor' (1999).

(Above, right)
Brett Leonard's striking
'The Lawnmower Man' (1992)
draws from videogame imagery
to visualise virtual spaces.

violent action of first-person shooter games. Like *The Thirteenth Floor*, the film
plays with levels of reality, all of which are presented as regular cinematic
space. We begin in a reality in which lead game designer Allegra Gellar
(Jennifer Jason Leigh) is debuting her new game 'eXistenZ'; the preview is
disrupted by a pro-reality agitator who tries to kill her, and she ends up on
the run with marketing intern Ted Pikul (Jude Law). During their adventures,
the pair enter a deeper level of game space that is an exaggerated version of
their own reality. In 'reality' Allegra's gamepod is a squishy, biological mass
that makes animal-like noises as it operates, derived from a combination
of IT hardware and genetic engineering; in the game-within-the-game,
this technology is harvested from mutant amphibians that are graphically
slaughtered in a strange factory/fish-farm hybrid. This visceral and fleshy
technology echoes the imagery of Cronenberg's earlier *Videodrome* (1983),
which explored the danger of media penetrating one's mind like a virus,
altering our experience of reality and indulging dangerous appetites
for excess. *eXistenZ* takes this one step further, the pod technology
literally penetrating its users with umbilical-like cords that insert into
their bioports and interface directly with the nervous system. In the VR
game, this technology becomes bloody and ugly, literalising the anxieties
about desensitisation to violence associated with immersion in VR.

In the film's final minutes, Allegra and Pikul emerge into yet another
layer of reality, in which the pair are test marketers of a 'real' game,

(Above)
Oliver Stone's conspiracy
thriller miniseries 'Wild Palms'
(1993) explores our fading
sense of what is real and
what is media manipulation.

(Below)
People enter a virtual
world that is the recorded
memory of another person's
experience in Kathryn Bigelow's
'Strange Days' (1995) .

'transCendeZ'. This reality replays the opening sequence, but now they are the pro-reality fighters and kill the 'real' game designer. The final shot is them facing the camera, guns raised, just after another player says, "Tell me the truth: are we still in the game?" More than just a gimmick, this dialogue questions the difference between game play and real life in a more fundamental way than did *The Thirteenth Floor*: throughout, Pikul was disturbed by the "game impulses" his body seemed compelled to follow while Allegra, in her character of game designer, praised the gap between his instincts and his actions, the embrace of "new and previously unimagined taste sensations" capturing the film's critique of the addictive quality of virtuality. The odd graphemes for eXistenz and transCendeZ suggest existence and spirituality reduced to trademarked banality as we embrace the easy pleasures and violent scenarios of most digital games. The film offers no compelling alternative space and seems to ignore how its own medium is implicated in such fantasies.

Videodrome interrogated the dangers of television as a reality that enters our private, domestic space – an intimacy stunningly captured in the image of Max (James Wood) penetrating the fleshy screen of his pulsating television set as he kisses Nicki's (Deborah Harry) televised lips. The conflation of television and VR is also explored in Oliver Stone's surreal miniseries *Wild Palms* (1993), which features a cameo by William Gibson as himself, set in a near-future America in which VR broadcasts displace television.

A conspiracy thriller about the political rivalry between libertarian Friends and totalitarian Fathers, *Wild Palms* explored our fading sense of what was real and what was media manipulation in the early days of network culture. In his sweeping *Informal Age* trilogy (1996-98), sociologist Manuel Castells argues that contemporary experience had become one of "real virtuality", in which people's entire material and symbolic existence is captured on the screen and communicated through information media, a constructed and partial world of representations that we take to be reality. *Wild Palms* is a paranoid vision of such a world, a bizarre mix of surrealism and dream space, in which the right-wing Fathers construct 'Church Windows', a VR program that projects television characters into the space of viewers' living rooms, while the drug mimozene creates the illusion of tactile interaction. Senator Anton Kreutzer (Robert Loggia) plans to take over people's minds through this medium and to live forever through the 'go chip' that will enable him to live entirely in the virtual. The Friends, a group of freethinkers and artists, organise a successful resistance and ultimately capture the public's support by showing the truth about political manipulation. It concludes with protagonist Harry (James Belushi) defending the 'paradise' of real-life experience over the escapism of VR fantasy.

This faith in the transformative power of truth also shapes a number of representations of VR on the big screen. Kathryn Bigelow's *Strange Days* (1995) anticipates today's world of ubiquitous recording via smartphone cameras. A response to the LAPD beating of Rodney King, captured on camera by bystanders, the film posits a future of Superconducting Quantum Interface Device (SQUID) technology in which people can enter a kind of VR that is the recorded memory of another person's experience, complete with their emotional responses. The film's conspiracy narrative involves police attempts to cover up their murder of a black political activist, captured on such a device. When the truth is finally revealed, it has a transformative effect on public perception of the right-wing political order, similar to the conclusion of

(Above)
Max (James Woods) penetrates
his television set to kiss Nicki's
(Deborah Harry) lips in David
Cronenberg's 'Videodrome'
(1983), in which media literally
enters the mind like a virus,
altering perceptions of reality.

(Right)
Allegra Gellar (Jennifer Jason
Leigh) and Ted Pikul (Jude Law)
move through different levels of
virtual reality in Cronenberg's
'eXistenZ' (1999).

(Opposite, top)
Jeff Bridges as Kevin Flynn, the software programmer abducted into the world he programmed in 'Tron' (1982).

(Opposite, bottom)
Nanotechnology is used to replace the brain's neural tissue in 'Gamer' (2009), allowing gamers to play human bodies as characters.

Wild Palms, in which the manipulative Church of Synthiotics is shown in ruins, while Harry escapes with his restored heteronormative family.

The more recent film *Gamer* (2009), by Mark Neveldine and Brian Taylor, has essentially the same plot and conclusion as *Wild Palms*, but with updated technology. In this case, gaming and reality are conflated by Ken Castle (Michael C. Hall) through nanotechnology that replaces the brain's neural tissue with synthetic tissue capable of receiving signals, allowing gamers to play human bodies as characters, either in the hypersexualised world of 'Society' or in the violent war game 'Slayers', whose avatars are all convicted criminals. Like Kreutzer in *Wild Palms*, Castle has a fantasy of world domination through control of this medium, in this case by having his own brain tissue replaced by a kind of nanotech that can send signals, thus enabling him to control anyone through his thoughts. *Gamer* concludes with hero Kable (Gerard Butler) figuring out and revealing this conspiracy – which began as a military research experiment, perhaps a nod to Chris Carter's short-lived VR television series *Harsh Realm* (1999) – defeating Castle's control over him by the power of love for his imperilled daughter and broadcasting his victory to change public opinion. The film ends with Kable reunited with wife and daughter and driving out of the dystopian city – almost the exact conclusion of *Wild Palms*.

This saccharine conclusion should encourage us to be more sceptical of the reality we take as real – as both Baudrillard and Castells suggest, in their different ways. The thematic parallels suggest that although we have become more immersed in virtual spaces in the intervening 15 years, our anxieties about individuality and ethical behaviour requiring a 'real' site of experience remain the same.

Trouble in mind

If VR is not represented as an extension of game space – by far the more dominant representation – it is shown as an extension of one's subconscious, visualising the inside of the mind just as *Tron* visualised the inside of the computer. This theme is explored most fully in the television series *VR.5* (1995), in which a young VR researcher, Sydney (Lori Singer), tap into people's minds to solve crimes, eventually uncovering a conspiracy that has to do with her father's research. Sydney phones her subjects and when they answer puts the receiver in her VR modem to enter their minds, an image that perhaps inspired *The Matrix*'s use of then-outmoded telephones. Sydney's VR is more advanced than contemporary research, and is visualised, like the rest of the series, not as graphic animation, but with over-saturated colours that cue it as a surreal, dream-like space. Another VR of the mind, Alejandro Amenábar's *Open Your Eyes* (*Abre los ojos*, 1997) – remade by Cameron Crowe in English as *Vanilla Sky* (2001) – is structured similarly to *eXistenZ*: we spend most of the film thinking we are in a reality that in the conclusion proves to be virtual, the nightmarish vision of a young man in cryogenic sleep. Following a disfiguring accident, he killed himself and contracted to be reborn in an idealised virtual version of his life. He chooses at the end to leave this space and be reborn in a physical body, reinforcing the preference for reality, however difficult, over its simulation. This conflation of VR with subconscious spaces privileges a straightforward concept of truth and anticipates cautionary films about editing one's memories as if they were fictional media, such as Michel Gondry's *Eternal Sunshine of the Spotless Mind* (2004) and Christopher Nolan's *Inception* (2010).

Science-fiction films of VR are thus simultaneously fascinated by and fearful of the enhanced and edited realities they project. Like *The Matrix* they spend most of their screen time – and offer their most

visually arresting images – in the reality offered by the blue pill of virtuality. Yet almost without exception, they tells us that in the end we should, like Neo, take the red pill – leave the theatre and return to an often difficult but also emotionally rewarding physical reality.

Many of these films emerged in the 1990s, the early days of VR research during which we anticipated the risks and rewards of technology to come. In our contemporary world of ubiquitous social media, the actual experience of VR has so far proven very different to the one envisioned by these films: rather than entering into the virtual space, we take our portable technologies with us into the material world and filter our experience of this reality through such technologies. As Baudrillard argued, reality and simulation cannot fully be separated. Nowhere is this more evident than in military technology such as remotely piloted drones, which their operators experience as a kind of virtual simulation, but which nonetheless drop real bombs. Thus it is not surprising that one of the most recent appearances of VR on the big screen is in Gavin Hood's *Ender's Game* (2013), based on Orson Scott Card's 1985 novel, in which Ender (Asa Butterfield) believes he is merely training in VR when he wins a decisive victory by slaughtering an entire alien race, only to discover that he was in fact remotely piloting real forces. Although such experiences of VR are not like the immersive ones anticipated in film, they remind us that the choice between the blue pill and the red is one we live with today. ●

Clothes to come: between sci-fi costume and fashion

by Marketa Uhlirova

Science-fiction cinema and fashion have always mirrored each other in their drive to herald the future's new look, to articulate visually that which is yet to appear. Both court the unfamiliar, relying on the power of imagination to break away from known reality and recast it anew. It is hardly surprising, then, that the two have long enjoyed a reciprocal relationship. Whether it is costume designers pushing current fashions towards cinematic hyperbole, or fashion collections borrowing from outlandish sci-fi fantasies in a bid to express the 'cutting edge', both spheres have provided a blueprint for one another. The following are some of the most iconic examples of sci-fi costumes with strong affiliations to fashions of their time.

Aelita: Queen of Mars (1924)

Yakov Protazanov's film remains one of the most ambitious endeavours of Russia's silent cinema and a remarkable showcase of its avant-garde design. The film's peculiar brand of futurism was a joint artistic vision of Isaak Rabinovich, Viktor Simov, Sergey Kozlovsky and Aleksandra Ekster who together asserted a seamless scenographic unity between the sculptural sets and costumes. With no prior experience in film, Ekster especially was an interesting choice for Protazanov. Prior to *Aelita*, she had already enjoyed a career that was both multifaceted and international in its reach. As a painter in Paris she developed her style in the futurist and cubist traditions; later she was also associated with Russian constructivism. From 1916 she worked for the theatre. She also temporarily turned to fashion, which in Soviet Russia became a heavily politicised form.

Ekster's designs for the Martian scenes in *Aelita* have much in common with the constructivist aesthetic. They are kinetic (Aelita's headdress and her maid's metallic jupe-culotte) or at least suggestive of kinetism, and also expose basic elements of their own construction. They foreground hard, industrial materials such as metal sheets and foils, celluloid and plexiglass – all being light-reflective or transparent materials ideal for the cinematic effect. Costumes in *Aelita* are conceived less as conventional garments than three-dimensional compositions of converging geometrical forms, material surfaces and textures. Rendering the body as a composite of separate geometric parts, they convey it as distinctly machine-like. This is most salient with the uniforms of the underground guards who assist in the freezing of workers for later reuse – Ekster here created a spatial version of Fernand Léger's 'mechanical' paintings.

Ultimately, though, Aelita's costuming reveals a conflict between a constructivist orthodoxy of utilitarianism and a penchant for formal opulence. All of the film design is rather flamboyant, and was largely seen as betraying the constructivist ideal, with the costumes especially criticised for being too decorative and painterly – the glamorous queen Aelita (Yuliya Solntseva) most of all. As the most 'human' Martian, she wears two outfits which are arguably more plausible as wearable fashions and rely on more conventional couture materials such as silver lamé, diamanté, sequins and beading.

High Treason (1929)

High Treason's grandiose architecture is modern and sleek, less a metaphor of oppression, as in Fritz Lang's *Metropolis* (1927), than an aspirational showcase of the deco style – and this is just as evident in its décor and costuming. The costumes were designed by the American commercial artist Gordon Conway, who by 1933 had become the executive dress designer at Gaumont-British, heading the first British studio costume department. Working for leading women's magazines of her time,

(Above)
Aleksandra Ekster's designs for
'Aelita: Queen of Mars' (1924)
reflect the constructivist
aesthetic, and make the
body appear machine-like.

(Previous page)
Jane Fonda in a Jacques
Fonteray-designed costume
for 'Barbarella' (1968).
The photograph was taken
for the cover of 'Life'
magazine in 1968.

Conway spent much time depicting contemporary couture collections. Her chic, slender female figures, drawn with elongated silhouettes, nonchalantly posing in luxurious outfits, appealed to the growing market of the 'new woman' as perfect embodiments of urban fashionability.

Held in the BFI's Special Collections archive are Conway's sketches of costumes worn by women in the film's dance party scene – its fashion parade moment. They mesh contemporary fashion trends with formal elements derived from the pre-war avant-gardes, especially futurism – they are clean-lined and asymmetrical, constructed from fabrics with different surface effects, emphasising the diagonal and contrasting fabric inserts *à la* futurist Giacomo Balla. Conway proposed a dynamic look for emancipated women who wear trousers underneath their dress skirts. The skirts are constructed from geometric panels of various lengths and shapes, sometimes cleverly overlaid, and feature large central slits, appliqués and inserts. Conway made use of materials such as silver lamé, reflective satin and 'American cloth' (in gold, silver and copper colours) whose strong shimmering effect would lend garments in motion an industrial edge as well as a sense of glamour and drama.

Things to Come (1936)

The costumes in William Cameron Menzies's film, designed by John Armstrong, Cathleen Mann (as the Marchioness of Queensbury) and René Hubert, are relatively tame as far as the futuristic effect goes. Their role was to remain relaxed and rather civilian-looking; to humanise the majestic, starkly modernist sets of 21st-century Everytown.

H.G. Wells, on whose 1933 book *The Shape of Things to Come* the film is based, prophesised that clothing of the enlightened future would be "austerely beautiful", efficiently machine-made-to-measure and utterly disposable. Wells elaborated more on the social and cultural conditions at the root of the new fashions than questions of style *per se* – those he brushed away with a non-specific "according to the fashions of the time". After he was approached by the film's producer Alexander Korda, Wells negotiated a contractual right to write the script and be involved in all aspects of the production, including those of the art department – causing him to clash with Menzies, himself an acclaimed art director.

The final part of the film, set in the future, is a daring visualisation of Wells's technotopian vision, which was in some ways specific, yet abstract enough to let the designers do their bit of magic. Wells proclaimed a "higher phase of civilisation", with a new kind of city that is more "pellucid and clean", and a human race that is more united, equal, wealthier – although inconspicuously so – and leisurely. In his script and memos to the production team, Wells also included some general notes on the clothing, in which he demanded that the film show no signs of oppression, strain or decay caused by mechanised civilisation, and expressly rejected all futuristic clichés of previous cinema. The final decision to use cloth, as opposed to more radical avant-gardist materials, must have come from this line of thinking.

The film's first whiff of modernity is delivered in 1970, by the architect of the new world order, John Cabal. He cuts an impressive, if alien, figure in a black airman suit consisting of a giant bubble helmet – "suggestive of Buddha against a circular halo", in Wells's description – and a tight uniform with a stiff shiny bodice (presumably rubber) with large sculptural armholes "ribbed like a scallop shell" that exaggerate the shoulders. Although the look of the most distant future, 2036, was meant to be in sharp contrast to the airman's uniform ("In an age of mechanical perfection there is no need for overalls and grease-proof clothing"), and is predominantly

(Above, left)
The costumes designed by
Gordon Conway for Maurice
Elvey's 'High Treason'
(1929) were a showcase
for the art deco style.

(Below, right)
The costumes for 'Things to
Come' (1936) were designed
by John Armstrong, Cathleen
Mann and René Hubert,
visualising ideas in H.G.
Wells's source novel.

(Top)
Anne Francis models an unused costume designed by Helen Rose for her character Altaira in 'Forbidden Planet' (1956).

(Above)
The high hemlines of Helen Rose's costumes for Altaira anticipated the miniskirts that became popular in the 1960s.

white, the motif of a stiffened bodice and exaggerated shoulders is carried through. This is a less utilitarian, more serene and formal look which blends modernist geometry, rationality and standardisation with the heroism of warrior wear and the quiet dignity of ancient Greece and Rome, via 1930s 'classical' fashion such as that seen in Madeleine Vionnet or Jeanne Lanvin.

There is a sweeping uniformity to looks seen in 2036, but it is the male wardrobe that more radically departs from established conventions of modern-day wear and becomes more memorable. The dominant motif here is a triangular bodice or vest with manifestly extended shoulder line (modelled on the 'kataginu' garments of Japanese samurai), offset by narrow waists cinched by wide belts. Adorned with subtle wearable tech, these garments are worn with draped cloaks, shorts, bare legs and sandals – a look that is as regal as it is far-fetched.

Forbidden Planet (1956)

The blue-grey boilersuits worn by the all-male crew of the spaceship in MGM's *Forbidden Planet* were created by Walter Plunkett, one of Hollywood's doyens of costume design. Their ribbed chest panels, prominent shoulder pads and utilitarian belts hardly make them realistic attire for space travel, but their comic-book and military references sufficiently convey the assertiveness of future space colonisers, American style. The dresses for the female lead Altaira (Anne Francis) were the responsibility of Helen Rose, the studio's chief costume designer since 1947. Although Altaira is not exactly an earthling (she was born on the 'forbidden planet'), her wardrobe is devoid of obvious futuristic references, as if to emphasise that she is, after all, a fully-fledged human. Rose initially proposed much more outlandish looks for Francis. In her memoir *'Just Make Them Beautiful': The Many Worlds of a Designing Woman*, Rose remembers wanting to develop silver spray-on garments, an idea that was quickly discarded. Other 'futuristic' clothes she designed also never made it into the film. Francis believed this was because they were too revealing but it is just as likely they were too high-tech-looking. One remarkable unused outfit, known from production photographs, was a clinging silver lamé jumpsuit worn with a plastic overcoat. As Francis described it: "It was long sleeved and covered me from neck to toe [although in the photographs it ends below the knees], with silver cuffed gloves to match. It also had a skull fitting lamé hood … Over this was to be worn a see-through coat that was knee length and belted in at the waist. Specially made see-through shoes were to adorn my silver feet [they were in fact open-toe silver boots with a central zip fastening and asymmetrical heels]. It was sexy for sure…".

The dresses Altaira wears in *Forbidden Planet* highlight her youthful naivety as well as her feminine allure. They are relatively plain, elegant creations, so short they barely cover her buttocks. Made from silks and silk chiffons (Rose's preferred fabrics) in black, white, pastels and metallics, sometimes bejewelled for extra sparkle, they are ideal vehicles to showcase the unique tonalities of Eastmancolor. With the exception of one ankle-length gown, Altaira's legs are fully on display, anticipating the short hemlines that would become fashionable during the next decade. Indeed, Rose states in her memoir – presumably to settle the notorious dispute between the fashion designers Mary Quant and André Courrèges – that it was she who introduced the first miniskirts.

The Tenth Victim (1965)

Italian-French sci-fi *The Tenth Victim* revolves around the kind of premise more recently popularised by *The Hunger Games* – a future establishment has turned killing into officially sanctioned mass entertainment, for which rules are set and killers selected by the state. Except director Elio Petri treats the subject in a style that is decidedly more satirical and cartoonish than chillingly dystopian, and its highly stylised – and often deliberately gimmicky – 'pop' fashions and décor quickly bring this home. The film opens with a long chase sequence through the streets of New York, in which a young woman, Caroline (Ursula Andress), skilfully dodges the bullets of her male hunter. She wears a black-and-white cow-print dress and cape, black tights and contrasting white accessories, including boots with prominent cut-outs. Her strong and chic look signals canniness and a wild side, suggesting she is more a huntress than victim. After she has momentarily escaped her killer in a club (appropriately named 'Masoch'), she ends the scene with a triumphant assassination conceived as the climax of her striptease act: she shoots two bullets through a spiky metal bra, which brandishes gun muzzles for nipples.

Caroline's first black-and-white costume sets the tone and colour palette for the fashions of all the other characters (even furniture removal men wear white dungarees over black T-shirts). The film's sharp graphic wardrobe blends perfectly into the sets and décor, all of which reference modernist architecture and design alongside the more current op and pop art movements. Perhaps the strongest visual statement is made in the Colosseum scene (an obvious reference to ancient Roman spectacles) where Caroline shoots her tenth victim, Marcello (Marcello Mastroianni), in a grand televised finale of her 'Big Hunt'. She is framed by a chorus of dancers in white and black ensembles, with front-slitted skirts and sleeveless hooded cropped tops emblazoned with a single black line running both vertically and horizontally. Such monochrome blocks with contrasting stripes à la André Courrèges are the film's uniform, echoed throughout, including in Marcello's own collarless white-trimmed black suit. Designed by former illustrator for French *Vogue* Giulio Coltellacci, the costumes tapped into the progressive 'space age' fashion which Courrèges championed alongside Paco Rabanne, Pierre Cardin and Rudi Gernreich, among others. Their ultramodern, futuristic aesthetic was a rebellion against traditional tastes of luxury couture and heralded maverick materials such as plastics and metals, new forms of dress construction and fastening, stark geometric designs in monochrome primary colours and wacky details such as cut-outs (for which *The Tenth Victim*'s Elsa Martinelli is a great poster-girl). It is only Caroline who, having fallen for Marcello, is eventually allowed to wear a more conventionally sensuous dress – a device that sets her off against the rest of the institutionalised crowd.

Barbarella (1968)

The costumes worn by Jane Fonda in Roger Vadim's film testify to a time in which a fascination with technological possibilities of the future had spilled out of the realms of the military and science, and into mainstream politics and culture. The film was based on Jean-Claude Forest's racy comic serial which detailed the adventures of a beautiful 'cosmic queen' dressed in skimpy leotards and body-hugging suits.

Barbarella's costumes, designed by Jacques Fonteray, with 'inspiration' from Paco Rabanne, are comic-book gear through and through, and like Coltellacci's costumes for *The Tenth Victim*, are remarkably in line with fashions of the time. Many 60s classics, including the chain-mail fabric, minidresses, go-go boots and second-skin full body tights are in evidence here, albeit transformed into a distinctly kinky superhero

(Above)
Ursula Andress in outfits designed by Giulio Coltellacci for her character in 'The Tenth Victim' (1965). Top to bottom: the black-and-white cow-print dress worn in the opening scenes; the spiky metal bra with gun muzzles for nipples; in a more conventionally sensuous dress, framed by monochrome dancers, in the film's climactic scene at the Colosseum.

(Above)
Marina Levikova's designs
for 'Liquid Sky' (1982) are
an exuberant display of the
fashions seen in downtown
New York clubs circa 1980.

style that exaggerates Barbarella's sex goddess attributes.

One such outfit has become iconic since Fonda donned it for the cover image of *Life* magazine in 1968 – a black fabric bodice featuring a central cut-out with a plastic stomach and in the chest area fastened to a hard shell of interlinked plastic strips moulded over what seems like prosthetic breasts. The shaped plastic was most probably Rhodoïd, a material that had already been used by Vincent Korda for the furniture in *Things to Come* and that Rabanne pioneered in his accessory and clothing designs. Such references to armour (Rabanne's trademark chain-mail being another one) are commonplace in a wardrobe that constantly oscillates between extreme protection and extreme revelation. The copious use of plastic in the film's sets and costumes serves a similar purpose, for the transparent material proves an ideal vehicle to 'dress' while simultaneously affording dramatic and titillating views of the actress's body. In a future world where sex is dealt with by means of popping a pill, even nudity becomes a viable costume: having shed her space suit during the opening credits, the stark-naked Barbarella proceeds to have a video-phone conversation with the (male) president of Earth.

Liquid Sky (1982)

Slava Tsukerman and Anne Carlisle's sci-fi-meets-Brechtian-theatre extravaganza is a brilliant visual manifesto of New York's 'new wave' scene. Often cited as a key influence on the more recent Electroclash scene, it is a film that has won cult status largely thanks to its characters' outlandish looks. Diverting from the conventions of the genre, the clothes here do not envision future mankind or alien entities (who in this film are present but without bodies); rather, they serve, in a metaphorical sense, to denote one's inner alien.

Liquid Sky is an exuberant parade of alternative fashions of its time, designed by Marina Levikova and derived from the severely individualistic, bricolaged gear on display in New York's downtown clubs *circa* 1980. The film openly declares its fascination with these sartorial styles and, more generally, with fashion as a kind of modern theatre. Its two major fashion-themed scenes provide an opportunity for characters to pose in bizarre designs that have transformed avant-garde art into fierce 'anti-fashion' chic: an asymmetrical orange jacket with three multi-coloured lapels on one side; a yellow-tinted plastic vest worn with a purple waist-coat, white jacket and a bow-tie painted with geometric forms; a protruding triangular collar in the same yellow plastic featuring a rainbow motif. Both fashion scenes are filmed at night, lit so the acid colours of the costumes gain an eye-popping luminosity against the dark backgrounds.

It is possible that for these 'fashion' looks Levikova drew on the work of New York-based designer Julia Morton whom Carlisle, her friend and model, had originally approached about *Liquid Sky* (Morton stepped down). In her collections from the late 1970s and early 1980s, Morton presented brightly coloured clothes that, influenced by constructivism, featured unconventional materials (including plastic table cloth), exaggerated silhouettes, geometrical details and unfinished edges – all of which are also seen in the film. Another creative figure Carlisle brought in to the film was the make-up artist and hair stylist Marcel Fiévé, whose contribution became absolutely essential. Treating the face, and sometimes neck, as a canvas on which to paint abstract-art masks, his make-up for *Liquid Sky* is a take on the experimental looks of the club kids as well as other professional make-up artists, most notably Richard Sharah.

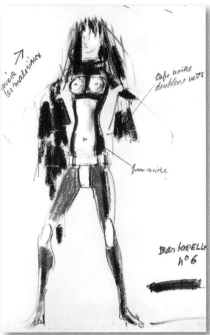

(Above)
A sketch and two designs
by Jacques Fonteray for
'Barbarella' (1968).

(Above, right)
Jean-Paul Gaultier's
distinctive aesthetic is
seen in the costumes he
designed for Luc Besson's
'The Fifth Element' (1997).

(Above)
For 'The Hunger Games:
Catching Fire' (2013), designer
Trish Summerville approached
design labels to contribute
clothing and accessories.

(Below)
Jennifer Lawrence in
the 'Girl on Fire' glossy
warrior suit designed by
Judianna Makovsky for
'The Hunger Games' (2012).

The Fifth Element (1997)

French fashion's *enfant terrible* Jean-Paul Gaultier seemed like a natural choice as costume designer for Luc Besson's film, a visually excessive spectacle populated by a pantheon of exaggerated characters. Highly regarded for mixing *haute* elegance and skilful tailoring with 'lowbrow' and risqué influences from popular culture, Gaultier's ostentatious, irreverent and precisely executed clothes were already favoured by fashionistas, music performers and arthouse film directors alike.

For *The Fifth Element* Gaultier was responsible for around 1,000 costumes – a mammoth task, for which he mined his own collections as well as a reservoir of sketches he had been compiling for a number of years. Visualising the future was for Gaultier largely an opportunity to update, not radically transform, existing fashions: "I didn't think of the costumes as automatically futuristic... I saw them instead as an evolution of the clothes we wear today." Indeed, the continuity between the film's costumes and Gaultier's fashion designs is visible, with many of the designer's trademarks and themes in evidence: excessive campness (DJ Rudy Rhod), androgyny (Leeloo's and DJ Rudy Rhod's looks), body consciousness and lasciviousness (the provocative cut-outs of air hostesses' uniforms, Mangalore's thongs under a plastic miniskirt), tongue-in-cheek humour (McDonald's uniform), bondage (Leeloo's orange rubber harness), use of unconventional materials such as rubber (Korben Dallas's vest), plastic (Zorg and his men's head plates) or neoprene (air hostesses' uniforms). It's no surprise the film launched several instant fancy-dress classics.

The Hunger Games series (2012-)

Like *Liquid Sky*, *The Hunger Games* films are among the rare breed of sci-fi cinema which spotlights fashion and the power of image as one of the central themes. Here we are presented with a future in which young adults are paraded on national television, having been transformed into showpieces by professional 'stylists'. The costumes for the first film were designed by Judianna Makovsky who also set the tone for Trish Summerville's designs for the second instalment. With many distinct looks, few of which are conventionally futuristic, Makovsky brought together references of old Americana, high-performance clothing, warrior wear and contemporary fashion. The film's contrasting looks serve above all to display economic and social inequalities of the city and the provinces, but they also indicate more subtle psychological states of the characters, especially manifest in the deliriously over-coordinated glamour of the Capitol's corrupted population.

Despite their differences, there is a coherence to all of Makovsky's costumes in that they display a quintessential touch of quirkiness, edge and glamour which makes the films feel so contemporary. One of the strongest looks is Katniss's 'Girl on Fire' glossy warrior suit made from a novelty stretch fabric with an embossed plastic. Whereas Makovsky was inspired by high fashion both old and new (she cites Alexander McQueen, John Galliano and Elsa Schiaparelli) for some of her looks, Summerville went one step further. Taking on the role of the fashion editor, she approached design labels (including Alexander McQueen, Tex Saverio, Cerre and Anjhe Mules at Lucas Hugh) to contribute clothing and accessories. Then, timed for the film's release, the online retailer Net-a-porter launched a 16-piece line of garments and accessories designed by Summerville herself – a textbook example of the kind of commercial tie-in between cinema and fashion that dates back to the silent era. ●
(This chapter is dedicated to Roger K. Burton)

FILM INDEX

CONTRIBUTORS

Laura Adams is events programmer at BFI Southbank and the BFI London Film Festival

Stephen Baxter is among the pre-eminent SF writers of his generation. His many novels include the Destiny's Children series, the Flood novels, the Time Odyssey series (with Arthur C. Clarke) and the Long Earth series (with Terry Pratchett)

Josephine Botting is a curator of fiction film at the BFI National Archive, and is currently writing a PhD thesis on British film director Adrian Brunel

Mark Bould is reader in film and literature at the University of the West of England, and the editor of *Science Fiction: The Routledge Film Guidebook*, founding co-editor of *Science Fiction Film and Television Journal*, co-author of *The Routledge Concise History of Science Fiction*, and author of the BFI Film Classic on *Solaris*

Ashley Clark is a freelance writer and programmer, and a regular contributor to *Sight & Sound*. He programmed the BFI Southbank's 'Inside Afrofuturism' season, part of the BFI's 'Sci-Fi: Days of Fear and Wonder' project

John Clute is co-editor of *The Encyclopedia of Science Fiction* and author of *The Illustrated Encyclopedia of Science Fiction*. He was one of the co-founders of *Interzone* magazine and is the author of the novel *Appleseed*

Bryony Dixon is curator of silent film at the BFI National Archive. She specialises in British silent cinema, and is the author of the BFI screenguide *100 Silent Films*

Mark Fisher writes regularly for *frieze*, *New Statesman*, *Sight & Sound* and *The Wire*, where he was acting deputy editor for a year. He is a visiting fellow at Goldsmiths, University Of London, and maintains one of the most successful weblogs on cultural theory, k-punk (http://k-punk.abstractdynamics.org). His books include *Capitalist Realism: Is There No Alternative?* and *Ghosts of My Life: Writings on Depression, Hauntology and Lost Futures*

William Fowler is curator of artists' moving image at the BFI National Archive where he undertakes film restoration projects and programmes the 'Essential Experiments' strand at BFI Southbank. In 2014 he curated 'Queer Pagan Punk: Derek Jarman' plus 'This Is Now: Film and Video After Punk' in association with artists' moving image agency LUX

Ken Hollings's writing has appeared in a wide range of periodicals such as *The Wire*, *Sight & Sound*, *frieze* and *Strange Attractor Journal* as well as numerous catalogues and anthologies.

His books include *The Bright Labyrinth: Sex, Death and Design in the Digital Regime*, *Welcome to Mars: Fantasies of Science in the American Century, 1947-1959* and the novel *Destroy All Monsters*

Simon Ings is the author of *Wolves* (Gollancz, 2014). He reviews for the *Guardian* and edits the culture pages of *New Scientist*

Helen Lewis is deputy editor of the *New Statesman*. She tweets @helenlewis

Roger Luckhurst is professor of modern and contemporary literature at Birkbeck College, University of London. His publications include *The Mummy's Curse: The True History of a Dark Fantasy* and BFI Film Classics monographs on *The Shining* and *Alien*

Kevin Lyons is a documentation editor at the BFI, and editor of the website www.eofftv.com (*The Encyclopedia of Fantastic Film and Television*)

Sophie Mayer is the author of *The Cinema of Sally Potter: A Politics of Love* and co-editor of *There She Goes: Feminist Filmmaking and Beyond*

Kim Newman's fiction includes *An English Ghost Story* and the *Anno Dracula* novels; his non-fiction includes *Nightmare Movies* and BFI Film Classics monographs on *Cat People* and *Quatermass and the Pit*, and a TV Classic monograph on *Doctor Who*. His official website is www.johnnyalucard.com

John Oliver is a curator of fiction film at the BFI National Archive

Vic Pratt is a curator of fiction film at the BFI National Archive. He co-founded and co-programmes *The Flipside*

Alastair Reynolds's novels include the Revelation Space Trilogy: *Revelation Space*, *Redemption Ark* and *Absolution Gap*. His many other novels include *On the Steel Breeze* and *Blue Remembered Earth*. He has a Ph.D. in astronomy, and gave up working as an astrophysicist for the European Space Agency to become a full-time writer

Jonathan Rigby is the author of several books, among them *English Gothic: A Century of Horror Cinema* (2000), *American Gothic: Sixty Years of Horror Cinema* (2007) and *Studies in Terror: Landmarks of Horror Cinema* (2011)

Adam Roberts is professor of 19th-century literature, Royal Holloway University of London. He is the author of 15 science-fiction novels, some of which have won prizes

PICTURE CREDITS

Adam Rutherford is a scientist, writer and broadcaster. His official website is www.adamrutherford.com

Mark Salisbury is a screenwriter, journalist and author of more than a dozen books, among them *Burton on Burton*, *Writers on Comics Scriptwriting*, and the art/making of companions for *Prometheus*, *Elysium*, *Alice in Wonderland* and *Frankenweenie*

Graham Sleight is the managing editor of the Hugo Award-winning *Encyclopedia of Science Fiction* (www.sf-encyclopedia.com). He has written about sf for the *Washington Post*, *Interzone*, *Locus* and *Strange Horizons* among others. His official website is www.grahamsleight.com

Matthew Sweet is a writer and broadcaster. His books include *Shepperton Babylon: The Lost Worlds of British Cinema* and *Inventing the Victorians*. He has written several *Doctor Who* audio plays and short stories

Marketa Uhlirova is a senior research fellow at Central Saint Martins College, University of the Arts London, and director of the Fashion in Film Festival where she oversees all of its programming. She has recently edited *Birds of Paradise: Costume as Cinematic Spectacle* (Koenig Books, 2013) and contributed articles to publications including *Fashion Theory* and *Aperture*

Sherryl Vint is professor of Science Fiction Media Studies at the University of California, Riverside, where she co-directs the Science Fiction and Technoculture Studies program. She is the author of *Bodies of Tomorrow* (2007), *Animal Alterity* (2010), *The Wire* (2013), and *Science Fiction: A Guide to the Perplexed* (2014). She co-edits the journals *Science Fiction Film and Television* and *Science Fiction Studies*

George Watson is a film booker at the BFI

All images courtesy of BFI National Archive/Special Collections except: p59 © Center for Visual Music, Los Angeles; p31, p33 (bottom), p41, p50 (bottom), p57 (top), p103, p106 (bottom), p116, p122 (bottom left), p129, p132 (top), p137, p150 (top) courtesy of the Kobal Collection; p37 (top left), p42, p81, p96, p141 (bottom) courtesy of the Ronald Grant Archive; p79 REX/Huw Evans, courtesy of REX; p80, p81, p82, p83 courtesy of the BBC; inside cover, p111 courtesy of Photofest; p145 Carlo Bavagnoli/The LIFE Picture Collection/Getty Images, courtesy of Getty Images; cover courtesy of BFI National Archive/20th Century Fox; p150 all images courtesy of Slava Tsukerman.

ACKNOWLEDGEMENTS

Thank you to all of the contributors. Thanks for their advice and assistance to Laura Adams, Nigel Arthur, Stuart Brown, David Edgar, Nick James, Roger Luckhurst, Kim Newman, Stephanie Redstone, Isabel Stevens, Heather Stewart, Darren Wood. Special thanks to Lisa Kerrigan, Jamie McLeish, Rhidian Davis, and to Christopher Brawn, this book's designer. Particular thanks to Rob Winter.

ALSO IN THE BFI COMPENDIUM SERIES

SCI-FI: DAYS OF FEAR AND WONDER SEASON

Together with

1895
H.G. Wells publishes *The Time Machine*
1896
H.G. Wells publishes *The Island of Dr. Moreau*
1898
H.G. Wells publishes *The War of the Worlds*
1902
Georges Méliès's *A Trip to the Moon* is released. It depicts a spacecraft fired to the moon from a giant cannon – an idea borrowed from Jules Verne
1904
Georges Méliès's *Voyage á travers l'impossible* is released
1906
W. R. Booth makes *The ? Motorist*, in which a driver drives off the Earth for a trip to the sun and around the rings of Saturn
1910
J. Searle Dawley makes the first screen adaptation of Mary Shelley's *Frankenstein*
1912
Arthur Conan Doyle publishes *The Lost World*
1914
Heinrich Galeen makes *The Golem*, with Paul Wegener playing the automaton. He will reprise the role in 1920, in a film he also directs. H. G. Wells publishes *The World Set Free*, in which he prophesises the atomic bomb
1921
Czech novelist and playwright Karel Capek stages *Rossum's Universal Robots*, which popularises the word 'robot'. André Deed makes *L'uomo meccanico*
1923
René Clair's *Paris qui dort* visualises a Paris frozen by the invisible ray of a mad scientist. *Weird Tales* magazine begins publishing
1924
Yakov Protazanov's *Aelita: Queen of Mars* is released
1926
Fritz Lang's *Metropolis* is released. *Amazing Stories*, the first US magazine to be devoted to science fiction, is launched

'The Incredible Shrinking Man' (1957)

under the editorship of Hugo Gernsback
1929
Maurice Elvey's *High Treason* imagines a futuristic London of 1940. Fritz Lang's *Frau im Mond* offers an early realistic vision of rocket-powered space travel
1930
The futuristic musical *Just Imagine* is released. It follows a man of 1930 who is struck by lightning and wakes up in the New York of 1980
1931
James Whale's classic *Frankenstein* is released, starring Boris Karloff
1932
Erle C. Kenton makes *Island of Lost Souls*, based on Wells's *The Island of Dr. Moreau*. Aldous Huxley's *Brave New World* is published
1933
James Whale makes *The Invisible Man*
1936
William Cameron Menzies's *Things To Come* is released. H. G. Wells writes the screenplay, based on his 1933 book *The Shape of Things to Come*. The popular *Flash Gordon* series starts in the US

1937
Olaf Stapledon publishes *Star Maker*, which will influence Arthur C. Clarke among others. Katharine Burdekin's *Swastika Night* is published
1938
Orson Welles's radio dramatisation of *The War of the Worlds* causes mass panic
1939
Science-fiction fans gather for the First World SF Convention in Manhattan
1947
An alien spacecraft is reported to have crashed at Roswell, USA, and sparks a rush of UFO and 'flying saucer' sightings
1949
George Orwell's *Nineteen Eighty-Four* is published
1950
George Pal's *Destination Moon* is released. It reflects the increasingly realisable possibility of space travel. Isaac Asimov's *I, Robot* is published. It contains Asimov's three laws for the safe programming of robots (originally published in 1941)
1951
Two classics of 1950s science-fiction

cinema are released: Robert Wise's *The Day the Earth Stood Still* and Christian Nyby's *The Thing from Another World*. John Wyndham's *The Day of the Triffids* is published, as is Arthur C. Clarke's *Sentinel of Eternity*, later the basis for Stanley Kubrick's *2001: A Space Odyssey*

1952

The groundbreaking US anthology TV series *Tales of Tomorrow* begins. It paves the way for such series as *Science Fiction Theater* (1955-57) and *The Twilight Zone* (1959-64)

1953

Byron Haskin's adaptation of H. G. Wells's *The War of the Worlds* is released. Jack Arnold makes *It Came from Outer Space*. *The Quatermass Experiment*, written by Nigel Kneale, is broadcast by the BBC

1954

Two classic films inspired by contemporary fears of nuclear war and mutation are released: Gordon Douglas's *Them!* and Honda Inoshiro's *Gojira* (*Godzilla*)

1955

Don Siegel makes *Invasion of the Body Snatchers*. It is claimed as a denouncement of both McCarthyism and of communism

1956

Forbidden Planet, a galactic version of *The Tempest* directed by Fred Wilcox, introduces the popular character of Robby the Robot, who will reappear in both *The Invisible Boy* and the TV series *Lost in Space*. Ursula Andress stars in Elio Petri's sylised 'pop' sci-fi *The Tenth Victim*

1957

Several films about radioactive mutations are released, including Jack Arnold's *The Incredible Shrinking Man*, Bert Gordon's *The Amazing Colossal Man* and Roger Corman's *Attack of the Crab Monsters*

1960

Wolf Rilla makes *The Village of the Damned*, an adaptation of John Wyndham's *The Midwich Cuckoos*.

The East German/Polish co-production *The Silent Star* is released

1961

Val Guest's *The Day the Earth Caught Fire* is released. The BBC TV series *A for Andromeda* is broadcast

1962

Chris Marker's *La Jetée* is released

1963

Doctor Who is first broadcast by the BBC

1965

Jean-Luc Godard uses Paris locations to stand in for a future urban dystopia in *Alphaville*. Frank Herbert's *Dune* is published. The BBC's science-fiction series *Out of the Unknown* is broadcast

1966

Star Trek is first broadcast, with William Shatner's Captain Kirk at the helm of the Starship Enterprise. François Truffaut adapts Ray Bradbury's *Fahrenheit 451* into a film starring Julie Christie and Oskar Werner

1967

Roy Ward Baker's *Quatermass and the Pit* is released, scripted by Nigel Kneale

1968

'The ultimate trip', Stanley Kubrick's *2001: A Space Odyssey*, is released. Jane Fonda stars in her then-husband Roger Vadim's *Barbarella*. Charlton Heston stars in Franklin J. Schaffner's *The Planet of the Apes*

1970

George Lucas makes *THX-1138*

1971

Stanley Kubrick directs *A Clockwork Orange*, adapted from Anthony Burgess's novel of a violent future dystopia

1972

Andei Tarkovsky adapts Stanislaw Lem's *Solaris*. Douglas Trumbull directs *Silent Running*

1973

Richard Fleischer's *Soylent Green* imagines a future in which human corpses are recycled as food. Woody Allen's sci-fi comedy *Sleeper* is released. French director René Laloux's sci-fi animation *Fantastic Planet* is released

1974

Sun Ra appears in John Coney's film *Space Is the Place*, its title taken from one of Ra's own compositions. John Carpenter makes *Dark Star*

1976

David Bowie stars as the alien in Nicolas Roeg's *The Man Who Fell to Earth*

1977

George Lucas's *Star Wars* is released, to runaway success. Steven Spielberg revisits and updates the sci-fi movies of the 1950s with *Close Encounters of the Third Kind*. Peter Hyams's *Capricorn One* portrays a faked Mars landing by NASA

1979

Ridley Scott's *Alien* is released, starring Sigourney Weaver as Ripley, and with designs by H.R. Giger. Douglas Adams publishes *The Hitchhiker's Guide to the Galaxy*

1980

David Cronenberg makes *Scanners*. Mike Hodges remakes the 1930s TV serial *Flash Gordon*. Ken Russell's *Altered States* is released

1982

Harrison Ford stars in Ridley Scott's *Blade Runner*, adapted from Philip K. Dick's novel *Do Androids Dream of Electric Sheep?* Slava Tsukerman makes the stylish *Liquid Sky*. Steven Spielberg's *E.T. The Extra-Terrestrial* becomes a box-office hit. Disney's *Tron*, directed by Steven Lisberger, pioneers the use of computer graphics in science-fiction cinema. David Cronenberg makes *Videodrome*. John Carpenter remakes *The Thing*

1983

Lizzie Borden's feminist sci-fi *Born in Flames* is released

1984

John Sayles makes the low-budget *The Brother from Another Planet*. David Lynch adapts Frank Herbert's *Dune*. Arnold Schwarzenegger stars in James Cameron's *The Terminator*. William Gibson's *Neuromancer* is published

1985

Terry Gilliam's *Brazil* is released.

CHRONOLOGY

Marty McFly (Michael J. Fox) travels back to 1955 in a DeLorean in Robert Zemeckis's *Back to the Future*
1986
David Cronenberg makes *The Fly*. Margaret Atwood's *The Handmaid's Tale* is published
1987
Paul Verhoeven's *RoboCop* is released
1988
Otomo Katsuhiro's *Akira* becomes the first Japanese anime to achieve international success
1989
Tsukamoto Shinya's techno body-horror *Tetsuo: The Iron Man* is released
1990
Richard Stanley makes the low-budget cyberpunk film *Hardware*. Paul Verhoeven makes *Total Recall*
1991
James Cameron's *Terminator 2: Judgment Day* breaks ground in its use of digital special effects
1993
Steven Spielberg's *Jurassic Park* pioneers computer-generated special effects. Chris Carter's *The X-Files*, starring Gillian Anderson and David

'District 9' (2009)

Duchovny, is first broadcast. Haile Gerima's time-travel film *Sankofa* is released
1995
Kathryn Bigelow's *Strange Days* is released
1996
Roland Emmerich's *Independence Day* depicts an alien invasion. John Akomfrah makes *The Last Angel of History*
1997
Jodie Foster stars as an astronomer contacted by alien life in *Contact*, based on a novel by Carl Sagan. Paul Verhoeven adapts Robert Heinlen's *Starship Troopers*. Luc Besson makes

The Fifth Element, with costumes designed by Jean-Paul Gaultier
1999
The Wachowskis' *The Matrix* is released. George Lucas's *Star Wars* prequel *The Phantom Menace* is released to a mixed reception
2002
Tom Cruise stars in Steven Spielberg's *Minority Report*
2004
Jim Carrey and Kate Winslet star in Michel Gondry's *Eternal Sunshine of the Spotless Mind*. Shane Carruth's micro-budget time-travel film *Primer* is released to critical acclaim
2005
Doctor Who is revived on the BBC by writer Russell T. Davies
2006
Alfonso Cuarón adapts PD James's *Children of Men*. Bong Joon-ho makes *The Host*
2009
James Cameron's 3D epic *Avatar* is released. It will become the highest-grossing film of all time. South African Neill Blomkamp releases *District 9*. Duncan Jones's *Moon* is released. J.J. Abrams reboots *Star Trek*
2010
Gareth Edwards's low-budget debut *Monsters* is released
2011
A South London housing estate faces an alien invasion in Joe Cornish's *Attack the Block*
2012
Jennifer Lawrence stars in *The Hunger Games*, adapted from the novel by Suzanne Collins
2013
Scarlett Johansson plays an alien in Jonathan Glazer's *Under the Skin*. Tatiana Maslany plays all 12 clones in the TV series *Orphan Black*
2014
Christopher Nolan's epic *Interstellar* is released

'Fantastic Planet' (1973)